Challenging the Civil Rights Establishment

Challenging the Civil Rights Establishment

Profiles of a New Black Vanguard

Joseph G. Conti
and Brad Stetson

PRAEGER

Westport, Connecticut
London

Library of Congress Cataloging-in-Publication Data

Conti, Joseph G.
    Challenging the civil rights establishment : profiles of a new
black vanguard / Joseph G. Conti and Brad Stetson.
        p.   cm.
    Includes bibliographical references and index.
    ISBN 0–275–94460–3 (alk. paper)
    1. Afro-American leadership.   2. Afro-Americans—Civil rights.
3. Civil rights movements—United States—History—20th century.
I. Stetson, Brad.   II. Title.
E185.615.C663   1993
323.1'196073—dc20   92–31851

British Library Cataloguing in Publication Data is available.

Library of Congress Catalog Card Number: 92–31851
ISBN: 0-275-94460-3

First published in 1993

Praeger Publishers, 88 Post Road West, Westport, CT 06881
An imprint of Greenwood Publishing Group, Inc.

Printed in the United States of America

The paper used in this book complies with the
Permanent Paper Standard issued by the National
Information Standards Organization (Z39.48–1984).

10 9 8 7 6 5 4 3 2 1

Dedicated, in admiration and gratitude,
to the New Black Vanguard.

CONTENTS

PREFACE

Since the end of the Vietnam War, American civil discourse has become progressively more preoccupied with issues surrounding race. A puzzling feature of this preoccupation is the pronounced one-sidedness of opinion assigned to black America by the media and African-American political leaders and spokespeople.

This phenomenon was, by and large, reinforced and amplified by the panels of black scholars and activists assembled by television and print media to frame the meaning of the searing cataclysm that was the Los Angeles riot of 1992. The panel choices were quite predictable. Few black advocates were invited to speak who dissented from the generally accepted version of the causes and solutions to the problems of inner-city blacks. In this way, a kind of "black political correctness" was tacitly professed and enforced, and the illusion of homogeneity of opinion among black intellectuals and social scientists was perpetuated.

By all standards of civil discourse, this is rather strange. On any given social issue one expects to hear, and does hear, a variety of opinions and comments. And yet, sui generis, this principle of public discourse is habitually suspended on black issues. The resultant impression of unanimity absurdly belies the rich diversity of opinion held by African-Americans on social issues. This book aims to unfold some of that diversity.

The subjects of this book boldly reject the authority and cogency of the "official story"—represented in the views of civil rights luminaries—regarding the path to black advancement. They offer an alternative message: *It is a message of self-reliance, in the context of a dignified community, trusting its own ability to exercise freedom with responsibility and thereby provide for itself the moral and social resources that breed and sustain independence*. This book examines the controversial axioms and controlling principles of these dissenters, and explicates their forceful critique of mainstream black leadership.

While these black dissidents do not presume to "speak" for black America, they would be heard. Unfortunately, aside from the flashbulb coverage accorded them following the nomination of Clarence Thomas to the Supreme Court, they have largely inhabited the obscurity reserved for the political fringe.

Although the purpose of this book is to draw attention to what we see as common themes and outlooks among the dissidents here profiled, we by no means want to give the impression that their thought is monolithic. While we do strive to separate these figures and do justice to their individual thought, a full-scale delineation of their differences is beyond the scope of this book. Seeing as, to our knowledge, there is no study extant explaining the often subtle disagreements among these black dissidents, we can only refer the interested reader to the primary sources— the work of the dissidents themselves.

This is more than a book about race. The thinkers here profiled touch on matters fundamental to human society: the individual, the community, social responsibility, freedom, and human dignity. This book is the first attempt to afford a hearing to them, the New Black Vanguard, a social force in ascendance.

South Central Los Angeles
Summer 1992

ACKNOWLEDGMENTS

We are indebted to a number of people and organizations who, through their comments, criticisms and other forms of assistance, contributed to the formation of this work. We thank especially Dallas Willard, Robert Rector, Mike McKenzie, James Q. Wilson, the staff of the Hoover Institution, the National Center for Neighborhood Enterprise, Emmanuel McLittle, Elizabeth Wright, Robert L. Woodson, Donna Lewis, Glenn C. Loury, Clint Bolick, Ezola Foster, William B. Allen, Jesse Peterson and the men and women of the Brotherhood Organization of a New Destiny, Bob and Gretchen Passantino, John and Carol Stetson, Shelby Steele, Lawrence Mead, David Hayes, Marvin Olasky, Steve Bivens, Alfred Regnery, *The Los Angeles Sentinel*, the Capital Research Center, the Institute for Contemporary Studies, Praeger Publishers, Anne Kiefer, Nina Stetson, and the graduate faculty of the School of Religion and Social Ethics at the University of Southern California. Of course, none of these individuals or groups are responsible for any errors contained in this book.

Challenging the Civil Rights Establishment

——— 1 ———

THE COMING BATTLE FOR BLACK LEADERSHIP

Arguments, like men, are often pretenders.

Plato

It is not a sign of weakness, but a sign of high maturity to rise to a level of self-criticism.

Rev. Martin Luther King, Jr.

Socrates' rhetorical method of question, answer, and counterquestion effectively devastated many a philosophical opponent. By showing the implicit assumptions and necessary consequences of a given viewpoint, Socrates was able to unmask the true character of ideas. What at first seemed cogent and sensible might be revealed to be fallacious and incongruent with human experience. Indeed, if the corpus of Socratic dialogues reveals a general truth about human beings, it is that the pretensions of human argument are hard to overestimate.

This book is about thinkers who claim that in the wake of the 1960s civil rights victories, ideological pretension has overrun clear thinking and the empirical data of human experience when it comes to discussions of race and culture. It seems to them that the construction of public policy has devolved into a kind of "ethnic cheerleading" that exalts race and ethnicity above personal character and behavior in determinations of what is fair and fitting. In addition, they are alarmed by the stark decline in the *quality* of racial discourse conducted by black leaders. On the six o'clock news, on talk shows, in university classrooms, and in political debate, they are startled to find that the rhetoric of black lead-

ership, popular and political, often resembles a bizarre Orwellian doublespeak, as when:

—A black intellectual, who fought passionately for civil rights in the 1960s,
is called an "anti-Negro Negro" and "reassigned" from a black studies
department, because he dared assert his civil right to dissent from the
"politically correct" black viewpoint in the department.

—A black college-educated female "raptivist," Sister Souljah, insists in
national media that an evil white power structure is oppressing American blacks, although black college-educated females currently earn 125
percent of what white college-educated females earn.

—The Rev. Jesse Jackson defends Sister Souljah's public philosophy of
race, although she said to the press, "This is a race war" and rationalized
the Los Angeles riots by saying, "If black people kill black people every
day, why not have a week and kill white people?" Jackson called her
critics divisive, and said that Bill Clinton's criticism of Souljah was indicative of a character flaw in *Clinton!*[1]

—Of black babies, 62 percent are born out of wedlock (and in some neighborhoods, well over 80 percent), and an essayist for "the largest black-
owned newspaper in the West" sarcastically dismisses calls for a discussion of values as "playing the moral values card."

—A twenty-year member of the NAACP says Clarence Thomas's opposition to affirmative action programs was "enough to oppose him,"
because "that's what Martin Luther King died for."[2]

—The Los Angeles black leadership, following the 1992 riots, informs the
nation that there is a lack of educational opportunity for South Central
Los Angeles youth, even though the City of Los Angeles has nine community colleges (one of these in the central riot area), which require no
high school diploma for entry, each charging about $5 for a unit of
instruction, with low-interest loans available.

—When 90 percent of black parents in Milwaukee, responding to dismal
test scores and rocketing dropout rates, come out in favor of a parental
choice plan, the chief litigant *against* the plan is the local chapter of the
NAACP.

—A popular rapper, whom the *Los Angeles Times* described as a "positive
role model," announces after the riots: "I am privileged and honored
to be living at [a] time [when] people are looting and robbing and stealing, because . . . now it's time for [whites] in this country to understand
what [blacks] are going through."[3]

The New Black Vanguard, and many average, fair-minded Americans,
are weary of these kinds of regular violations of common sense that
characterize discussions of race in America.

The thinkers who comprise the New Black Vanguard are a dissident voice among black intellectuals and activists. Indeed, their very designation as "activists" is novel, inasmuch as their message is addressed inward, toward the black community itself, rather than toward the megastructures of government and politics, the habitual targets of liberal black activism. This interior activism bespeaks a clear paradigm shift in the quest for remedies to problems that have dogged the black community.[4] Conspicuously absent, here, are appeals for increased government assistance through affirmative action, forced integration, "race-norming" of test scores, and expanded welfare entitlement programs.

The oddness of this absence lies in the fact that such policies are seen by some as identical with black interest, so much so that to oppose them is often seen to be, if not racist, then racially insensitive. This goes for both white and black opponents, except that in the case of the latter the offense is particularly sinister, since it is viewed as a grievous disservice to one's racial heritage, an Iscariot-like betrayal of the sacred bonds of ethnicity. For nearly three decades such pressure to conform has effectively quashed the kind of self-criticism Dr. King knew to be a sine qua non of vital public discourse.

But the New Black Vanguard is undissuaded by allegations of racial disloyalty, and maintains that the traditional methods of advancing black interests are effete, if not iatrogenic. This is a provocative idea, but it is only a small part of the Vanguard's forceful and polyangular critique of racial discourse in America today.

Now, these ideas are not "new" in the sense of having never been heard before. Indeed, some of the greatest black thinkers in the history of this country advanced ideas thoroughly consonant with those of the thinkers profiled in this book. Frederick Douglass, in his 1848 speech, "What Are the Colored People Doing for Themselves?" spoke in terms so evocative of today's black dissidents, that in many ways his remarks serve as a summary of their social philosophy:

> The fact that we are limited and circumscribed ought to incite us to a more vigorous and persevering use of the elevating means within our reach, rather than to dishearten us. . . . Our oppressors have divested us of many valuable blessings and facilities for improvement and elevation, but thank Heaven, they have not yet been able to take from us the priviledge of being honest, industrious, sober and intelligent.[5]

Similarly, Booker T. Washington (1856–1915) wrote presciently when he discerned the kind of opportunistic leadership that would ill serve his people, in his day and thereafter:

> There is another class of colored people who make a business of keeping the troubles, the wrongs, and hardships of the Negro race before the public. Having learned that they are able to make a living out of their troubles, they have grown into the settled habit of advertising their wrongs—partly because they want sympathy, and partly because it pays.
> Some of these people do not want the Negro to lose his grievances, because they do not want to lose their jobs.[6]

But despite this rich historical precedent, the New Black Vanguard is "new" in the sense that today it stands in stark opposition to, and has the potential to end, the longstanding political hegemony of the "civil rights establishment." Our use of the phrase "civil rights establishment" is patterned after the definition advanced by Clint Bolick, author of *Changing Course: Civil Rights at the Crossroads*.[7] Bolick, who is an attorney specializing in education and employment issues, understands the "civil rights establishment" as a core of groups and organizations committed to advancing, through political means, a revised agenda, not of civil rights, but of social entitlement and privilege.[8] The primary ideas of the civil rights establishment revolve around: a commitment to political expediency over principles, if the latter threaten to undermine the former; the privileging of government efforts over individual or private efforts to solve social problems; the primacy of equality (as they understand it) over freedom and individuality; the equation of equality of opportunity with equality of result.[9]

Now, although Bolick's rubric "civil rights establishment" includes a host of groups—NAACP, Urban League, Southern Christian Leadership Conference, Mexican-American Legal Defense Education Fund (MAL-DEF), NOW, Alliance for Justice, People for the American Way, and ACLU—our focus is primarily on those groups specifically focused on the advancement of African-Americans.[10]

Much of what follows makes the case that those segments of the civil rights establishment devoted to black advancement—groups we often term mainstream, or conventional, black advocates—have transformed their goals and methods so drastically that their work now has a negative effect on their putative beneficiaries. It is clear that the term "civil rights" no longer means what it once did, and that the goals of black advocacy are no longer what they once were. Bolick writes of the emergence of this change in course, or what he calls a "revised agenda":

> Recently, thoughtful commentators have challenged this illusion. Columnist William Raspberry, for instance, proclaims that "the Civil Rights

Movement is over." The civil rights struggles of a quarter-century ago, he argues, achieved the movement's goal of securing the political rights and basic opportunities necessary to enjoyment of the fruits of American citizenship.

The question, then, arises: What is it that has taken the civil rights movement's place? The answer is disturbing. What has emerged during the past two decades is no longer a civil rights "movement" at all, but an establishment dedicated to perpetuating itself and expanding its power. The civil rights establishment differs from its predecessor movement in a critical way. What gave the traditional civil rights movement its moral legitimacy was the universality of the rights it sought to establish, but the modern civil rights establishment has abandoned this moral claim by transforming the meaning of civil rights from those fundamental rights we all share equally as Americans into special benefits for some and burdens for others.

Still the establishment continues to enjoy a monopoly over the civil rights mantle; and it continues to dictate the terms of the debate, even as it distorts the traditional meaning of civil rights, to the detriment of most Americans—and perhaps especially to the detriment of its purported beneficiaries.[11]

Indeed, perhaps the most poignant testimony to the effete nature of the civil rights establishment today is the tragic state of nearly one-third of black America, the black poor:

—In big-city ghettos, the black youth unemployment rate often exceeds 40 percent.

—Over one-quarter of young black men in the critical age group of 20 to 24 have dropped out of the economy.

—In urban centers, the vast majority of all black babies are born out of wedlock. Nationally, 62 percent of all black babies are born to unwed mothers.

—Blacks, though little more than a tenth of the population, constitute approximately half of the imprisoned felons in the nation.

—Roughly 40 percent of those murdered in the United States are black men killed by other black men.[12]

So as it moves into the twenty-first century, with a sharp and painful consciousness of the urban problems threatening what semblance of national tranquillity may remain, this country is hearing the debate between two sets of ideas that are vying to direct the future of American blacks—and possibly the country as a whole.

WHO ARE THE NEW BLACK VANGUARD?

In a prescient article at the beginning of the 1980s, sociologist Murray Friedman wrote in *Commentary* of the emergence of "the new black intellectuals":

> These men do not share a common social and political philosophy. At important points, they differ sharply from one another. What permits them to be classed together, however, is that in their work on poverty they have avoided generalized indictments of American society and eschewed purely racial explanations of the plight of poor blacks.[13]

Ten years since Friedman wrote this, several of the figures he discussed, including Thomas Sowell, Glenn C. Loury, Walter Williams, and William Julius Wilson, have indeed attracted the attention he predicted. Sowell emerged as arguably the leading anti–affirmative action theoretician and polemicist of the 1980s. In his assault on what he termed the "self-anointed 'moral leaders' "[14] of a calcified civil rights establishment, he was recognized in some circles as "a leading contender in the bitter contest over who speaks for American blacks," though Sowell himself has no such pretentions.[15] Clarence Thomas, in an interview given shortly after his nomination to the Supreme Court, acknowledged Sowell as an early and important mentor. Thomas's initial reading of Sowell's works and those of other dissenters in the early 1980s came as a happy surprise to him. With his waxing disenchantment with what he perceived to be the narrow agenda of the prevailing "civil rights ideology,"[16] he was excited to discover that a new kind of black advocacy was in the works. "It was like pouring a glass of water on a desert," he recalls. "I just soaked it up."[17]

Loury, a political economist, continued to develop his increasingly influential communitarian argument at Harvard and Boston universities, as a corrective to what he saw as an unhealthy cleaving of rights from responsibilities in the rhetoric of the civil rights establishment. He recognized an odd cognitive dissonance in the black leadership's habitual denunciations of social irresponsibility among whites, but relative silence on social irresponsibility among blacks. Urging black leadership to a more self-critical and objective approach, Loury wrote of "an inherent link between these two sides of the 'responsibility coin'—between acceptance among blacks of personal responsibility for our actions, and acceptance among all Americans of their social responsibilities as citizens."[18] Loury, with Sowell, was an early critic of "black political correctness," which has held sway in university black study departments for the last quarter-century.[19]

Walter Williams, an economist at George Mason University and a social commentator of the most provocative sort, continued to press his libertarian argument through the 1980s, resisting demands for "economic rights" beyond those guaranteed by the Constitution and blaming the wrong-minded black leadership for its part in fomenting dangerous demands, and supporting public policies that undermine virtue. "People actually choose welfare," objected Williams, "because it is their 'right'."[20] Controverting the civil rights establishment's demands for more state intervention on behalf of blacks, Williams has insisted that "black people are primary victims of state intervention."[21] Williams has continued to sting the left with his characteristically jarring inversions of conventional wisdom, going so far as to claim that liberals have done more harm to blacks than the Ku Klux Klan. He also inverts the claim that "hopelessness" sparked the Los Angeles riots in the spring of 1992. "To the extent that hopelessness explains anything," he writes, "most of it stems not from the fact of hopelessness but that it is created in the minds of our youth by civil rights leaders like Jesse Jackson."[22]

Still, Williams does share a few views with the liberal William Julius Wilson, a sociologist at the University of Chicago and fellow dissident; both have argued against forced busing and preferential treatment. In the early 1980s Wilson's *Declining Significance of Race*[23] shook many on the left (who had long maintained that black ghettos were chiefly perpetuated by ongoing "structural racism") with its controversial thesis that class position now plays a much larger role than race in determining black chances for economic advancement. Indeed, soon after the book won the American Sociological Association's prestigious Spivak Award, the outraged Association of Black Sociologists published a censure of Wilson, blasting the book's thesis, which, they held, could lead to "further suppression of blacks."[24] In 1987 Wilson again stirred things up, with *The Truly Disadvantaged*; its significance in the field was such that a conference was convened in 1989 to examine its thesis, one which drew a constellation of America's most noted social scientists.[25]

Other rebel voices have been heard:

—Anne Wortham, a sociologist whose debunking of "ethno-race consciousness" in *The Other Side of Racism* preceded Shelby Steele's *The Content of Our Character* by nearly a decade.

—Steele himself, who on the basis of his personal experiences and observations, has constructed an original and insurgent psychological model to account for the perversities of racial dynamics in America today.

—A cultural critic, Stanley Crouch, a writer for the *Village Voice*, whose panning of Spike Lee's movie *Do the Right Thing* ("for all its wit, the sort of rancid racist fairy tale one expects of the racist, whether or not Lee actually is one") scandalized the *Voice*.[26]

—Robert L. Woodson, architect of "neighborhood enterprise" projects in low-income areas across America, who has sought to expose what he views as the folly of anticapitalist solutions to black poverty advanced by the civil rights establishment.

—Jesse Peterson, a community activist, whose controversial Los Angeles radio show—which had boldly aired New Black Vanguard themes, including his view that antiwhite prejudice is rife and counterproductive—was pressured off the air by black ministers.

—Wisconsin state representative Polly Williams, whose "parental empowerment" school initiative in Milwaukee triumphed over "educrats," whose manic focus on desegregation, she argued, ignored the real educational needs of the poor.

—Emmanuel McLittle, whose audacious *Destiny* magazine counters "the destructive rhetoric of self-appointed black leaders" with articles that have regularly debunked affirmative action, rap music ("the most destructive phenomenon to hit the ear drums of Black American Youth"), and black victimization. ("It's high time we stopped acting like a victimized minority and started making meaningful inroads into the mainstream of American life.")[27]

—William Allen, a political scientist and former director of the U.S. Commission on Civil Rights, who is an eloquent voice in academia calling for African-Americans to resist race-consciousness and its balkanizing force and return to a full and vigorous participation in the American civil community. Allen's current (1992) candidacy in California for the U.S. Senate is conspicuously void of the racial themes so common in black political campaigns.

A wider and more diverse list of dissenters would include Orlando Patterson, Harvard sociology professor; Julius Lester, poet and academic; columnist William Raspberry; J. A. "Jay" Parker, founder of the Lincoln Institute; Bob Teague, New York television journalist; Allan Keyes, former resident scholar at the American Enterprise Institute, and president of Citizens Against Government Waste; Rev. Buster Soaries of New Jersey; Rep. Gary Franks of Connecticut; Ezola Foster, founder of Black Americans for Family Values; Randall Kennedy, Harvard law professor and editor of *Reconstruction* magazine; Elizabeth Wright, editor of *Issues and Views*; Stephen Carter, Yale law professor and author of *Reflections of an Affirmative Action Baby*. These thinkers have challenged many of the descriptive and prescriptive *fait accompli* of the civil rights establishment.

THE DEBUNKING PROJECT OF THE NEW BLACK VANGUARD

In light of all this diversity, both in tack and viewpoint, how can we speak of a coherent "New Black Vanguard"? While recognizing that their foci are diverse, we find a common intellectual disposition in these thinkers. At its most fundamental level, theirs is a *debunking project*. It is a protestation concerning the dominant, routinized racialist philosophy at work in America. It rejects the conventional wisdom that a liberal political agenda is identical with the best interests of black Americans, challenging the kind of thinking reflected in *Today Show* host Bryant Gumbel's statement that a "racism quiz" he was administering on a television special would indicate "if you're a racist or a liberal."[28]

In their unanimous opposition to preferential treatment policies, the rubric "neoconservative" has been carelessly appended to these black dissidents. Though the label does not sit well with all of them, and some, including Shelby Steele, have explicitly rejected it,[29] its application is not wholly inappropriate, at least when applied to selected aspects of their thought. For instance, most of them voice a definite distrust of, and dissatisfaction with, governmental instigation of political remedies—with "government-knows-best" policies, in Woodson's phrase. Moreover, they generally hold to a "constrained vision" of the human being that emphasizes "the moral limitations of man in general, and his egocentricity in particular."[30] This makes them leery of the social engineering of "intellectual-bureaucratic mandarins" (Sowell), who insist that their civic proposals are unflawed by self-interest.[31]

But perhaps the most telling feature many of them share with neoconservatives is their disillusionment with the radicalism of the 1960s and early 1970s, and the common lessons they personally gleaned from those dizzying years "at the barricades," in Steele's term. Many are, as the sarcastic phrase goes, "liberals who have been mugged by reality."[32] Some of their "second thoughts" on the black political culture of those times are encapsulated in Peter Collier and David Horowitz's *Second Thoughts: Former Radicals Look Back at the Sixties* (1989), which features retrospectives from Loury and Lester. Lester, an influential columnist in the 1960s for the New Left newspaper *The Guardian*, discussed in

Second Thoughts his surprise and disillusionment at the enforcement of "political correctness" in the Movement, after the honeymoon period.

> Second thoughts abounded now like wildflowers. Both the Black and White movements attacked individuals within their ranks more viciously than they attacked the administration in Washington. The personal had become political, and the gray-flanneled conformity of the Fifties was replaced by a blue-jeaned and Afroed totalitarianism.[33]

It is this perceived cognitive orthodoxy that the New Black Vanguard speaks against, with different, though similarly impassioned, voices. One cannot help but admire the sincerity of these voices; they are a minority within a minority, criticizing certain now-entrenched attitudes that, in the 1960s, spoke with romantic passion. The years have transformed those espousing these once-revolutionary viewpoints into what the New Black Vanguard perceives as imperious and doctrinaire sentinels of "proper" racial attitudes.

Black dissidents are unpopular underdogs, voicing opinions they know will be identified as from the enemy camp. "It has not been a pleasure to write this book but a necessity," begins Thomas Sowell in *Civil Rights: Rhetoric or Reality?* He adds, soberly, "Nothing is more certain than its distortion."[34] Writing well over a decade ago in *The Other Side of Racism*, Wortham began:

> Some people may conclude that my criticism of Negroes is a manifestation of hatred or contempt for these people of my own race. Or it may be interpreted by some as a confession of shame I might feel in being a Negro. But any sensible person knows that criticism of Negroes cannot be automatically equated with antiblack sentiments. And only a moral coward would hold back valid criticism merely to escape the charge of being antiblack.[35]

Though charges of race betrayal continue to hound these dissenters into the 1990s, there is some indication that the tenor of the criticism is changing, partly as a response to the anti–political correctness movement of the early 1990s. On the editorial pages of major black newspapers across the country, something of a phenomenon has been emerging that may foretell a larger social trend; while writers are still very critical of many New Black Vanguard figures and themes, their diatribes are now regularly mitigated by nods to the reality of political diversity within the black community. This may not seem like much, but it is a definite break from the cavalier *ad hominem* dismissals of dissidents as turncoat "Uncle Toms," that characterized many such editorial pages in the past.

Of course, credibility is hard won in an intellectual climate as politicized and intellectually stifling as today's liberal academy. For example Andrew Hacker, in his bestselling tome on the immorality of America, *Two Nations*, can muster no more than one small paragraph in explanation of black conservatism. Alleging that black conservatives are nothing but the dupes of heartless white conservatives, Hacker gravely notes:

> Since [white conservatives] see themselves as bearing no onus for whatever problems blacks face, they do not really care if blacks feel aggrieved or unfairly treated. To support their position, they cite black conservatives . . . who assure them that blacks have played the victim too long and must be judged by the same standards as other Americans.[36]

What can we say to Hacker's unreflective and wholesale dismissal of these thoughtful scholars? Is the Hoover Institution stupid to keep Sowell, this servant on the plantation of white conservatism, around? Are the faculties of Harvard and Boston universities too politically unaware to recognize that Loury's thought functions only to palliate the consciences of white conservatives? Hardly. We can only conclude that, paradoxically, it is Hacker who is using black conservatives, as chessmen in his heroic polemic against white conservatives.

But for their part, the dissidents insist that they do not intend to fashion a new procrustean bed of "orthodox" thought. According to Sowell, the dissidents desire "to explore alternatives, not to create a new orthodoxy with its own messiahs and its own excommunications of those who dare think for themselves."[37]

Though this book draws on the works of scores of dissident thinkers, its special foci are those of Sowell, Loury, Steele, and Woodson. Their emphases amount to a holistic and complementary analysis of the state of African-American welfare and advocacy, from a dissenting vantage. In the next few pages, we briefly profile each of these authors.

Thomas Sowell

Unquestionably, the father of this intellectual rebellion against civil rights orthodoxy is Thomas Sowell. "Mr. Sowell," affirms social critic Michael Novak, "shatters more icons and clichés per chapter than any heretic in recent memory."[38] For over a decade, Sowell has been regarded in conservative and libertarian circles as something of a one-man wrecking crew of Potemkin villages. Among his regular targets: Marxism, the "knowledge class," and entitlement programs, such as Penn State's innovative plan to pay each black student $580 for subtle grade improvements, such as from C to C+.[39]

It is in the old scholastic motto "The perfect is the enemy of the good" that we have something like the watchword of Sowell's debunking project. He argues that the "expert solutions" to social problems supplied by liberal policy analysts (whom he regularly scorns in his syndicated column as "the deep thinkers") are rooted in an anthropological optimism that is counterempirical. In contrast with this "unconstrained vision" of human being, which drives toward the alleged perfectibility of society, Sowell argues for a "constrained vision" of human potential that acknowledges human limitations and self-interest, and for social policy that incorporates these.[40]

A "constrained vision" patently informs Sowell's views on affirmative action. Studying affirmative action from a transnational perspective, Sowell found a disturbing constant in the data: racial anger and violence is intensified in countries where these policies have been pursued. Sowell's conclusion: By providing special privilege through law to certain groups of people, race-conscious policies work to rend the social fabric of a society.[41] What the optimistic "unconstrained visionaries" do not take into account, Sowell maintains, is the latent resentment generated by race-based policies. Based on these transnational findings, Sowell's prognosis for race relations in America is dire, should affirmative action continue to proliferate.

Currently a senior fellow at the Hoover Institution at Stanford University, Sowell has taught economics at Amherst, Cornell, Brandeis, and UCLA. Of poverty in America he writes, "[Poverty] statistics we hear thrown around by deep thinkers and moralizers do not represent permanent classes of people. Being poor is not like being left-handed or brown-eyed. You are not that way for life."[42] In his "political glossary" he ironically defines a matter of principle as "a political controversy involving the convictions of liberals" and an emotional issue as "a political controversy involving the convictions of conservatives."[43]

Glenn C. Loury

Political economist Glenn C. Loury is a conservative who is profoundly disappointed with the lack of passion he sees in some other conservatives on the issue of the underclass. Loury regards such passionlessness as a betrayal of a compassionate stance, as he is convinced that a vital conservatism is best suited to solving underclass problems. Still, his frustration with the right is matched by his annoyance with the left—with liberals who believe that "compassionate conservatism" is a cruel oxymoron, and who dismiss, a priori, antipoverty talk by conservatives as naive or hypocritical. The latter impression especially piques Loury, as illustrated in the following acerbic exchange between him and Michael Myers, a proponent of affirmative-action solutions and founder of the Research & Advocacy Center for Equality (RACE):

> M.M.: I think that the record is very clear, and the effect of Mr. Reagan's policies on the poor people Professor Loury appears to have an interest in . . .
>
> G.L.: Oh, of course I don't *really* have an interest in them. I'm just feigning interest in them. But someone like you, who happens to be a liberal, is *really* interested in poor people.[44]

Loury's sarcasm is clearly pointing to what he perceives as an underlying assumption, one that he finds objectionable: that liberals naturally have the moral high ground in black advocacy and that conservatives are dealing in subterfuge. In other words, conservatives, merely by virtue of their conservatism, have ulterior motives and are not truly interested in helping the poor.

One of the primary themes of Loury's work is the distinction he makes between the "enemy without" (racism) and the "enemy within." He defines the latter as "the dysfunctional behavior of young blacks that perpetuates poverty and dependency."[45] Another critical theme in his work is dignity. When Loury exalts dignity as a personal and social good, he intentionally distinguishes it from invocations of "black pride." Instead, he prefers the language of classical communitarianism, which values associations and shared commitments just as it values self-determination and autonomy.

Raised on Chicago's South Side, Loury taught at the John F. Kennedy School of Government, Harvard University, before his move to Boston University in 1990. On neighborhood deterioration, he writes:

> Those of us who, with trepidation, return to the places where we were raised, now communities unlike any we had known, who look despairingly at the tenements which once housed poor families in dignity but no longer do, and who, having found a long though unsatisfying list of whites to blame for this state of affairs are still bewildered at the profound changes

that have occurred in less than a generation, [should speak out]. We remain unwilling to express that bewilderment, or to ask today's residents: *"How can you live like this?"* We are a part of this conspiracy.[46]

On scapegoating he writes:

We act as though the historical fact of slavery and the associated culpability of America have endowed us with a fully paid insurance policy excusing whatever behavior now ensues: Every personal failing of blacks (even the illegal behavior of corrupt politicians) becomes evidence of the discrimination of whites, every individual success is taken to be an exceptional event. And in this we have been encouraged by the Left.[47]

Shelby Steele

While journalistic accounts of Shelby Steele's work tend to concentrate on his debunking of preferential treatment, Steele's most original contribution to race-relations discourse is his discussion of the experience of American blacks from an existential frame. Intrinsic to the existential critique of personal existence is the perception of life as individually lived and individually determined. Within the broad tradition of existentialism (both theistic and atheistic) there is an essentially wholesale rejection of behavioral determinism. Neither race nor class nor religion nor even law is a legitimate usurper of individual choice and the moral accountability inseparably tied to it. In light of that perspective, Steele regards the deterministic idea that racial identity is a critical element of personal identity—a primary assumption of the civil rights establishment—as completely absurd.

A demonstration of Steele's accessible existentialism can be found in a fascinating exchange of letters published in *Emerge* magazine between Steele and poet-playwright Amiri Baraka (formerly LeRoi Jones), a leading light of the 1960s Black Power movement. This exchange illustrates, in brief, the ideological confrontation in the black community.

Baraka: Steele . . . tells us, like David Rockefeller, that "the only way we will see advancement of black people . . . is for us to focus on developing ourselves as individuals and embracing opportunity." . . . Of course it has long been the whine of house Negroes that they are individuals, not to be confused with *common* field niggers. It is the cry of the most reactionary sector of the bourgeoisie, that they, indeed, ain't with the rest of us woogies. All black and poor and stinking like that! . . . For the mass of us the struggle continues, not because of our "bad attitude" but because we are being oppressed. And it is Steele's backward class stance that is expressed when he openly describes his alienation from the historic and just struggle of the African-American masses. He sees the black national revolutionary stance as a "wartime" stance. It is!

Steele: Amiri Baraka, that mad Marxist rapper, thinks of me as a neo-con "twit." . . . But only one of us can be right, and I think Baraka has stayed too long at the barricades. . . . Am I saying that racial oppression no longer exists, that white racism has vanished from the American landscape? Hell, no! . . . [Yet] I believe we are freer than we think, and that the white man is nowhere as omnipotent as he used to be. Can he hurt us? Of course. Can he stop us for long? No way. Will it be as easy for us to advance as it is for him? No. Can we advance anyway? Yes. Is this fair? Not at all. Is this reality? Absolutely.[48]

One of Steele's most important analytical components is his exposition of what he calls "the harangue-flagellation ritual." This cycle of black accusations of racism and white confessions of guilt produces an inveterate "victim identity" that supersensitizes blacks to discrimination, resulting in what Steele calls "a new class of supervictims who can feel the pea of victimization under twenty mattresses."[49] Perhaps something of this supersensitivity can be seen in a comment by Jesse Jackson during his post-riot tour of Los Angeles. When told by a reporter that some residents had seen an opportunistic motive for his visit to the city (where, among other things, he appealed to church groups for funds for his Rainbow Coalition), Jackson replied that he had been "speaking to thousands and giving them hope," that he "had been in public leadership for thirty two years," and that the very suggestion of his being opportunistic had "racist assumptions."[50] But why "*racist* assumptions"? Is the charge of opportunism so rarely leveled against political figures that, when applied to Jesse Jackson, it must carry something other than its prima facie meaning, that is, it can only be a racist remark, masquerading as a serious criticism?

Steele is a professor of English at San Jose State University in San Jose, California. On white liberals he writes:

Watch out that your closest friend may be your greatest enemy, is my feeling about liberals, because they encourage us to identify with our victimization. It is one thing to be victimized; it is another to make an identity out of it.[51]

On the effects of racism upon blacks he writes:

I think being lower class has a much greater impact [than racism]. You and I both know, as a middle-class black you can send your kid to any school you want. But if you and I were on the South Side of Chicago and not doing very well economically, then clearly you would not be able to send your kid to whatever school you wanted.[52]

Robert L. Woodson

Robert L. Woodson, founder of the National Center for Neighborhood Enterprise, is perhaps the most widely quoted advocate of "interior activism" in America today. Woodson's activism seeks to deploy the resources of the voluntary sector to solve neighborhood problems. Called the "dean of self-help activism,"[53] Woodson holds that one of the worst results of "government-knows-best" policies for black Americans is that they have buried, under a mountain of paltry welfare checks, the rich legacy of black entrepreneurship in America. At the turn of the century, he points out, blacks owned and controlled more than $60 million in Harlem real estate.[54] He argues that this heritage of vital black capitalism, thriving even in adversity, provides a template for a contemporary renascence in black "neighborhood enterprise," which he sees as the best hope for the underclass. "Above all," argues Woodson, "the black community must disentangle itself from the welfare professionals whose primary objective has become the maintenance of clients."[55]

Woodson is a former fellow of the American Enterprise Institute and currently chairs the Council for a Black Economic Agenda, in addition to directing the National Center for Neighborhood Enterprise.
On poverty programs he writes:

It is the government bureaucracy which feeds and shields the welfare state. Since Lyndon Johnson's War on Poverty began in the 1960's we have spent more than a trillion dollars in . . . aid to the poor. Twenty years ago, if you had predicted that such generous aid would fail to cure the problem, you would have been ridiculed. . . . Ironically, we are now faced with the problem of how to help the poor survive their champions.[56]

On black politicians and corruption he writes:

When they get caught engaging in illegal actions, they pull out their "civil rights credit card" and charge that off, saying, "We want to be exempt from this." A lot of the civil rights folks said, "We want to be 'judged by the content of our character, not by the color of our skin.' But when they get caught stealing money intended for poor folks, they say, "No, no, no!

We want to be judged by the color of our skin—because if we are judged by the content of our character, we won't make it."[57]

NOTES

1. "Jackson Sees Clinton 'Flaw' in Rapper Attack," *Los Angeles Times*, 19 June 1992.

2. *Los Angeles Times*, 12 August 1991, p. B8.

3. *TV Etc.* 4, no. 6 (June 1992): 8.

4. It should be pointed out that some of the dissidents, notably Anne Wortham, see their ideas as directed not to the black community as such, but toward all people. Thus, these thinkers would be uncomfortable with the designation "interior" activism.

5. For a description of the contributions of Booker T. Washington, Frederick Douglass, and W. E. B. Du Bois, see Ethelbert W. Haskins, *The Crisis in Afro-American Leadership* (Buffalo, N.Y.: Prometheus, 1988), pp. 71–126.

6. E. L. Thornbrough, ed., *Booker T. Washington* (Englewood Cliffs, N. J.: Prentice-Hall, 1969), p. 57.

7. Clint Bolick, *Changing Course: Civil Rights at the Crossroads* (New Brunswick, N.J.: Transaction Books, 1988).

8. Clint Bolick, *In Whose Name? The Civil Rights Establishment Today* (Washington, D.C.: Capital Research Center, 1988), pp. 7–8.

9. This summary is patterned after Anne Wortham's discussion in *The Other Side of Racism* (Columbus, Ohio: Ohio State University Press, 1981), pp. 302–333.

10. Although these groups bear no explicitly articulated common goal, aside from the general goal of 'advancing black interests,' they do have common philosophical allegiances, as we have described. Even though these groups frequently are involved in separate projects, when their efforts are united, they constitute powerful social force. Their frenzied assault on the Supreme Court nominations of Robert Bork and Clarence Thomas are the most notable recent examples of their uniting forces.

11. Bolick, *In Whose Name?* p. xi.

12. Glenn C. Loury, "Black Dignity and the Common Good," *First Things*, June/July 1990, p. 13.

13. Murray Friedman, "The New Black Intellectuals," *Commentary*, June 1980, p. 46.

14. Thomas Sowell, *Pink and Brown People* (Stanford, Calif.: Hoover Institution Press, 1981), p. 22.

15. "Thomas Sowell," in *Current Biography*, edited by Charles Moritz (New York: H. W. Wilson), 1981, p. 390.

16. Robert Detlefsens's phrase in *Civil Rights under Reagan* (San Francisco: Institute for Contemporary Studies Press, 1991).

17. *Newsweek*, 10 September 1991, p. 27.

18. Loury, "Black Dignity and the Common Good," p. 18.

19. See Glenn C. Loury, "A New American Dilemma," *New Republic*, 31 December 1984, pp. 14–22.

20. Walter Williams, *All It Takes Is Guts* (Washington, D.C.: Regnery-Gateway, 1987), p. 111.

21. Walter Williams, "Reply to Dan Smith," in *The Fairmont Papers* (San Francisco: Institute for Contemporary Studies Press, 1980), p. 104.

22. Walter Williams, "Rioting Must Be Met with Strict Force," *Orange Country Register*, 6 May 1992.

23. William Julius Wilson, *Declining Significance of Race: Blacks and Changing American Institutions* (Chicago: University of Chicago Press, 1980).

24. Loury quotes from the A.B.S. in "The 'Color Line' Today," *Public Interest*, no. 80, (Summer 1985), p. 97.

25. The papers presented during this conference were collected in Christopher Jencks and Paul E. Peterson, eds., *The Urban Underclass* (Washington, D.C.: Brookings Institution, 1991).

26. Stanley Crouch, *Notes from a Hanging Judge* (New York: Oxford University Press, 1990), p. 239.

27. *Destiny*, December/January 1990–1991.

28. *Media-Watch*, April 1991, p. 7.

29. See "Shelby Steele Replies," *Dissent*, Fall 1990, p. 522. Steele rejects the neoconservative tag in his reply to a critique of his work by Martin Kilson. See Martin Kilson "Realism About the Black Experience: A Reply to Shelby Steele," *Dissent*, Fall 1990, p. 522.

30. Thomas Sowell, *A Conflict of Visions* (New York: Morrow, 1987), p. 20.

31. Sowell, *Pink and Brown People*, p. 49.

32. Stuart M. Butler and Anna Kondratas, *Out of the Poverty Trap: A Conservative Strategy for Welfare Reform* (New York: Free Press, 1987), p. 2. Of course some, for example Anne Wortham, never subscribed to the popular civil rights ideology in the first place. She is an interesting figure in that, from the time she first began writing on civil rights issues in 1963, her concerns have been primarily philosophical rather than pragmatic. Writing in defense of individualist liberalism, she considers herself distinct from neoconservatives, pragmatic conservatives, and existentialists.

33. Julius Lester, "Beyond Ideology," in *Second Thoughts: Former Radicals Look Back at the Sixties*, edited by Peter Collier and David Horowitz (New York: Madison Books, 1989), p. 218.

34. Thomas Sowell, *Civil Rights: Rhetoric or Reality?* (New York: Quill, 1984), p. 1.

35. Wortham, *The Other Side of Racism*, p. xi.

36. Andrew Hacker, *Two Nations: Black and White, Separate, Hostile, Unequal* (New York: Scribner's, 1992), pp. 51–52.

37. Thomas Sowell, "Politics and Opportunity: The Background," in *The Fairmont Papers*, p. 4.

38. "Thomas Sowell," in *Current Biography*, p. 391.

39. George F. Will, "The Stab of Racial Doubt," *Newsweek*, 24 September 1990.

40. Sowell, *Conflict of Visions*, pp. 19–25.

41. See Emile Durkheim's idea of society's "collective conscience," as discussed in Peter Berger, *The Precarious Vision* (Garden City, N.Y.: Doubleday, 1961), pp. 102–4.

42. Thomas Sowell, *Compassion versus Guilt* (New York: Morrow, 1987), p. 98.

43. Ibid., p. 126.

44. "Pride and Prejudice: A Scholar and an Activist Face Off," *Esquire*, December 1986, p. 234.

45. Glenn C. Loury, "Black Dignity and the Common Good," p. 15.

46. Glenn C. Loury, "Black Political Culture after the Sixties," in *Second Thoughts: Former Radicals Look Back at the Sixties,* edited by Peter Collier and David Horowitz (Lanham, Md.: Madison Books, 1989), p. 141. Emphasis in the original.

47. Ibid., p. 142.

48. *Emerge*, February 1991, pp. 44–49.

49. Will, "Stab of Racial Doubt," p. 86.

50. *Los Angeles Times*, 6 May 1992, p. A5.

51. *Time*, 12 August 1991, p. 6.

52. Ibid., p. 8.

53. Vanessa Gallman, "Self Help." *Destiny,* December/January 1990–1991, p. 29.

54. Robert L. Woodson, *On the Road to Economic Freedom* (Washington, D.C.: Regnery-Gateway, 1987), p. 4.

55. Ibid., p. 22.

56. Robert L. Woodson, "Poverty: Why Politics Can't Cure It," *Imprimis*, a publication of Hillsdale College, Hillsdale, Michigan. 17, no. 7 (July 1988): 1.

57. *Tony Brown's Journal*, 11 August 1991.

2

ASPECTS OF NEW BLACK VANGUARD THOUGHT

intimations of racism in every leaf that falls
Jim Sleeper, *The Closest of Strangers*

During 1970 and 1971 angry black leaders were in demand on the lecture circuit. [One of them] traveled to Detroit and Baltimore to display his rage to admiring audiences.
Scott C. Davis, *The World of Patience Gromes*

As noted, the New Black Vanguard is not a monolithic voice. The spectrum of opinion includes elements of neoconservative, libertarian, populist, and liberal thought. So it is that none of the following axioms necessarily represents a unanimity of opinion by dissenters from the civil rights establishment. Nevertheless, their body of dissent from the civil rights ideology does exhibit some coherent themes, as follows:

1. The New Black Vanguard rejects the deterministic notion that race unavoidably conditions individual thinking.
   Those who oppose the usual civil rights methods regard the charge of racial betrayal—the charge that expressing opposing opinions serves whites not blacks—as an illegitimate insistence that only certain thought patterns and ideas are appropriate for those who are black. As such, the usual civil rights thinking constitutes a kind of tyranny of the mind, a muzzling of alternative, and potentially salutary, ideas. Denying that their dissent from the civil rights establishment constitutes a disservice to the black community, the New Black Vanguard stands that charge on its head: By overrelying on resources exterior to the black

community, the popular viewpoint is inherently limited in what it may accomplish. Opposing the myth of racial betrayal, the dissenters hold that the opening-up of discourse to include alternative, *minority*-minority voices creates a healthy tension among ideas that works to advance black interests.

An example of the sort of criticism directed at the dissenters can be found in a remark by journalist Carl T. Rowan on the work of Thomas Sowell: "Vidkun Quisling in his collaboration with the Nazis surely did not do as much damage to the Norwegians as Sowell is doing to the most helpless of black Americans."[1] Rowan's criticism is paradigmatic, both in rhetoric and presupposition, of the kind of remarks directed at dissident black viewpoints. As such, it bears some scrutiny.

One can only marvel at this nearly revolutionary flash of racial partisanship on the part of Rowan. Does he really believe that the state of race relations in America today is tantamount to genocidal oppression?[2] If so, perhaps he should put down his pen, don a bandanna, and lead a mob to sack the capitol. But of course Rowan's intentions are not so grand, and his analogy not literal. But the symbolism of his analogy betrays the extreme nature of his guiding presupposition, which is that the interests of blacks can only be faithfully served by one particular set of opinions. So those who disagree with Rowan, like it or not, must assume the mantle of racial quisling. They are damned by their very thoughts, and not by any empirical demonstration of inaccuracy or evidential substantiation of personal ill will.

It seems that the effective contention of Rowan, and those who think like him, is that true black advocacy is cognitively monolithic, that is, univocal in its understanding of the nature of black interests and the consciousness that results from "the black experience." This dominant view insists on a *specific* ideological disposition from each individual black woman and man. It represents a kind of collective identity that subsumes any individual objection or disaffection, the result being that those who reject, on the basis of personal conscience, the dominant view are seen not as a well-intentioned cognitive minority, but rather as a seditious threat to the family of race. A clear example of this was cited in *Outrage: The Story Behind the Tawana Brawley Hoax*, coauthored by six reporters from the *New York Times*. At one point, black journalists who had reported facts that called into question the authenticity of Tawana Brawley's "nightmare" were confronted by angry Brawley supporters, who called them "Uncle Toms" and "traitors" for not rubber-stamping Brawley's story.[3] To them, the reporters were guilty of a heinous race-betrayal for merely questioning the words of a black woman. Such a response recalls sociologist Peter L. Berger's idea of ideology—in this case, a racial ideology—as "constitut[ing] the official self-interpretations of entire social groups, obligatory for their members on pain of excommunication."[4] Apostates from an unquestioning ideology of victimhood in the eyes of Brawley's supporters, the reporters were to be "excommunicated" from the body of authentic black consciousness.

The commitment to racialist ideology is seen in Rowan's remark as well. Rowan's charges are reminiscent of the early 1960s racist charge of "nigger-lover" that white bigots levelled at pro–civil rights whites who joined Afro-Americans in freedom marches in the South. Like today's black dissenters, these courageous whites were charged with betraying the interests of their own race and damaging their collective social posture, merely for stating facts. Nat Hentoff writes of one such instance:

> I remember . . . Herbert Hill, the fierce labor secretary of the NAACP [in the 1950s] who relentlessly—with reams upon reams of facts—exposed racial discrimination in the trade unions, and that meant nearly all of them. Some of the labor leaders were surprised, and even more angered . . . when they found out that Herb was white.[5]

Similar pressures to conform are exerted on blacks by the dominant orthodoxy of today's black leadership. Thus, the contrary views of the New Black Vanguard are regarded as a kind of philosophical Trojan Horse. The dissidents are seen as representing the interests of the mistrusted "white establishment" even though they outwardly bear the marks of racial qualification.

Julius Lester sees this enforcement of political correctness in the black community as a fairly recent phenomenon. As he recalls in *Falling Pieces of the Broken Sky*,

> Twenty-five years ago . . . the Reverend Dr. Martin Luther King, Malcolm X, Adam Clayton Powell, Roy Wilkens, Whitney Young, James Farmer, and the Student Nonviolent Coordinating Committee, among others, argued and publicly debated the philosophies, tactics, and strategies of the civil-rights movement. The arguments were bitter, but the fact of disagreement was accepted as normal.
>
> Such debate and diversity of opinion are absent today. When a student at the School of Art Institute in Chicago exhibited a painting satirizing the late mayor Harold Washington, the school removed the painting after an

angry reaction from blacks. Yet, neither the Reverend Jesse Jackson nor any other black leader objected.[6]

Closer to home, black colleagues at the University of Massachusetts asked in 1988 that Lester be "reassigned" from his teaching position in the Department of Afro-American Studies to another department. Though the stated reason was the alleged "deliberate misrepresentation" of James Baldwin in Lester's then just-published *Lovesong: Becoming a Jew* (which described his conversion to Judaism), Lester finds a more credible explanation in remarks from the chair of the Department of Afro-American Studies, quoted in the *Amherst Bulletin*: "We have nothing against his Judaism, . . . but when one develops a vicious attitude toward blacks and black organizations, Jackson, Baldwin, and civil rights, there is some question as to the appropriateness of his remaining in the department."[7] Lester never denied the heterodox character of his viewpoint vis à vis that of his department colleagues—but, he asked, was not "the role of the intellectual to be independent of ideology so as to be better able to describe whatever aspect of reality he or she chose to examine"?[8] Such questioning would prove his undoing in the department. After a long period of "shunning," whereby colleagues in the department made it known that he was not welcome among them, Lester joined another department at the university.

The ostracism of black thinkers who dissent from the civil rights establishment becomes especially curious in light of surveys that show that, on key policy issues, the black public also dissents from its putative leadership. For instance, when *Washington Post* pollsters asked whether minorities should receive preferential treatment to make up for past discrimination, 77 percent of black leaders said yes, while an equal percentage of the black public said no. Asked about the death penalty, 55 percent of the black public favored it, but only 33 percent of black leaders. On forced school busing, 68 percent of black leaders approved, while 53 percent of the black public disapproved. On the other survey questions, the black public persistently dissented from its leaders.[9]

Surprise at this incongruity would seem to confirm Walter Williams's contention that the media regularly misrepresents diversity of viewpoint among the black public by reifying the sentiments of 30 million people into that media archetype, the "black spokesperson," whose Black Viewpoint, says Williams, is a predictable species of social liberalism. Alternative viewpoints are tacitly diminished as pseudo-black. He notes sardonically:

When Jesse Jackson feeds the reporters a line like, "We're going from the outhouse to the White House," or "From disgrace to amazing grace," or some other inane rhyming preachment there's never a reportorial query, such as "What does that mean?" But let Dr. Thomas Sowell or me say, "Our investigations show the minimum wage has a devastating unemployment effect on black youth," and the media people ask all kinds of searching statistical and theoretical questions about our evidence. In fact, they even dig into our personal, financial, and educational backgrounds, the way they dig at . . . other leaders who dispute the views of the black "leadership."[10]

Remarks by a Harvard professor, Orlando Patterson, during the Clarence Thomas confirmation hearings also speak to this sorry reification. Noting the propagation of "a new form of racism that finds it hard to imagine African Americans not as a monolithic group," he makes an obvious point, but one at odds with the media's imaging of the Black Viewpoint, that African-Americans are a "diverse aggregate of perhaps 30 million individuals with all the class differences, strengths, flaws and ideologies we find in other large populations."[11]

The veiling of this diversity of opinion clearly serves the ends of civil rights groups, by allowing them to confront corporate sponsors with the Black Viewpoint, and on that basis, solicit financial support. Remarks Bolick, a keen observer of the sociology of civil rights organizations: "The civil rights establishment has been very effective at convincing corporations that access to the black community must be channelled through the civil rights groups."[12] Consequently, in 1985 the 25 largest corporations that revealed their philanthropic activities donated upwards of more than $2.6 million to mainstream civil rights organizations. This beneficence is in stark contrast to the $9,000 allowed the free market Lincoln Institute and Woodson's National Center for Neighborhood Enterprise.

2. *The New Black Vanguard argues that a chilling silence has been spread around a ghetto-specific culture by black advocates who fear that discussions about it will play into the hands of enemies of the black community. Such taboos on discussion, those in the Vanguard argue, at best conduce to ineffective social policy—at worst, to social engineering fiascoes.*

A benchmark moment in the history of American racial discourse occurred in 1965 with the publication of the commotion-causing *The Black Family: The Case for National Action* by Daniel P. Moynihan, now the Democratic senator from New York. Noting a sudden sharp rise in the number of single-parent black families, Moynihan suggested that this trend posed a threat to black progress in the coming years and would effectively close opportunities newly opened by civil rights victories.[13] For this analysis and prognosis, Moynihan drew heavy criticism, even vilification. Many academics, including William Ryan, a psychologist, accused him of "blaming the victim."[14] Others accused him of crypto-racism.

In a 1986 retrospective piece on the Moynihan controversy titled, "The Family, The Nation, and Senator Moynihan," Loury argued that the chilling effects of this caustic censuring had been felt in the social sciences for decades, effectively dissuading against bold critical discourse on black family issues.[15] In the rhetorical calculus of the late 1960s and early 1970s, for instance, a sociologist's call for attention to widespread unwed pregnancy would not infrequently be descrambled as "genocide." Rather than risk costly charges of crypto-racism, however unfounded, many academics played it safe, and shied away from controversial analyses. In this way, a multitude of topics related to black welfare were cordoned off from free inquiry, and nonconformist viewpoints suppressed. Of course, a good many scholars were genuinely persuaded by Ryan's rebuttal to Moynihan's thesis, but as a matter of record, says Loury, many dissenters were simply cowed into silence.

The sad irony, according to Loury, is that two decades after Moynihan's censure, the prescience of his thesis is beyond dispute.[16] William Julius Wilson, at odds with Loury on many issues, agrees with him on this one. "Aside from some problems in historical accounting," writes Wilson in *The Truly Disadvantaged,* "Moynihan's analysis . . . proved to be prophetic."[17] A broad consensus in agreement with Wilson and Loury has developed on the matter. The scoffing at Moynihan's thesis was not without consequence. James Q. Wilson notes, "Two decades that could have been devoted to thought and experimentation had been frittered away."[18]

The plausibility of Moynihan's hypothesis that rising out-of-wedlock pregnancies would have the effect of limiting the life-chances of many blacks, just when new opportunities were opening up, is emphatically confirmed by current demographic data. In 1959 about 2 percent of all black babies were born out of wedlock; today the percentage has risen to over 60 percent.

Robert L. Woodson believes this reflects an alarming deterioration in community ethos, and that it offers a damning commentary on the quality of black advocacy during the 1970s and 1980s. A radical "course correction" is needed, he argues, that particularly seeks the vitality and stability of the black family and boldly cautions black youth that poor personal choices may block opportunity as much as, or more than, the machinations of racists.[19] Reflecting on the present strategy of black leadership, which he sees as largely discredited by its track record, Shelby Steele argues that "their impulse is to be 'political,' to keep the larger society on edge, to keep them feeling as though they have not done enough for blacks."[20]

The media, especially, is kept "on edge," argues Sowell. Reporters, eager to avoid embarrassing and costly charges of masked racism, are inclined to handle issues in ways consonant with the civil rights establishment's vision of race relations in America, which means perpetuating the idea that "structural racism" is the biggest obstacle to black progress. Relative to race-related issues, the objections of dissidents, black or white, rarely make the six o'clock news; instead, dissidents are treated, says Sowell, as benighted "yokels or fascists."[21]

What does make the news is the rhetoric of victimization, which goes conspicuously unchallenged by reporters, who are desperate to avoid charges of racial insensitivity, even at the expense of objectivity. Such distortion was obvious in media coverage of the 1992 Los Angeles riots. One of the capital ironies of the coverage was the absence of the expres-sions "racially motivated violence" and "hate crime" on local Los Angeles news broadcasts during the seventy-two hours of bedlam—though these same expressions had long been nightly on the tongues of grave news anchors, with furrowed brows, reporting yet more minority victimization. The straitjacketing control of political correctness would not allow the suggestion that racism can be practiced by blacks.

But beyond this, says Sowell, the media deliberately supports the civil rights establishment—so much so that there "is a positive hostility to analyses of black success, when these cut across the grain of the civil rights vision."[22] Sowell's thesis finds confirmation by a team of social scientists in *Media and Business Elites* (1981) and *The Media Elite: America's New Power Brokers* (1986). S. Robert Lichter, Stanley Rothman, and Linda Lichter, investigating how journalists' ideological values influenced their reporting, interviewed 240 journalists affiliated with several major outlets comprising the "media elite," including the *New York Times*, the *Washington Post*, and the three television networks. Of these "media elite" journalists, 80 percent favored affirmative action for blacks.[23] In another survey, the three social scientists asked journalists "where they would turn for reliable information" if they were doing a story on welfare reform. The reporters' choices were "weighted heavily toward the liberal end. Three out of four journalists mention at least one liberal source [as a reliable guide to welfare reform]. In sharp contrast, fewer than one in four cites a conservative source."[24]

In addition to ideological fidelity, media coverage of racial issues is shaped by pressure tactics, according to Clint Bolick. "I see the media as being extremely intimidated. They like to be politically correct as much as possible." For instance, says Bolick, when self-styled "community representatives" protested the *Washington Post*'s failure to portray blacks in a "positive" light in its Sunday magazine, the pressure paid off instantly; now every third issue of the *Washington Post*'s Sunday magazine has a "positive" cover story of a black subject. Bolick comments, "It's amazing how quickly they will knuckle under—it doesn't matter if these groups don't really represent anyone. They are perceived as doing so."[25] Of course, the community representatives' concept of what is a "positive" image of blacks is partisan, skewed to the left. It is unlikely they would find Sowell's opposition to their self-appointment "positive."

At the heart of all these phenomena there is a distorting racial protocol. Reporters, usually quick to dig for evidence of hypocrisy and deception, often check their scepticism at the door when the news conference inside has bee called to air claims of minority victimization. This suspension of journalistic rigor is partly due to the sensational copy to be had (victims and conspiracy theories cadge large audiences) and partly due to the fear that critical scrutiny of such claims could be labeled "racially motivated."

This idea is clearly articulated in the following comment from investigative reporter Chris Blatchford, winner of the prestigious Peabody Award:

> In twenty-two years as a broadcast journalist in a number of major cities in the United States, and somebody who has covered a lot of investigative news and a lot of political news, there is no question in my mind that white reporters and black reporters (but white reporters in particular) have often refrained from asking the tough questions of black politicians or black activists, for one simple reason: fear of being branded a racist. . . . At times when sent to do a story in a minority community, I have been told, "Make sure you put a positive spin on it." Nobody ever says that about anything else.[26]

Earlier we referred to the "blaming the victim" syndrome, as conceived by William Ryan. Ryan's *Blaming the Victim* (1972) was intended, at least in part, as a reply to the famous "culture of poverty" thesis expounded by sociologist Oscar Lewis. This is the core of Lewis's controversial thesis, in Lewis's own words:

> Once the culture of poverty has come into existence it tends to perpetuate itself. By the time slum children are six or seven they have usually absorbed the basic attitudes and values of their subculture. Thereafter they are psychologically unready to take full advantage of changing conditions or improving opportunities that may develop in their lifetime.[27]

Ryan found Lewis's conclusion "very disturbing." While appreciating the disclaimer that only one in five of America's poor is actually caught in a "culture of poverty," Ryan regarded Lewis's central thesis as driving toward unjust public policy—in brief, it "blamed the victim":

> If poverty is to be understood more clearly in terms of a way of life of the poor, in terms of a lower class culture, as a product of a deviant value system, then money is clearly not the answer. We can stop right now worrying about ways of redistributing our resources more equitably, and begin focusing our attention on where it belongs—on the poor themselves.[28]

Civil rights leaders joined in Ryan's rebuke of Lewis's "culture of poverty" thesis, agreeing with Ryan that ghetto residents were being held back by material disadvantages, not by a chimerical, self-generating "culture of poverty." Ryan and others were especially outraged at the suggestion that high rates of illegitimate births among the poor could be attributed to features of a ghetto subculture. Ryan insisted that should "access to the knowledge and resources required for family planning" become available to the poor through family planning programs, teenage pregnancy rates among the poor would decline significantly.[29]

But, say the dissenters, pregnancy rates have not declined, despite the wide availability, in the quarter-century since Ryan's writing, of free birth control information in low-income neighborhoods, and the wide availability of free or nominal-cost contraceptives to residents. This macrosociological evidence, say the dissidents, contradicts Ryan's diagnosis. And on a microsociological level (where personal interviews are especially valued as evidence), Ryan's debunking of Lewis's "culture of poverty" thesis appears equally shaky. Here dissidents point to the evidence of streetwise studies, such as Leon Dash's year-long investigation into teenage pregnancy in 1984 for the *Washington Post*. At the outset of his study, Dash shared Ryan's belief that "the high incidence of teenage pregnancy among poor, black urban youth nationwide grew out of youthful ignorance about birth-control methods and reproductive capabilities."[30] He was disabused of this misconception, he confesses, during his first few interviews. His conversation with sixteen-year-old Tauscha was typically enlightening:

> For an hour I kept asking questions about what teenagers know, don't know, or misunderstand about contraceptives. Obviously tiring of my probing, Tauscha leaned forward over the coffee table and looked at me as if I were a naive child.
> She spoke in a husky voice: "Mr. Dash, will you please stop asking me about birth control? Girls out here know all about birth control. There's too many birth control pills out here. All of them know about it. Even when they twelve, they know what [birth control] is. Girls out here get pregnant because they *want* to have babies! You need to know what's going on inside people's homes these days!"[31]

A particularly remarkable corollary to Tauscha's reporting was supplied by a black businessman on a Los Angeles talk show in the wake of the 1992 riots. The interviewee, who owned several fast-food restaurants in South Central Los Angeles that had been looted and burned, reflected on family breakdown in the area and its role in creating the conditions that gave rise to the social collapse. He related a conversation he had had with a customer before the riots. She was a pregnant fifteen-year-old girl whose mother had given birth to her, out of wedlock, when *she* was fifteen, and whose grandmother had given birth to her mother when *she* was fifteen and unmarried. When asked about this trend, the young girl responded with a glint of defiant pride, "It's a tradition!"[32]

Finding similar indications from other studies persuasive, many black dissidents regard Lewis's "culture of poverty" analysis as generally credible. While not denying that external forces are factors in black poverty, the dissidents believe that certain features of ghetto-specific culture dissuade many ghetto residents from taking full advantage of the opportunities opened up by civil rights victories. Loury asks:

> Does anyone seriously argue today that the current illiteracy rates in excess of 40 percent among young black mothers arise because of racism? Are we to understand the growth in welfare dependency in this population, to the point that in most cities more than one half of all black children are supported in part by AFDC, as the consequence of an external, societal failure?[33]

As is clear in Loury's question, the dissidents are frustrated by what they regard as obscurantist denials of a "culture of poverty." They have been further astonished and alarmed when these "denials" have been transfigured into passionate panegyrics to "street culture" by activists and sociologists. Harvard sociologist Orlando Patterson marvelled at this trend, which bloomed during the 1970s:

> Black American ethnicity has encouraged the intellectual reinforcement of some of the worst sociological problems of the group and an incapacity to distinguish the things that are worthwhile in black life from those that are just plain rotten. The "street culture" of petty crime, drug addiction, paternal irresponsibility, whoring, pimping and super-fly inanity—all of which damage and destroy only fellow blacks—instead of being condemned by black ethnic leaders has, until recently, been hailed as the embodiment of black "soul."[34]

The dissidents generally see the denial and/or rhapsodic treatment of the "culture of poverty" as a strategic move on the part of certain strands of black advocacy. For the civil rights establishment to admit the existence of an injurious "culture of poverty" would be to falsify its own claim that the black underclass is essentially a passive victim-class, blocked at every turn by "structural racism." As such, recognition of a ghetto-specific culture would make the civil rights establishment's trademark "external activism" appear misdirected.

Consistent with denial of a "culture of poverty," a black advocacy of "external activism" typically advances public policy initiatives that take a "value free" approach to helping the poor. But "value free" social policy, contends Loury, often buttresses the very values and cultural forces that fuel poverty. He points to the debate in 1984 over the New York Board of Education's proposed course of instruction in "Family Living Including Sex Education for Grades K–12." Conservative local clergy protested that the course's dogmatically nonnormative perspective was a contradiction in terms, and that it would redound to the devaluation of the traditional family. But the *New York Times* defended the course, editorializing that instruction favoring intact families would offend many students, since according to public health care surveys, around 79 percent of Harlem children had mothers who were not married. Loury objects to the underlying presuppositions of the *Times'* position, questioning whether the 79 percent rate were something the public school should simply present as a fact about the world,

Or does it, rather, call for a concerted effort to teach the values of the traditional family even (or perhaps especially) to those children least likely to see them confirmed in their private lives at home? Can there be an effective family policy which takes *no* position on such an issue?[35]

Essentially, what the civil rights establishment is discouraging in a multitude of ways, assert the dissenters, is a serious discussion of the flip side of social entitlement, which is personal responsibility. Journalists, television reporters, and newscasters all play along, not venturing to ask hard questions. A chilling silence ensues, further forbidding discussion. This strikes Loury as an updated version of the "Moynihan treatment":

To invoke such terms as "values," "character," or "social pathology," in speaking about the poor (black or otherwise) is still today to invite the charge of blaming the victim or, if the speaker is black, of being an Uncle Tom. Remarkably, one still encounters the same line that was used to dismiss Moynihan twenty years ago—namely, that acknowledging a behavioral basis to economic deprivation feeds stereotypes about blacks and provides grist for the racists' mill. It is as if the facts about inner-city life, staggeringly evident to anyone with eyes to see, could be blunted by simply banning any discussion of them from polite society.[36]

Jesse Peterson, founder of the Brotherhood Organization of a New Destiny (BOND), agrees with Loury. Based in Los Angeles, Peterson's organization is dedicated to "reclaiming an outlook within the black man, one that emphasizes objectivity and personal initiative."[37] Peterson claims that many black leaders have a vested interest in hushing public discussion of ghetto dysfunction and a "culture of poverty" because they can get more political mileage out of rousing community resentment against "enemies" outside the community than by objectively and self-critically discussing dysfunction within.[38] Sowell agrees. "Politicians who represent slums or ghettos are not going to get cheers or votes by saying that the basic problems of these communities are in the communities themselves."[39]

Peterson makes this specific:

Illiteracy and out-of-wedlock pregnancies are tearing our community apart. They just give an extra spin to the cycle of poverty and welfare dependence. But instead of facing this problem directly, and seeing it as a failure *within* the black community, we blame "the system" or white racism. How can we honestly blame white people, for instance, for black teenage pregnancies? When we do that, we are basically saying that we have no moral authority over our own children. Perhaps we have to face the unpleasant possibility that we *have* lost authority over them.[40]

Typically, according to Peterson, government policymakers either do not have the insight to recognize the attitudinal roots of teenage pregnancy or, under political pressure, downplay their significance. This results in a tangle of misdirected social initiatives. Sowell writes, "When very serious problems facing the poor are mistakenly diagnosed, the cures prescribed can make their situation worse."[41]

Jewish ethicist and religious broadcaster Dennis Prager, who interviewed Peterson following the Los Angeles riots of 1992, found refreshing Peterson's refusal to exculpate black rioters for their racism and criminal violence. Prager commented on Peterson's value-laden approach to community building, and by extension, the approaches of the other black dissidents:

> The single most important problem in black life—as it is in white life, Hispanic life, Norwegian life, and every other life I can think of (with the exception of those being oppressed by Nazi- or communist-type regimes) is *internal*. It's the personal moral values of its constituents. To the extent that leaders of a community focus their community's attention onto external problems rather than onto the moral development of their constituents—to that extent they have succumbed to demogoguery, rather than [showing] leadership. Jesse Peterson is different.[42]

3. *The New Black Vanguard maintains that racism is not a sufficient cause for ghetto poverty and other social problems experienced by the black poor, though the belief that it is, effectively demotivates the poor.*

Many black leaders continue to assert that racism is the primary cause and the sustaining force of black poverty in America. Argues Jesse Jackson, "Ronald Reagan took the shame out of racism," and, "Racism is now so powerful again in our domestic and foreign policy that it threatens the soul of our nation and our status in the Free World."[43] Alphonso Pinkney agrees with Jackson: "Reports of the ongoing oppression of Afro-Americans are commonplace."[44] The exact way this expansive national racism is supposed to manipulate and control the fortunes and destinies of American blacks is commonly left underdeveloped and unsystematized.

Undeniably, statistical disparities exist between blacks and whites in many areas, including income, education, and occupations. But, Sowell asks, do these disparities necessarily represent "moral inequities" caused by "society"? That is the view of what he calls the "civil rights vision." According to this perspective, statistical dissonance is automatically indicative of these moral inequities.[45] In other words, the civil rights vision reflexively and habitually identifies racial discrimination as the root cause of these disparities. It assumes that there is a seamless garment of oppression covering the black experience, rendering it a uniformly victimized condition.

But there are problems with this view. Beyond its implausibly absolutistic and highly general nature, it cannot account for the emergence and continued rise of the black middle class; and it ignores correlative differences in "human capital" and performance as they relate to social mobility. These factors, over the last thirty years, have been exerting an economically polarizing effect on black America, highlighting the distinction between the middle and lower class.

While 30.7 percent of America's 30 million blacks have incomes below the poverty line, the population of middle-class and affluent blacks has been dramatically expanding.[46] "You've got one segment moving up, and the other stuck at the bottom," says William O'Hare, a social demographer at the University of Louisville.[47] Of those moving up, nearly one in seven black families had an annual income of $50,000 or more in 1989, according to O'Hare's study, compared with only one in seventeen in 1967.[48] In addition, since the 1960s the percentage of affluent African-Americans has more than doubled.[49] The initial skepticism about this trend, as proof of cynical "tokenism," has grown less and less credible through the years.

Sowell accounts for this economic polarization among blacks in terms of differences in "human capital" and occupational choice. He notes in *The Economics and Politics of Race* that by the late 1960s, black males from families with a library card, magazines, and other literature in the home reached high-level occupations as often as white males with a similar background.[50] As further counting against the hypothesis of an economically crippling national racism against blacks, Sowell has pointed to definite economic progress among blacks who, by their own efforts, have increased their "human capital" through education. For married couples outside the South, black family income was 78 percent of white family income in 1959, 91 percent in 1969, and 96 percent in 1970. Black female-headed families have had declining real incomes during this period, while black husband-wife families have had rising real incomes, both absolute and relative to white families. (Few have put the logic of this decline more succinctly than social analyst Charles Murray. "A poor woman who wishes to get out of poverty ought not have a baby out of wedlock. This is not a moral statement but an empirical one."[51]) Failure to note these class distinctions skews aggregate income figures for blacks downward, giving a misleading picture of overall black progress.

But what of disparities in pay scales for black and white professionals with Ph.D.'s? Is Sowell not aware, ask his critics, that blacks with Ph.D.'s make less, on average, than whites? Sowell replies that such "evidence" of widespread and gross discrimination, frequently pronounced on the six o'clock news as definitive proof of America's indefatigable racism, amounts to statistical legerdemain. The economic value of a Ph.D., he points out, is related to its field of expertise. A large percentage of these blacks have Ph.D's in education—not a very lucrative field, relatively speaking. Had these blacks taken Ph.D.'s in fields more typical of non-blacks, such as engineering, computer science, and mathematics, this "shocking" evidence would evaporate, along with the "gross disparities."

Sowell believes that the society-wide presumption in favor of racism has acquired a nimbus of authority and an indisputable cogency. Anyone who challenges this socially inveterate opinion invites charges of racism, insensitivity, and ignorance. Rather than challenge the routinized conclusion that black poverty is substantially the result of white racism, and thereby risk charges of bigotry, public figures usually play it safe. They are rewarded with admittance into the huge social clique of the sophisticated and politically sensitive.

Rejecting racism on empirical grounds, as omni-explanatory, the New Black Vanguard is convinced that there are other and more credible causes of black poverty, not least of which is the pervasive *belief* that "the System" is egregiously racist and discriminatory. This tends to discourage full-scale economic effort and instead to encourage embitterment and resentment, emotions that are demotivational and lead to economic withdrawal.

The System, as conceived in the minds of ghetto youngsters, according to Jesse Peterson of BOND, is an octopus-like beast controlling every facet of black life, resisting black success at every turn.[52] By such grand assumptions, black youth are fitted with the lenses of racial oppression, which lead them to see the events of their lives as a testimony to society's racial vendetta against them. From working with black youngsters, Peterson learned that they take as social fact the theatrical representations of black oppression regularly presented in rap videos. For instance, the Public Enemy video fantasy "Can't Truss It" equates blue-collar jobs for blacks today with antebellum plantation work. Rerun often on MTV and music video programs, the video opens with black factory workers filing into work under the scornful eye of a white supervisor. The scene then shifts to the same men as plantation slaves, under the whip of the same white supervisor. The message is clear: Nothing has changed in centuries for blacks in America. To work for a company owned or supervised by a white person is to slave for The Man, to sell out to the evil System.

The "can't trust it" mood of much of rap culture is hardly the full explanation for ghetto alienation, but it does have a significant effect. Jeffrey Clayton, the director of a minority-oriented Upward Bound program at the University of Southern California, says that his work with youth in South Central Los Angeles has convinced him that rap plays a much larger role in such alienation than most outsiders imagine. Says Clayton, the "faith of hate-rap," to borrow from a title from Norman Mailer, insinuates a deep, vitriolic prejudice against whites and all things imagined to be exclusively white—including, sadly, a steady job and an education.[53] This prophecy is disasterously self-confirming. Clayton tries to show them an alternative view.

> I tell them that they can get into the system and make it work for them. They *can* go to college, nobody's stopping them. When I tell them that, I'm saying something that they don't normally hear from people in the neighborhood. It seems to have a special meaning to them when they hear it from a black man. What they get from their peers is, "Let's burn this place down."[54]

Clayton's thesis that "fight the Power" rap is powerfully demotivational among inner-city youth is hardly farfetched in light of recent historical precedent. Social theorists regularly affirm a pussiant dialectic between the counterculture of the 1960s and its music. The difference is that hippie youth who had second thoughts about their emigration to Woodstock Nation could usually "retrieve their mistakes" (as Charles Murray said in a different context) with the help of the tidy bank accounts of suburban parents. But ghetto teenagers who have been influenced to spend their youth shadowboxing with "the Power," instead of gradually improving their lot, enjoy fewer exemptions than suburban white teens from the consequences of their bad choices. Jim Sleeper enlarges on this point in his perceptive meditation on race relations in New York City, *The Closest of Strangers*. "These youngsters and blacks of all ages interacting daily on a footing of rough equality with white peers, enjoy none of the rhetorical and moral exemptions granted to black leaders by the media, liberals, and the left.[55] Widespread promulgation of the belief that the System is inveterately antiblack is also making a normally bad situation, inner-city public education, even worse. Many inner-city schoolchildren reflexively view the school system—a primary symbol of structured society—as an arm of the System that wishes, they have been assured, to oppress them. For many of these youth, full and successful participation in school is seen as a capitulation to the oppressive and antiblack character of American society. So defined, the school becomes a locus of rebellion, and many black students, intending to be "racially faithful," withdraw and refuse to fully participate in it. Chuck D of Public Enemy, whose "Afro-fascist rap," (in Stanley Crouch's phrase) is widely influential among inner-city youth, spoke with perverse pride to *Village Voice* interviewers about rap's part in this alienation:

> You know, you walk into a fourth or fifth grade black school—quote unquote black school—today, I'm telling you, you're finding chaos right now, 'cause rappers came in the game and threw that confusing element in it, and now kids is like, Yo, fuck this.[56]

Racial fidelity, as many of these youngsters understand it, also obliges them to actively oppose those of their race who "sell out," that is, enter into behavioral cooperation with the school system. Among other things, this amounts to a pervasive ethic of anti-achievement. This phenomenon is chronicled in an important study by John Ogbu and Signithia Fordham, focusing on the attitudes of students at a predominately black high school in Washington, D.C.[57] For our purposes, the primary import of the Ogbu and Fordham study is that in some black schools there is a perverse equation of academic achievement with "acting white." This social fiction has a tragically debilitating effect on the black community as a whole, especially in the long run.

An instance of this anti-achievement bent is found in the chilling experience of fourteen-year-old Za'ketotha Blaylock. A top student in her Oakland, California, middle school, she has regularly been harrassed by anonymous telephone threats assuring the bright girl, "We're gonna kill you." The threats are the work of a gang of black girls at her school whose special charter it is to intimidate black students who achieve academic excellence. "They think that just because you're smart, they can go around beating you up," Za'ketotha explained. By virtue of her good grades, she has been the target of the most potent weapon in her antagonists' verbal arsenel: she has tried to "act white."[58]

The psychological oppression represented by Za'kettha's antagonists, and by fight-the-Power "raptivists" like Public Enemy, who clearly delineate the black-white power dynamic, serves only to encourage and legitimate withdrawal from mainstream American life. This amounts to a powerful move for a "dis-assimilation," as it were, which perversely disempowers already impoverished African-American youngsters, who mortgage their futures for the sake of associating with the dominant antiwhite ideology. Whatever social enlightenment the rapper-politicos may have in mind by so proseletizing youth, their actual effect is to create a motivational vacuum. By voiding mainstream society and the bourgeois values integral to it, such as diligence, thrift, and respect for traditional religious values, they leave unfilled the young person's need for a practical value system. One fifteen-year-old Los Angeles gang member who, after he sang the praises of the antiwhite lyrics of one group, was asked, "What do they tell you to do with your life?" was seized with a puzzled look and flatly said, "They don't tell us to do nothing. They just give us knowledge."[59] A prominent feature of this young man's "knowledge" is virulent prejudice. "I hate *all* white people," he told one of the authors, affirming that blacks were right in beating and killing white strangers during the Los Angeles riots.[60]

On a more general level, the dissidents are also specially concerned with what they regard as lopsided media presentations of race relations and the psychopolitical effects of the "victim-identity" they believe it encultures. Writes Sowell:

> How are you going to tell a young black man to work hard, or study hard, in order to get ahead, when both the media and many so-called "leaders" are constantly telling him that everything is rigged against him? Why knock yourself out on the job, or miss the Saturday night party in order to study, if whitey is just waiting in ambush to pull the rug out from under you anyway?
>
> There have always been racists, but there has not always been racial hype on the scale that we are seeing.[61]

Dissidents point to findings from media bias studies such as Edith Efron's pioneering *The News Twisters* and Rothman and Lichter's *Watching America*, as warrant for their proposition that television news and entertainment routinely depict American race relations as a Manichaean struggle, a "crude racist cartoon—with noble blacks pitted against evil conservative white America."[62] Quite against the pervasive comment that "media portrays blacks in a negative light"—and that, therefore, their climb up the socioeconomic ladder is made more difficult—are the findings of *Watching America*. The book surveyed the plots, themes, and characters of 620 television programs aired over three decades of prime time. "Over the past thirty years," the authors write, "nine out of ten murders on television were committed by whites. During that period, only three in one hundred murders [on television] were committed by blacks. . . . [B]lacks on television are about eighteen times less likely to commit homicide than in real life."[63] In light of this dramatic lopsidedness, it hardly seems tenable to believe that media constantly demonizes blacks.

On the contrary, television images school the public in the supposition that black suffering is the product of white oppression. Ethelbert W. Haskins, writing in *The Crisis in Afro-American Leadership* (1988), argues that black leaders who point to white racism as the major cause of ghetto poverty find a ready ally in the major news media:

> The ideologues . . . merit discredit . . . for the climate of despair they keep alive in the center city. Imagine the cyclone of frustration created by the authoritative voice of lamentation chanted in the ears of an entire generation! And, unfortunately, the mainstream news media reinforce the ideologues' contention.[64]

Alluding to this same social construction of reality, Justice Clarence Thomas, speaking at a college commencement, ironically told graduating black seniors:

> You all have a much tougher road. You now have a popular national rhetoric which says that you can't learn because of racism, you can't get up in the mornings because of racism. Unlike me, you must not only overcome the repressiveness of racism, you must also overcome the lure of excuses. You have twice the job I had.[65]

Just as the dissidents' views on self-help are typically caricatured as "bootstrapism" (a discussion of which is forthcoming in Chapter 3), so their thinking on the "lure of excuses" is regularly treated reductively. Writing in *Savage Inequalities*, Jonathan Kozol states:

> There is a belief advanced today, and in some cases by conservative black authors, that poor children and particularly black children should not be allowed to hear too much about [inequality]. If they learn how much less

they are getting than rich children, we are told, this knowledge may induce them to regard themselves as "victims." ... But this is a matter of psychology—or strategy—and not reality.[66]

Kozol's simplification of "black conservatives" ignores their nuanced perspective on social oppression. No black conservative scholar has suggested that history lessons should be redacted to explain away inequality, past or present. It is true that Sowell and others would not have the social science teacher reflexively pull the weary rabbit of racism out of the shiny hat of statistical analysis. But this is not because of some "psychological" or "strategic" purpose, as Kozol has it, but rather because the dissidents are not convinced it is true. To Sowell in particular, statistical disparities do not ipso facto constitute racial oppression. To profess otherwise—in the classroom, on the political stump, or in the popular media—is to engage in a reductionistic sociology that enlightens neither the student, the citizen, nor the public at large.

Kozol is correct in his assertion that "black conservatives" understand "victim-thinking" as a psychological mode, and one that is motivationally debilitating. But Kozol mischaracterizes the dissidents' viewpoint when he implies that their recognition of victim-thinking as a psychic reality, amounts to a denial of the reality of any victimization. "Black conservative" Loury's insistence that "so many black kids' chances, actual life chances, are so miserable that fundamental questions of justice, racial justice, are raised" hardly sounds as if Loury regards inequality as social maya projected by liberal propagandists.[67]

At its best—and Loury's work is a case in point—the dissident perspective grasps that no omnipresent racist Behemoth is choking black progress, and yet it remains painfully sensitive to the harsh realities of ghetto life and ghetto anger. When conservative community activist Jesse Peterson listens to black youngsters tell of police harrassment, he understands their anger, having been the victim of police harrassment himself. Indeed, the personal histories of virtually all the dissidents contain experiences of the raw bigotry and serrated racism that has scarred American history. William B. Allen recalls: "I was driving from California to Florida in that summer of '64, just after the Civil Rights Act had been passed. Then, for the first time in my life, I was able to contemplate stopping at any restaurant or motel I came across.[68]

Of course, the young teens with whom Kozol is concerned have also experienced insults coming from a mind-set they do not understand: the racist glare of a stranger driving through the neighborhood; the shopkeeper who trails the black teenager up and down the aisles; the woman who crosses the street as a black youngster approaches. Beyond their anger at such racial insults, youngsters in the inner city are also angered by the intrinsically frustrating character of life in dysfunctional neighborhoods, whether in the form of decrepit and barely functioning schools, dilapidated and decaying surroundings, a fractured family life, or the brooding presence of the gang banger and the drug pusher. Their childhood inclines them toward a palpable anger that, contra Kozol, the New Black Vanguard *has* factored into its social critique.

The dissidents maintain that it is possible, indeed essential, to weather such experiences, and the anger they generate, without developing a personally destructive victim-identity, constructed around the assumption that the particular affronts one experiences are merely stitches in a much larger and more comprehensive tapestry of national oppression. They know, from their own experience, that there is no impermeable wall separating the individual who grows up in a ghetto from full participation in larger society. Though individual hurts in an inner-city environment are inevitable, there is no insuperable social barrier preventing poor youngsters from prevailing over social impediments. But this message about self-determination, coming from "black conservatives," should not be construed, as it commonly is, to be a ratification of the status quo. As we shall suggest in Axiom 5 below, the dissidents would undo the sources of "structural poverty" as soon as practicable.

Finally, then, what are we to make of this dynamic of felt anger and its rhetorical expansion at the hands of raptivists and other community "spokesmen"?

It seems to us that the psycho-emotional challenge faced by inner-city youth, of self-determination in the midst of ghetto despair, is only made more difficult when the siren call of hate-rap, with its "lure of excuses," invites these youngsters to enlist in the ranks of the thoroughly alienated. Though the anger felt by black youth is not "merely the result of opportunistic agitprop," the fact is many are hobbled by hate-rap's deterministic message and embittered by its "defeatist undertoe that so misshapes [their] thinking regarding intellectual and career engagement."[69]

4. The New Black Vanguard objects on moral and pragmatic grounds to the civil rights leadership's reliance on the political capital of white guilt.

Black dissidents resist the temptation to harness white guilt for political purposes. They have a pragmatic reason for not drawing on the guilt many whites feel about racism: such an emphasis, as the record of the civil rights establishment shows, tends toward ineffective juridical and governmental solutions to the problems of blacks as a racial class. Rather than motivating individual poor blacks to self-improvement and a critical evaluation of their lives and of the course of their lives, it works to evoke an "It's their fault!" mentality. As Sowell and others argue, this has a stultifying effect, stagnating individual efforts to succeed in spite of obstacles. In *The Flip Side of Soul* (1989); veteran correspondent and anchorman Bob Teague asks:

> To achieve our ultimate goals, will we advance faster or slower if we consistently point a finger at Mr. Charlie as the root of all our troubles, never at ourselves? It is my guess that true progress now depends on abandoning our current posture of total innocence.[70]

Forming an interesting corollary to Sowell's notion of the political use of white guilt is Loury's idea that such "political capital" is most readily garnered by politicians who supercharge their rhetoric with images of the ghetto, the archetypal symbol of white oppression—even when they are stumping for policies that will primarily benefit middle-class blacks, not the poor:

> The growing black "underclass" has become the constant reminder to many Americans of an historic debt owed to the black community. I suggest that, were it not for this continued presence among us of those worst off of all Americans, blacks' ability to sustain public support for affirmative action, minority business set-asides and the like would be vastly reduced. That is, the suffering of the poorest blacks creates a fund of political capital upon which all members of the group can draw in the pressing of racially based claims.[71]

Both Loury and Sowell see many black leaders as intending to create a bottomless well of "political capital," which can then be harnessed to serve legislative interests as articulated by these black leaders. In this way, white guilt is used as fuel for what Sowell, Loury, and others see as the misguided programs and policies backed by traditional black leadership. Steele calls them "escapist racial policies": whites support these policies, he theorizes, to achieve a quick (but spurious) innocence.[72] Because "self-constrained guilt" is more interested in guilt-relief than in the efficacy of remedies, says Steele, it supports instant but ineffective "solutions" (e.g., preferential treatment) rather than effective but less dramatically expiating policies.[73]

This seizing of victim-capital by civil rights luminaries, and the regular accession to their demands by the media and the liberal political elite, has led, in the minds of some, to the diffusion of a perverse moral double standard, whereby African-Americans are not expected to observe the ethical norms applied to others. Following the Los Angeles riots, Walter Williams devoted a newspaper column to this general topic, titled "We Hold Black Rioters To a Lesser Standard." In their application of a moral double standard to the rioters, Williams suggested, "black politicians and civil rights leaders . . . demonstrate their [own] rapidly disintegrating moral values."[74] Ethicist Dennis Prager shares Williams's view that this relaxation of moral standards is not only ethically indefensible, but harmful to those groups accorded this dubious exemption, as such standards are necessary for community vitality:

> The laborious, unromantic, un-"revolutionary" work of developing character, personal ethical values, is the most important of any society, including and especially black society in America today. The only reason I say "especially" is that it is the community least expected to live by moral norms. That's because liberals, black and white, make exceptions for black behavior that they would never make for white.[75]

Prager's stern ethical rebuke of liberals, black and white, whom he sees as offering counterproductive exculpations—and who, by doing so, foster a moral insolvency in sectors of the black community—might be greeted with the objection. "How can a Caucasian, or any nonblack, normatively remark on problems facing black America?" Though this question is occasionally directly broached in the public square, it is more commonly a subtext of the frequent a priori rejection of such comments.

We answer this racialist objection by saying that neither black people, nor white people, nor any other people exist in a social vacuum, completely unaffected by others. Our destinies, as individuals and as members of a common society, are tightly intertwined. In our pluralistic society, everyone's interests are perforce united. Consequently, responsible reflection on political issues that really affect us all should not be seen as the special preserve of those who happen to be a particular color.

In this pluralistic society, and in this media-saturated and informationally sophisticated age, knowledge of other peoples is readily available. Such an education, empathetically applied, can lead to an enlightened understanding of people different from ourselves in culture and experience. This idea is foundational to the project of "multiculturalism," so influential in today's civil discourse. Indeed, as a philosophy of education, multiculturalism insists on the possibility of bridging sociocultural gulfs far greater than that separating black and white in America.

Regular assertions are made by conventional black advocacy that black/ nonblack, experiential and cultural gulfs are *absolutely* impassable, and that nonblacks should therefore refrain from reflection and comment on black behavior. Such assertions strain credulity. They are essentially political in character, meant to silence critical thought (as described in Axiom 2) and insulate blacks from normative criticisms by establishing a cognitive "Do Not Touch" sign around what are, by usual standards, episodes of objectionable behavior.

A clear example of this moral obfuscation was seen when 1992 presidential candidate Bill Clinton criticized raptivist Sister Souljah's exegesis of the thinking behind the Los Angeles riots: "If black people kill black people every day, why not have a week and kill white people?"[76] For daring to call attention to the obvious, that Souljah is a racist person, Clinton was immediately upbraided by certain intellectuals, including Ronald Walters, a professor at Howard University, who insisted that Clinton should have had the good sense to keep quiet. Clinton, and every other nonblack person who disagreed with Souljah, had not rightly understood the remark as expressive "street talk"; besides, "artists" such as Souljah, explained Walters, "exaggerate reality and we shouldn't be stupid enough to take what they say literally." Walters continued, asserting the inability of nonblacks to comprehend the labyrinth of the "black mind" and barring them from holding blacks responsible for their actions. "If you don't understand the culture, you have no business criticising it."[77]

A moment's reflection reveals the moral absurdities this line of thinking quickly leads to. Perhaps the four young African-American men, crowned the "LA Four," who were arrested for the attempted murder of white trucker Reginald Denny during the LA riots, were also artists, engaged, not in a racist assault, but rather in a fantastic *divertissement*, the symbolic expression of their creative angst and vision.

In our view, this rationalization by Walters well illustrates Berger's explanation of protected "subuniverses"—cultural enclaves made immune to common sense criticism and debunking "by various techniques of intimidation, rational and irrational propaganda (appealing to the outsiders' interests and to their emotions), [and] mystification."[78]

The very suggestion that nonblacks, because of environmental or constitutional differences, are unable to understand and critique problems facing African-Americans is highly deterministic. It assumes that one's physical makeup irresistibly steers one's thinking. This deterministic assumption seems to underlie much thinking about race in America today, and to largely shape the rhetoric of the civil rights establishment. For example, following the Rodney King verdict, when civil rights activists objected that the officers were not tried by a "jury of [Rodney King's] peers," there seemed to be at work the insistence that nonblack jurists would be absolutely unable to recognize the presence of a crime against a black man. Equating color with the ability or inability to discern the truth and fairly apply the law reflects a profoundly rigid understanding of human mental capacity. William B. Allen, who is a constitutional scholar, sees a danger in such color-coded thinking. He decries the widespread a priori belief in victimization of African-Americans as an unwarranted assumption of the inevitability of injustice. He writes:

> This is a way of proceeding in our country which leads to disaster. . . .
> The reason people do these things is because they are in the habit of
> thinking in terms of race, or gender—anything except of being an Amer-
> ican. Until we learn once again to use the language of American freedom
> in an appropriate way that embraces all of us, we're going to continue to
> harm this country.[79]

This drive toward an inclusive national ethos and a unified self-understanding as a nation is an earmark of New Black Vanguard thought. Allen and other dissidents believe in intellectual common ground among Americans of all colors; this is sharply at odds with the popular model of race relations, seen in remarks by film director Spike Lee. Angered over the reluctance of a bond company to further fund some of the production costs of his movie *Malcom X*, Lee charged that Hollywood is more willing to risk money on projects being supervised by white filmmakers. He lashed out at a black executive of the bond company, saying, "[She] is a black woman but Clarence Thomas is supposed to be black too. Skin color doesn't mean anything."[80] In light of what he intended it to mean, that last sentence is a great irony. Lee meant it to express his furious disapproval of those heretical African Americans who allow their minds to breach the borders of correct and truly authentic black thinking, but the true import of his statement and the intellectually stifling and censoring attitude it reflects is that *race means everything! It and it alone is deterministic of what one should think, and what one is justified in thinking.*

In contrast to the presumption toward determinism present in mainstream black advocacy, the New Black Vanguard believes that the individuality of each person enables that person to cognitively transcend the prescriptions of color-coordinated thinking. This transcendence makes possible the common moral project of a pluralist democracy. A denial of this transcendence is an invitation to racial balkanization.

Since, in the minds of the New Black Vanguard, this cognitive transcendence is possible and the national project it empowers worthy, reflection and comment on national problems across the racial spectrum is not only warranted, but imperative. Such a popular dialectic serves not only to preserve national vitality, but also as a hedge against individual hypocrisy and racial solipsism. But this imperative is going largely unobserved, for two reasons. First, liberals—muted by "white guilt" conjured up by liturgical recitations of the shibboleth, "four hundred years of oppression"—distance themselves from this imperative with anguished mea culpas. Second, conservatives, loath to be thought racist and obscurantist and mindful of economic repercussions, are cowed into silence by the threat of being ringed with the albatross of "racism."

This entire dynamic has an isolating and wearying effect on black apostates from the "civil rights vision." Perhaps especially disappointing to them is the reticence of white supporters, who, fearing the racism tag, fail to speak publicly in the dissidents' defense. "They want us to take the beachhead," says Anne Wortham. "I don't know what the toll is, but I do know that you [black individualists] tend to guard your privacy—so you go home and listen to music. You know you'll catch enough hell when you release your next bombshell."[81]

5. *De-emphasizing racism as the generator of black poverty, the New Black Vanguard ascribes the proliferation of the black underclass to other causes; including structural changes in urban economies, the effects of welfare work-disincentives, and elements of a ghetto-specific culture, which have "taken on a life of their own."*

As noted in Chapter 1, sociologist William Julius Wilson was attacked by the Black Sociologists of America when he published findings in *The Declining Significance of Race* challenging the routinized conclusion that racism is the omni-explanatory cause of ghetto poverty.[82] Wilson argued a "mismatch theory" of urban poverty in his award-winning *The Truly Disadvantaged.* Urban economies, he maintained, have been radically transformed in recent decades. Goods-producing industries have given way to service-providing industries; urban labor markets have polarized into low- and high-wage sectors, and many manufacturing industries have simply left the central cities for the suburbs.[83]

These structural economic changes could not have occurred at a worse time for urban blacks, Wilson insists.[84] Just as these changes were transforming American cities, a population explosion among minority youth was occurring in urban areas. The result: masses of unskilled young blacks, their employment prospects severely limited by a transformed urban economy, swelled the ranks of the underclass, tragically "mismatched" to new socioeconomic realities. In this way, says Wilson, poor neighborhoods take on the character of isolated enclaves, and "concentration effects" obtain. High levels of joblessness, welfare dependency, and out-of-wedlock births in a concentrated area tend to snowball into more of the same. Surrounded with dysfunction, the residents' own "social competence" (in political scientist Lawrence Mead's phrase) and capacity for mobility, declines.

Although Wilson's theory was at first excoriated by black intellectuals, today it exerts a palpable influence on the ideology of mainstream black advocacy. There are three reasons for this. First, given the proliferation of the black middle class and the growing weariness of white America with, in Jim Sleeper's phrase, the "intimations of racism in every leaf that falls," the civil rights leadership recognizes the political expediency in putting its imprimatur, at least in a moderate way, on Wilson's "mismatch" theory, with its deliberate deemphasis on discrimination and white racism as the Prime Mover of black poverty. Second, Wilson's theory of "concentration effects" recognizes internal dysfunction in black communities, though without the full "culture of poverty" implications so politically embarrassing to the civil rights establishment. Third, Wilson's social liberalism, which assigns a central role to government in neighborhood reform, coincides with the strategy of current civil rights leadership.

But while "many liberals contend that a mismatch between remaining jobs and low-skilled job seekers largely explains nonwork in the inner city," says Mead, " . . . research has failed to confirm these theories."[85] Although the mismatch aspect of Wilson's theory is called into question by Mead's statistics, Wilson's concept of ghetto-specific "concentration effects" appears to many as highly plausible.[86]

Now though a theory of snowballing "concentration effects" mainly comports with the theories of poverty of conservatives Thomas Sowell and Walter Williams, the picture drawn by Sowell and Williams of opportunity in poor neighborhoods, and its limitations, differs markedly from that drawn by Wilson. Many of these limitations, they argue, are state superintended and continue, by and large, with the approval of the civil rights establishment.

In *The State against Blacks*, Williams trains his analysis on statist curbing of opportunity among private entrepreneurs. As a case in point, he cites government enforcement of restrictive occupational licensing in urban areas. Many of these restrictions were unknown to turn-of-the-century immigrants, who used these occupations to get a foothold on America's economic ladder. It was in 1937 that New York City first required a licensure-medallion for each taxi in the city, with a single medallion costing $10. By 1992 the price of a New York city medallion has risen to about $60,000. This typifies, says Williams, the many "politically erected" barriers to employment that are depressing the life-chances of the black underclass.[87] These barriers prevent what Clint Bolick calls "economic liberty" and the upward mobility that such liberty facilitates.[88]

Inverting the nomenclature of oppression frequently deployed by the left, Williams terms these barriers and their effects "structural poverty."[89] Nevertheless, neither Williams nor Sowell believes that such "structural poverty" limitations adequately account for the pervasive nonwork in ghetto areas. Though black youth record the highest of all unemployment rates (typically over 40 percent), Sowell and Williams have argued that unavailability of employment does not account for the high incidence of nonwork for this group, nor that for inner-city blacks in general. They have also argued that steady employment, even at low-wage work, is a practicable route out of poverty—this contrary to the rhetorical deprecation of "dead-end" jobs by the civil rights establishment.

Contrary to the conventional wisdom, disadvantaged young black men generally report that minimum-wage jobs are easy to find.[90] According to a survey done by the National Bureau of Economic Research in the ghettos of Boston, Chicago, and Philadelphia in 1980, 71 percent of the youth surveyed said that it was easy or very easy to get a job at minimum wage.[91] Studies published in the volume *Black Youth Employment Crisis* suggest that although disadvantaged black youth are unemployed or out of the labor force twice as frequently as whites, one-quarter to one-third of that difference is due to the wages they insist on in order to work—they generally demand higher pay than nonblacks relative to their qualifications for employment. Their refusal to modify their demands keeps them unemployed.[92]

Moreover, when such jobs are taken, they are typically sufficient to raise employees who work a forty-hour week above the poverty level—

again, contrary to the conventional wisdom.[93] This principle applies to single mothers as well, assuming they work full time and claim all available "in-kind" government benefits.[94] Neither the availability of child care, nor its cost, oppose this principle. In one study, two-thirds of nonworking mothers affirmed that child care was available to them should they decide to work.[95] Moreover, expensive, center-based child care is not the norm;[96] in 1987, only one-third of working women using child care had to pay anything at all. The child care expenses of those who had to pay averaged less than 7 percent of family income.[97]

In light of such data, Sowell and Williams argue that nonwork and poverty in these neighborhoods are more plausibly attributed to a dialectic among circumstantial, ideational, and political forces, rather than to discrimination, unavailability of work, or prohibitively low wages. The forces involved in this dialectic include (1) entitlement programs, such as Aid to Families with Dependent Children (AFDC), which offer an alternative to work through cash and in-kind benefits; (2) a welfare-fostered breakdown of the inner-city black family, which often leaves black youngsters bereft of the guidance, discipline, and support that normally disposes toward work and achievement; and (3) the victim-rhetoric of community leaders, the media, and the icons of black youth culture—a rhetoric that enscribes economic passivity and dispiriting anger.

Many of the black dissenters discussed in these pages see the welfare system as a tender trap and the mainframe of "structural poverty." They argue that the proliferation and expansion of welfare benefits in the 1960s, however well intentioned, proved disastrous for inner-city blacks. Welfare, they argued, cracked the ridge-pole of the black heritage—the black family—and set into motion the dialectic among personal and social forces that is responsible for the cycle of welfare dependency seen in cities today. (Of course, blacks are not the only people hurt by welfare and the assorted problems seen in American urban centers.)[98]

Dissenters note that 80 percent of black economic progress between 1940 and 1980 was made before 1965, before the grand expansion of welfare spending and the ballooning of the "poverty industry," in Robert L. Woodson's acidulous phrase.[99] Between 1965 and 1975, the number of recipients of AFDC doubled.[100] In the early 1990s, with projections of eight out of ten black children born in 1980 winding up on welfare, the poverty industry is doing a booming business.[101] Says Woodson:

This industry accounts for hundreds of agencies and thousands of social workers, civil servants and other professionals whose business literally rides on the backs of the poor; about 75 percent of the aid to the poor goes not to them but to those who serve the poor.[102]

"The issue," says Sowell, "is not that the government gives too much help to the poor. The problem is that the government creates too much harm to the poor."[103] While black poverty had been steadily declining through the 1960s, during the 1970s, at the very height of the welfare state, this decline ceased, and black families experienced a rise in impoverishment.[104]

Sowell's pioneering work in the theory of an "intergenerational relay race" would seem to illuminate the mechanism of this financial devolution. Sowell's thesis recognizes the transfer, from generation to generation, of instrumental "human capital": the knowledge and skills, habits of mind, and values that eventuate in true autonomy, or what Mead calls "social competence."[105] The 1960s saw a dramatic change in the character of this "relay race" for many black Americans. By offering massive institutional disincentives to traditional family organization, welfare effectively began to plunder the hard-won capital of personal resourcefulness of blacks in the Old South, and as a result, sent deep fissures through what has always been the bedrock of the black community—the family.

"The black family," writes Sowell, "held together during centuries of slavery and generations of oppression. The large and growing numbers of one-parent, female-headed families have emerged in recent decades, as the welfare system has subsidized both male desertion and teenage pregnancy."[106] Sowell holds firm to the view that a government that stresses social entitlement courts a highly dependent clientele. There is nothing intrinsically "racial" about this, he points out, noting that currently more than half of the children born in Sweden, with its hefty welfare packages, are the result of unwed pregnancies.[107]

Bob Teague, a journalist, is personally appalled by the disintegration of the black family that welfare has wrought, and by the effect of this on the black community ethos. Teague, hardly a Pollyannaish apologist for white racism, as his early and militant *Letters to a Black Boy* (1968) emphatically proves, wrote in *The Flip Side of Soul* (1989):

It comes down once again to the disarray of minority families, doesn't it? Is it entirely Mr. Charley's fault that in 1987 more than half of black children were illegitimate, compared to only twenty percent twenty years ago? Who is responsible for the attitude of the welfare mom who said to her caseworker. "I've just had my sixth baby; what are you going to do about it?"[108]

Robert Woodson, too, locates the genus of this family decomposition and urban unrest in present welfare policies. Commenting immediately after the Los Angeles riots of 1992, he said:

> Welfare policies right now discourage family formation. People are made dependent, as food stamps determine what people can buy; public housing, where people can live; Medicaid, who their doctors will be; legal services, who their attorney is to be. You cannot have programs that treat people as impotent children and then expect them to act like responsible adults.[109]

In the view of conservatives, the eligibility rules and benefit packages attached to AFDC, the most important welfare program, have made work supererogatory and economically "enabled" the routinization of unwed motherhood.[110] Writes Robert Rector, an urban policy analyst:

> Current welfare may best be conceptualized as a system which offers each single mother a "paycheck" worth an average of between $8,500 and $15,000, depending on the state. The mother has a contract with the government: She will continue to receive her "paycheck" as long as she fulfills two conditions:
>
> 1) she must not work; and
>
> 2) she must not marry an employed male.[111]

Rector adds, "This is what I call the welfare incentive system from hell."[112] Two economists, Richard Vedder and Lowell Gallaway, estimate that the work disincentives built into welfare contributed to the unemployment of nearly 6 million Americans in 1984 alone.[113]

The family disintegration this leads to, say the dissidents, increases the probability that children will be raised in poverty. In a two-parent family, the probability that the family will be poor in any given year is 5 percent; for a single mother the probability goes up to 50 percent.[114] Not only do the children of such families directly inherit the dire economic conditions of their parents, but it is also demonstrably more likely that children of single parent families will themselves eventually head single-parent families.[115] Sowell's "relay race" is here transformed, from the passing down of the attitudes and habits that incline a person to achievement, into the burdening of younger generations with attitudes and habits that incline them toward social dysfunction. The result is an 8 percent increase in the total number of black babies born out of wedlock from 1980 to 1988, and a 25.9 percent increase from 1970 to 1988.[116] These staggering rates of unwed pregnancy cry out for explanation. In *Black Teenage Mothers*, we find a passage that we think speaks volumes about the insouciance and youthful myopia that is common in teen mothers:

> Tracy's energies were focused on her relationship with the fathers of her two children. She reported that she still saw both of them but that she prefers the seventeen year old father of her second baby. He is an entertainer in a group that sings and dances, which she described as successful and "hoping to make it big." Tracy wants to have four more children before she is thirty so that she will not be "too old" with her last child: "I want them to try to grow up with me, like my mother and me. Even though I wasn't there with her, it was still like I grew up with her." She expressed no aspirations for the two children she already has. When asked what ambitions she had for them, she said she had never really thought about it. Tracy completed tenth grade but did not return to school after the birth of her first baby. She aspires to be an accountant but has no definite plans to return to school. Tracy talked about both fathers of her children wanting more children. Of the father of her second child, she said, "A daughter would make his life complete."[117]

Comments from celebrated novelist Maya Angelou on teen pregnancy are direct and poignant:

> Young Black girls abandoned by their mothers, ignored by their fathers, untaught by their teachers, and uncared for by their politicians are having babies at a rate which startles and frightens us. Too frequently, they know too little about babies and even less about being mothers, and nothing at all about what being a Black American mother means. Rarely, do the young mothers have any hope of any support from the (also young) fathers. . . . [Both] are also ignorant of the success our forefathers and foremothers achieved.[118]

Angelou's forthright expression of discontent and critical concern is a rarity. Today's political climate invites a fourfold censure of those who would broach the difficult topic of reasons for the proliferation of black teen pregnancy. They are informed, first, directly or sotto voce, that their work constitutes a heartless diatribe against "the poor," reeking of self-interest and callousness; second, that they are attacking the "*black poor*"—here black dissidents are guilty of an especially heinous betrayal—and third, that they are attacking "black poor *mothers*" (no explanation necessary). But fourth, and the coup de grace, is the accusation that they have taken a stand against the *"children* of poor black mothers." As political terrain goes, this fourfold critique is a no-man's-land, and it is unremarkable that many politicians and civil rights leaders are silent on these matters, especially in the media.

Sowell, a veteran of this craggy terrain, sees the framing of such debates in these terms as a kind of "moral one-upmanship," whereby the tender concern of the ethically enlightened is counterposed to the blind greed of troglodytic self-seekers:

> There are grown men and women who seriously believe that the difference between them and other people who favor different policies is that they are . . . "compassionate" to the poor. . . . Presumably, others don't mind seeing . . . the poor starving. It's hard to be humble when you're the morally annointed. You start calling yourself things like "thinking people," "progressives," or believers in "social justice." Others don't think. They don't want progress; they would just as soon stagnate or go backward.[119]

For Sowell, programs which fly under the banner of compassion, are typically too simplistic, failing to address the full range of anthropological and economic issues. In this way, they are guilt assuaging but remain inefficacious. Occasionally, such ill-conceived compassion can be outright ruinous. Sowell would see Tracy and her children as casualties of "compassionate" welfare policy.

A notable example of a call for "compassion" comes from Marian Wright Edelman, founder of the Children's Defense Fund, in an article titled, "Dreams Shattered for America's Young Families." Citing rising poverty rates for "young black families" and finding responsibility for abating the destruction of black families to lie with "society," Edelman writes, "This crisis for young black families is contributing mightily to the tearing apart of the black community. This society cannot year after year increase the poverty and isolation and hopelessness of Black mothers and fathers and children—it can't keep turning the screws tighter and tighter."[120] In contrast to Edelman's assumption that the black poor are passive victims on whom "society" is turning the screws, the results of Mead's massive statistical analyses of poverty yield a quite different story: "Family poverty," writes Mead, "has risen mainly because poor single mothers fail to work regularly, and their departed spouses do not contribute to their support."[121] While Edelman is right that the impoverishment of young black families is devastating the black community, in her article she never grapples with "the enemy within," nor transcends the language of victimization and moral passivity. The New Black Vanguard believes this must be done if effective social policy is to be crafted. That is, gritty social facts must be exposed (e.g., the percentage of impoverished "young black families" comprised of single mothers and their children born out of wedlock, as well as the percentage of male desertion of these "young black families"). Once such social facts have been brought to light, the moral issues they raise, both civic and personal, must be seriously engaged.

Though the proliferation of single-parent families under current welfare policy has produced many bleak effects, inner-city education has been hit the hardest. According to one study, a child of a single-parent family, regardless of race or class, is three times more likely to fail in school.[122] Another study, of 18,000 students, sponsored by the National Association of Elementary School Principals, demonstrated that children from one-parent families habitually achieved less and were less well behaved than children from two-parent families. The missing parent was such a significant factor that youth from low-income, two-parent families did better in school than students from high-income, single-parent families.[123] How such an effect is multiplied when a majority or near-majority of a school district's children are on AFDC is yet to be determined, but in light of the above indications, such a social phenomenon would not seem to bode well for education. Majority and near-majority percentages of children on AFDC are currently seen in quite a few U.S. cities. For instance, 58 percent of the children enrolled in Newark's public schools are on AFDC; in New York the figure is 45 percent; in Chicago, 44 percent; in Philadelphia, 42 percent.[124]

Similar figures prevail at the site of recent and profound urban unrest. At the very epicenter of riot-torn Los Angeles, most black children are being raised in single-parent households—households frequently relying on AFDC. At a number of predominately black high schools in South Central Los Angeles, the welfare dependency rates are alarmingly high:

- Jordan High School, 78%
- Freemont High School, 58%
- Manual Arts High School, 53%

These statistics, provided by the Los Angeles Unified School District, are not readily attainable, as they clash with media-constructed realities about causes of black underachievement. Whatever the actual causes, it would seem hard to deny the presence of a link between the home life of these children and the violence and educational underachievement in their neighborhoods.

Frequently, such dysfunctions are attributed to inequities in educational funding—that is, inner city black schools are deliberately underfunded compared to suburban white schools. Of course, when comparing per pupil expenditures on education across schools in a large urban school district like Los Angeles, many factors must be considered. A critical factor, according to Lawrence Picus, professor of Education at the University of Southern California, is special federal funding provided under Chapter 1, the largest federal compensatory program. According to Picus: "If you consider programs like Chapter 1, many inner-city schools appear to have more money than suburban schools. *It is my sense at this time that in Los Angeles Unified School District, per pupil expenses are fairly comparable between black and white areas.*"[125]

It seems entirely reasonable to look to factors apart from school budgets for clues to educational failure. One factor that is seldom addressed but is undeniably essential to the educational development of a child, is reading in the home. Norma Anders, a branch librarian in Watts for five years and a children's librarian in South Central Los Angeles for ten years, comments:

> Inner city libraries are underused. It has been my general observation in 20 years of service here in the City of Los Angeles that African-American parents have not, unfortunately, used the library in a way that many other parents have. I don't see this, of course, as lack of love for their children— it may be that many parents just don't recognize the importance of early reading to children, for a number of reasons. It's painful to see this, because—as so many studies have pointed out, including Jim Trelease's classic *Read-Aloud Handbook*—that literacy and love for books starts with parents reading to their children at home.[126]

While such anecdotal evidence has its limits, it is reinforced by the testimony of others. In *Shut Up and Let the Lady Teach!* Emily Sachar reports the comments of Sharon, a fellow teacher at a predominately black school in the Bronx:

> Neither [the children] nor their parents have any concept of how reading can be a part of daily life. . . . Their parents never read to them. They never see their parents reading. And no one is communicating to these kids why school matters.[127]

While parental failure to read to children at home is certainly not unique to single-parent families, statistics in Detroit emphatically confirm that a special educational disadvantage is experienced by students from one-parent families, especially in the inner city. Of the 170,000 students in Detroit's nearly all-black school district, 70 percent are being raised by single mothers—and nearly two out of three boys entering high school in Detroit do not graduate.[128] A prominent black educator, Joe Clark, remarks:

> What can be done about the young who see no value in education and consequently learn nothing, who attack and denigrate authority, consort with criminals, take drugs, get pregnant, go on welfare, drop out, remain unemployed, and sink deeper into drugs and crime? Their children are raised in illiterate, anti-educational homes.[129]

Joe Clark and the dissidents would have the schools return to a deliberate emphasis on values and personal character. But under the yoke of the prevailing "value-free" (so-called) educational vision of the "experts," entering such discussions is generally verboten in public schools. In such schools, early educational dysfunction obscures the life-chances of inner-city youth, giving them the illusion of no hope for social mobility. This is shown in the irony of the worst urban mayhem in the United States during this century, taking place between two schools separated by a C+ average. Let us explain.

Located in South Central Los Angeles on Imperial Highway, Los Angeles Southwest Junior College is an institution offering AA degrees and general education—one of the nine low-cost junior colleges in Los Angeles. Like any junior college, one of Los Angeles Southwest's primary purposes is to convey students to colleges and universities. The nearest of these happens to be the University of Southern California, located 15 minutes away by car—a university consistently ranked in the top twenty-five in the nation in the professional fields of medicine, law, and engineering. The nine miles of acreage lying between the two schools was the primary arena of anarchy and violence during the riots of 1992. Now marred with ashen hulls, this part of the city has become a theater for somber politicians deploring, among other things, the "hopelessness" and "lack of educational opportunity," that led to the riots and, as the story goes, still rules today.

To our knowledge, no commentator on the "hopelessness" that spawned the "rebellion" took note of the longstanding fact that Los Angeles Southwest admitted any community member, with or without a high school diploma, at the rate of $5 per credit. Of course, as with any institution, student loans are available. But perhaps the most attractive feature of Los Angeles Southwest is the fact that USC has agreed to accept any of its transfer students who have maintained a C+ average in their course work. But given USC's $7,865 tuition per semester, such matriculation would probably seem truly "hopeless" for the average resident of South Central.[130] Not so. A USC admissions officer confirmed that, in an effort to recruit students from South Central Los Angeles, the university covers 100 percent of tuition costs for any transfer student from Los Angeles Southwest. Indeed, the worse an applicant's economic standing, the larger the financial award, even beyond tuition costs. At the current tuition rate, the value of a four-year scholarship (again, guaranteed to any Los Angeles Southwest student who can maintain a C+ average) is $62,920.

Given the modest (to say the least) prerequisite for such a sizeable award, not to mention the future benefits accruing to the university graduate, the rhetoric of "hopelessness" and "lack of opportunity" that hangs over the city hides manifold dereliction: on the part of the civil rights establishment, which has failed to publicize an opportunity that earlier generations strove for, instead inculcating an ideology of "hopelessness"; on the part of the parents, frequently unwed mothers and absent fathers, who have failed to supervise their children's schooling, perhaps unaware of the long-term benefits of higher education (90 percent of black children are born to mothers who have not completed a single year of college);[131] and on the part of the media, who have publicized South Central as an urban prison, and not a place where a C+ average at a community college is worth nearly $63,000.[132]

The publishing of opportunity does not seem to be a priority following the riots. At a newsstand two blocks from the university offering South Central youth this $63,000 opportunity, an edition of the *Los Angeles Sentinel*, the largest black-owned newspaper in the West, featured these lines from a regular columnist a few weeks after the riots:

> In column after column, I have tried to point out to my readers that the United States is on the verge of becoming a police state, if it is not there already. I have carefully described the many similarities between present day USA and early stages of the Nazi Third Reich in pre-war Germany.[133]

This columnist may have provided an object lesson of what Walter Williams earlier termed the "rhetoric of hopelessness." Rather than drawing this provocative historical comparison, the columnist might have better spent his column space carefully describing to his readership in South Central and greater Los Angeles the educational opportunity at Los Angeles Southwest and explaining how to take advantage of it.

Given the superabundance of defeatist rhetoric in these neighborhoods, it would seem imperative that public elementary and secondary schools provide the kind of inspiration and effective character formation that would equip youth to resist the lures to failure. But today's schools, argue the dissidents, are unable to fulfill this role, being constrained by the strict "value neutrality" cited in Axiom 2. Too often the child's school day is marked by stalled or hurried lessons, the grind and temptation of out-of-control classmates, and the uninspiring custody of harried teachers. As such, inner-city public schools form another truss in the "structural poverty" posited by the New Black Vanguard. The civil rights leadership, however, has consistently opposed the dissidents' specific program for neighborhood educational reform, one supported by most black Americans: a system of educational vouchers for inner-city parents and children. Indeed, the civil rights leadership led the unsuccessful effort to defeat a school voucher plan for the Milwaukee area, a plan sponsored by Wisconsin state legislator Polly Williams. Clint Bolick, an attorney who spent two years defending the voucher proposal throughout the Wisconsin state appellate process, said:

> I had the tremendous honor of defending that [school choice] plan all the way from the trial court to the Wisconsin Supreme Court. One of the things I found most shocking was that the local chapter of the NAACP allowed itself to be used by the teachers union as the lead plaintiff challenging the Milwaukee choice plan—despite the fact that it had 90 percent support within the black community, and the overwhelming percentage of its beneficiaries are black kids as well.[134]

Bolick continued, stating what he has found to be axiomatic of mainstream black leadership:

> Black leadership of the civil rights establishment are a single voice in the "special interest" chorus [in the above case, the teacher unions]. If the choice comes down to its constituency or special interest allies, I have never seen the NAACP, in particular, buck its special interest ties.[135]

In addition to linking educational dysfunction to a welfare system that encourages the formation of weak families, the dissidents generally recognize a link between the proliferation of single-parent families and the growth of criminal activity in the inner city. The nature of the link between single-parent families and rising crime rates is complex. One aspect of this link is ethical. The erosion of moral authority at home, according to Sowell, has led to the "re-barbarization" of neighborhoods.[136] He sees weak families—lacking in discipline and parental supervision—as tending to give rise to criminal behavior in youth. Though single-parent families do not inevitably and necessarily make for weak families, as Loury points out, in the inner city they avoid this dysfunction against the odds.[137] Studies indicate that, nationwide, children of single-parent families are more likely to engage in drug and criminal activities.[138] Children from single-parent families comprise 70 percent of youth currently in juvenile detention facilities.[139] One recently completed study tracked every child born on the island of Kauai in 1955 for 30 years and discovered that "five out of six delinquents with an adult criminal record came from families where [a parent] was absent."[140]

With specific reference to the black community, the dreadful effects of rising rates of out-of-wedlock births are becoming more apparent. In 1989, 23 percent of *all* African-American men aged 20 to 29 were either in prison or on probation or parole.[141] According to one study, one-fifth of all black males 15 to 34 now have criminal records.[142] Almost half of all African-American youth in Los Angeles County are involved in gang activity, according to a 1992 report.[143] Nearly 40 percent of those murdered in the United States are black men killed by other black men.[144] In Oakland, the city with the highest murder rate in California—and 43 percent of murder victims there are black—a neighbor of three recent murder victims commented on various reform ideas. "A curfew is not going to stop the killing. Most of the parents are under siege from their children."[145]

Given these assorted pathologies, it is hardly unreasonable to suggest that young unmarried women, like the above-mentioned Tracy, generally lack the parenting skills and personal emotional resources to control their children, especially during adolescence. Of course, these assorted social horrors are not solely due to the rising rates of out-of-wedlock births, but it is undeniable that there is a significant link between the two.

Aside from the myriad personal tragedies reflected by the aforementioned statistics, the socioeconomic consequences that flow from them are equally tragic, as whole communities suffer under a regime of fear. So frequent are gunshot wound cases at Martin Luther King Hospital in South Central Los Angeles that the U.S. Army sends medical personnel to train there. Nationwide, blacks are 70 percent more likely than whites to be victims of violent crimes.[146]

All of these statistics imply that the very real terror urban ghettos generate functions as yet another beam in "structural poverty." Social breakdown merely fosters further breakdown. Persistent gang harrassment drives many competent teachers from schoolrooms, and so lowers the quality of teaching, and as in the case of Za'ketta's harrassment, black students become oppressors of other black students. Criminal activity forces shops and businesses away from these neighborhoods, as the constant threat of robbery makes work hazardous and unpleasant, and for many the cost of insurance is prohibitively high. These costs are passed on to the poor, who can least afford them.[147] Middle-and upper-class blacks, the social core of black America, are reluctant to invest their dollars in enterprises in crime-ridden communities. Thus, the dominance of violence and fear in the inner city works to entrench poverty in poor black neighborhoods. And all the while, the black "leadership" continues to stress politics, eschewing intracommunity criticism.

Significantly, in public discussions about single motherhood—which is, as we have been arguing, a foundational cause of much urban dysfunction—a point frequently overlooked by media and liberal apologists for "alternative" family arrangements is the critical factor of a single mother's economic context.[148] Some middle-class women may be able to afford single parenting, but to hold them up as an example of the viability of the single-parent model as a "life-style choice" is to offer a sorry exculpation of a destructive inner-city phenomenon. This failure to mark the destructive force of unwed parenthood in the ghetto, and instead defend it as just another "option" for women, constitutes yet another impediment to overcoming structural poverty. But true to form, the *New York Times* offered such an apologia, a few days after Vice-President Quayle caused a media firestorm by suggesting a correlation between the rise in the number of single-parent families and the Los Angeles riots.[149] The *Times* article featured a New Orleans writer, Pat Friedmann, who at 28 chose single motherhood through artificial insemination and wrote an autobiographical account of her experience titled *The Exact Image of Motherhood*. In it she affirmed that by such choices women can "assert their identities."[150]

Kimi Gray, a nationally known black self-help activist who raised five children alone in dire poverty, is less sanguine than Friedmann about unwed motherhood as a form of self-actualization. (In Detroit, which is demographically similar to Gray's Washington, D.C., homicide is the leading cause of death of black males over ten, most of whom are fatherless.)[151] Rector relates Gray's preferred strategy for inner-city neighborhood revitalization:

> When she set about to reform her public housing complex, one of the first things she said was, "We had to get the men back in the family. You know, when we did get the men back, unwed pregnancy among our daughters went down, because the fathers were looking out for them, and refused to let the teenage boys do to them what they had done to other women when they were teenagers."[152]

Of course, we should remember that there are single mothers, like Gray, whose parental successes constitute heroic exceptions to the usual failure. The strength of her character, and the characters of many thousands like her, is hardly impugned, though, by pointing out that successful parenting under such circumstances has been accomplished against the odds.

Significantly, the black dissidents' factoring of family breakdown and personal morality into the poverty equation is regularly caricatured in the media as typical of benighted, "redneck" diagnoses. Los Angeles writer Ellen Snortland engages in such decoding in the following common polemic: " 'Traditional family values' is a right-wing euphemism for 'a white family where Daddy's the boss.' "[153] But merely to label an argument or, as with Snortland, to "reveal" its true meaning, is hardly to refute it. Words like "naive" and "simplistic," as Sowell says, "are used to dismiss instead of debate. These labels are not arguments; they are self-congratulations, which seldom foster either thoughtful foresight or prudent reconsideration."[154] It is in this way that the work of the dissidents is commonly dismissed by the media, as little more than rightist extremism in blackface. Robert Detlefsen, in *Civil Rights under Reagan* (1991), goes so far as to find a kind of Kulturkampf behind the eagerness to tag the "extremist Archie Bunker type" label on disbelievers in the efficacy of entitlement programs and "civil rights." On issues affecting blacks, "correct" views have assumed the currency of status symbols, says Detlefsen. One of these views is that the welfare system does not tempt to irresponsibility. Professions of this and other such views on matters of race, argues Detlefsen, are

> quite prevalent today, particularly among middle-brow, college-educated members of the "baby-boom" generation. Such persons are often not

thoughtful enough to probe the intricacies of the civil rights debate, much less to assimilate consciously the civil rights ideology. They have learned, however, from school and the media (especially television and its caricature of the quintessential "Low Rent" bigot Archie Bunker) that to dissent in any way from the orthodox shibboleths on matters of race is *déclassé*, the intellectual equivalent of wearing blue socks with brown shoes.[155]

Unintimidated by the *déclassé* insult, the dissenters find in these dynamics (and others we will explore) a complex set of intracommunity forces that, *apart from racism*, tend to keep the underclass down, and so constitute a species of tyranny.

Having limned something of the dissidents' "structural poverty" critique, it should be clear that their dissent from mainstream black advocacy hardly amounts to a ratification of the "tragic status quo," in Walter Williams' phrase.[156] The New Black Vanguard's picture of America under the influence of the civil rights establishment often takes on a Bosch-like texture, and as such confutes the view that civil rights leaders would "conserve" the sociopolitical system in its present form.

As noted in Axiom 3, the dissidents do not hold a deterministic view of human accomplishment. That is, they do not see the life-chances of inner-city youth as *unavoidably* shaped by ghetto conditions. The dissidents do not believe that inner-city blacks have the luxury of postponing their achievement until the civil rights establishment relaxes its grip on urban politics and conditions improve. Such passivity is morally indefensible, and indeed perversely mirrors the wait-on-the-government rhetoric that thinkers like Sowell and others find so repugnant. Their loathing stems from the counterdeterministic and individualistic tenor of their thought. Wortham encapsulates this view:

> [Frederick] Douglass made it. It stands to reason that somewhere, this day, there is a young black person determining that he will not be the next generation of his family on welfare. . . . The central idea of individualism is the autonomy and sovereignty of individual consciousness—that is, free will. And this is a feature of human *nature*, independent of historical or social circumstances.[157]

6. *The New Black Vanguard contests the practical relevance to the poor, as well as the morality, of preferential treatment policies based on race.*

Any consideration of preferential treatment policies must recognize from the outset that it is an element of what Bolick has called the "revised agenda" and is not coherent with the equal opportunity thrust of the original civil rights movement, which pressed for equality of opportunity

and not equality of result. Paradoxically, it is this heritage, now supplanted, that bears consonance with the history of black political
thought. For example, Robert Smalls, a U.S. congressman from Beaufort,
South Carolina (1874–86), declared, "My race needs no special defense,
for the past history of them in this country proves them to be the equal
of any people anywhere. All they need is an equal treatment in the battle
of life."[158]

But in our time and by degrees, says Sowell, a revisionist "civil rights
vision" began to insinuate itself, and its "rightness," into American
public life—against, he insists, the will of most black Americans, who
wanted equal opportunity and not race-based advantage.

As noted in Axiom 3, a major assumption of this transformed "civil
rights vision" has been that unequal representation of ethnic groups in
occupations and discrepant test scores are conclusive evidence of discrimination or bias. Sowell sees this assumption as unwarranted and
counterhistorical. It fails to take into account group differences in human
capital (e.g., attitudes, interests, work habits) while wrongly accenting
socioeconomic "advantage" or "disadvantage." Sowell disputes, for example, the tendency of the civil rights establishment to translate, for the
public's "edification," poor scores by blacks on certain tests into charges
of discrimination. Writing in 1983 in *The Economics and Politics of Race*,
Sowell reported that Black American, Mexican American, and American
Indian students did not score as high on the mathematics portion of the
Scholastic Aptitude Test as did Asian American students. The "obvious"
conclusion, as routinized in the media and energized by the "civil rights
vision," is that such disparities must be due to "socioeconomic disadvantage" befalling the poorer scoring groups. But as it turns out, the
cohort of Black American, Mexican American, and American Indian
students Sowell selected for this study were from families with *incomes
of $50,000 and up*, while the Asian American students were from families
with *incomes of $6,000 and below*.[159] Sowell's point: automatic equation of
low test scores with victimized treatment is a statistical fallacy, because
it ignores the influential role played by cultural differences.

Sowell finds similar statistical sleight of hand behind the reduction of
"equality of opportunity" into "equality of result." Nowhere on earth,
says Sowell, is there, in any given population, a proportionate equation
of ethnic affiliation with occupational choice.[160] Notwithstanding the
utopian ("eutopia" means "nowhere" in Greek) character of such a
perfect ethnic architectonic, it is the chimerical basis of preferential treatment policy in the United States.

Generally speaking, the dissidents' criticism of preferential treatment embraces at least four main ideas. First, they question its economic effectiveness. While many acknowledge that preferential treatment has furthered the careers of some blacks—as any policy of favoritism would—the dissidents find evidence that preferential policies have been irrelevant to, or have even damaged, the vocational hopes of the black underclass. Business owners are reluctant to locate in predominantly black neighborhoods because of preferential treatment standards. Incompetence comes in all colors, but firing a minority employee, according to these employers, is especially risky, as charges of racism may require significant financial resources to refute. For example, the owner of a small factory in Chicago, described by one columnist as "patently innocent of discrimination," was fined $148,000 for employing three blacks instead of the 8.45 blacks mandated for companies his size by the federal government.[161] "The huge legal liabilities," writes Sowell, "created by policies that make statistical 'underrepresentation' equivalent to discrimination create incentives for employers to protect themselves by putting distance between their companies and those communities from which they can expect large numbers of minority applicants."[162] In this way, businesses that could help a local economy (and so the poorest of blacks) are effectively discouraged from doing so.

Second, the New Black Vanguard objects to the moral perversity they see embodied in preferential treatment. "Live people," observes Sowell, "are being sacrificed because of what dead people did." This, according to the dissidents, represents an inherent moral incongruity. While the ill effects on whites of affirmative action are contemporary and presently felt, the advantage for which affirmative action is supposed to compensate is a past-tense privilege no longer in force in an official, statutory way. There is little doubt that the residual effects of centuries of white advantage are enjoyed today, by some whites more than others. But what is at issue is the relationship between culpability and residual advantage. It is morally problematic to punish someone who unwillfully benefits from a residual advantage secured by the willful misdeeds of an earlier generation of people, quite possibly unrelated to the one being punished. In fact, the descendents of "free persons of color" or of a black Harvard scholar may have more inherited capital than children of white manual laborers, making the arbitrary discrimination against the white laborer all the more problematic. Economic histories are not racially uniform, yet a policy of preferential treatment must assume that they are.

Is it morally justifiable to hold an individual of one generation responsible for the immoralities committed by individuals of previous
generations? Is the white fireman in Birmingham, Alabama, who is
passed over for promotion due to the sins of his "fathers" really being
treated fairly?[163] If discrimination is intrinsically wrong, then it seems
rather perverse to have public policy that intentionally codifies an immoral practice. The New Black Vanguard asks: In what other areas of
public policy are we willing to enact into law a practice we find morally
repugnant? But even beyond that there is an irony in the civil rights
establishment's pursuit of preferential treatment policies based on race,
since the removal of such policies was the very raison d'être of the
original civil rights movement. Writes Bolick, "The head-spinning swift-
ness with which the former champions of color-blindness embraced
color-consciousness once someone else's ox was being gored would have
been comic were it not so tragic."[164] Nathan Glazer, a political philos-
opher, comments on the irony of this revised agenda:

> In 1964, we declared that no account should be taken of race, color, national
> origin, or religion in the spheres of voting, jobs, and education. . . . Yet no
> sooner had we made this national assertion than we entered into an unex-
> ampled recording of the records of the color, race, and national origin in
> every significant sphere of [a person's] life. Having placed into law the
> dissenting opinion *Plessy v. Ferguson* that our Constitution is color-blind,
> we entered into a period of color and group-consciousness with a venge-
> ance.[165]

Third, the New Black Vanguard points to the indeterminate character
of affirmative action: its success point remains unarticulated and its
"finish line" unavoidably, and frustratingly, unmarked. When is racial
equality and parity achieved—when there are no poor minorities? But
what exactly are the standards by which progress will be measured, and
wherein lies the vindication, or warrant, for those standards? Unless
such guideposts and "finish lines" are cognitively erected, the condition
of absolute parity will be hard to recognize, acknowledge, and celebrate.
Fourth, the dissidents contend that affirmative action stigmatizes its
putative beneficiaries with self-doubt: in Steele's phrase, it sears with
the "stigma of questionable competence." A sociologist at the University
of California at Berkeley acknowledges "casualties" of affirmative action:
"minority kids who are depressed or feeling incompetent because of the
stigma." He tells of a black student who confided to him, "I feel like I
have AFFIRMATIVE ACTION stamped on my forehead."[166] Undermin-

ing the idea of personal merit, preferential treatment tends to make nonblacks suspicious of black achievement, and blacks themselves suspicious of others' suspicions. The antagonism this creates militates against interpersonal racial harmony.

But at the most fundamental level, laws such as preferential treatment policies violate the time-honored Kantian moral principle of treating people as ends in themselves, and not as means to ends, including social ends. Human dignity demands that people not be sacrificed for institutional efficiency—reduced to a number, some kind of statistical trophy. A Harvard professor, Michael Sandel, illustrates the moral oddness of this subjugation of human beings and their talents to social ends in the form of imaginary letters to successful and unsuccessful medical or law school applicants:

> *Dear (unsuccessful) applicant:* . . . It is not your fault that when you came along society happened not to need the qualities you had to offer. Those admitted instead of you were not themselves deserving of a place, nor worthy of praise for the factors that led to their admission. We are . . . using [all applicants] as instruments of a wider social purpose. You will likely find this news disappointing in the sense that your hopes of reaping the benefits given those whose qualities do coincide with society's needs at any given moment will not be realized. But this sort of disappointment occurs whenever an individual's preferences must give way to society's preferences, and should not be exaggerated by the thought that your rejection reflects in any way on your intrinsic moral worth; please be assured that those who were admitted were as intrinsically worthless as you.
>
> *Dear successful applicant:* . . . No praise is intended or to be inferred from this decision [to accept you], as your having the relevant qualities is arbitrary from a moral point of view. You are to be congratulated, not in the sense that you deserve credit for having the qualities that led to your admission—you do not—but only in the sense that the winner of a lottery is to be congratulated. You are lucky to have come along with the right traits at the right moment, and if you choose to accept our offer you will ultimately be entitled to the benefits that attach to being used in this way. . . . The notion of desert seems not to apply to your case.[167]

This reduction of the conditions and elements of desert to nothing more than fortuity strikes at what many people, including the black dissidents, find morally objectionable about affirmative action. Such a policy calls into question the validity and importance of those personal qualities our moral intuitions—and hopefully our schooling—tell us are the foundation of individual achievement: diligence, perseverance, and superior learning. It is disheartening, to say the least, if the grounds of my advancement and success are qualities I have no control over and no ability to influence, for example, my race and gender. Inequity resides in any policy that so radically perverts the idea of merit.

This general thought is illustrated in William Raspberry's account of an affirmative action policy-change at the University of Virginia Law School, and a young black woman's response to it. On the verge of making the *Law Review* by the standard criteria (grades and writing ability), she was about to become the first black to ever hold that position. But then a policy change was recommended and passed that supplanted merit-based criteria with assured slots on the *Review* based on other measures, including ethnicity and physical handicap. She was "catapulted onto the *Law Review*," writes Raspberry, "under the new dispensation." He continues:

> She said, "Why are you doing this to me?' . . . Students want to be on the *Law Review* because they know the big law firms look to [being on the] *Law Review* as an imprimatur. . . . But if you have two tracks, one for the white kids, and another for minority kids, the minority kid who makes the *Law Review* is forever having to defend and explain the door he came through. If he came through the door marked, "Minorities only," the value is gone from it."[168]

Loury sees affirmative action policies as at odds with "freely conveyed respect," which Loury sees as required by the high value of human dignity:

> If you want to be judged as equal, that requires performance. If the perception is that your achievement is the result of the policy of affirmative action, and not exceptional performance, then people will discount the achievement and won't credit you with the same degree of accomplishment as otherwise. It's an undignified posture, in that sense.[169]

7. *The New Black Vanguard emphasizes the importance of nonracial strategies to enhance the status of minorities, especially the development of human capital, mediating structures, and neighborhood enterprise.*

It cannot be denied that the New Black Vanguard speaks primarily in a critical voice. Some understand this thrust as mere carping and destructive cavil. Having declared against a political and juridical approach to black advocacy; against the educational bureaucracy; against the current welfare system; against a sociologism on the part of intellectuals that denies the centrality of personal responsibility in human development; against the language of victimization, doom, and discouragement used by the popular media and by rap culture; against the weak juvenile justice system; against a deterministic view of human consciousness based on race; and against preferential treatment policies based solely on skin color—since they are opposed to all this, it is hardly inexplicable that those of the New Black Vanguard are branded "negative."

But at least two replies may be made to this objection. First, the idea that the dissidents have no positive agenda is incorrect. Their positive proposals include welfare reform initiatives (e.g., mandatory workfare); service delivery through mediating structures; increasing the savings cap for those on public aid; school voucher plans; judicial interpretation that protects the "economic liberty" of small businesses; free enterprise zones; tenant management in public housing; and a youth subminimum wage. As the dissidents enter the political arena (we have in mind, here, the 1992 senatorial candidacies of Allan Keyes in Maryland and William B. Allen in California), they have spoken even more in a propositional voice, offering concrete policy proposals for public consideration.

Second, labeling the dissidents "negative" presumes that the origin of their solutions ought to coincide with the origins of the solutions of their critics—that they must reflect common assumptions about race, autonomy, family, government, and oppression. But the dissidents do not share these assumptions. Consequently, they press for dismantling many of the "positive" projects of the civil rights establishment and their ideological partners, arguing that these have proved ruinous to the axis of the black community, the black family. At this point in the historical development of unorthodox black advocacy, they find it necessary to engage in a concentrated social *via negativa* in order to shake the foundations of the longstanding hegemony of the "revised agenda."

Heading this social *via negativa* is the undoing of welfare laws that foster male desertion and unwed pregnancy. Contradistinctly, the civil rights establishment has consistently joined "welfare rights" groups (e.g., the National Welfare Rights Organization) in fighting for an "entitlement sans obligation" philosophy of welfare and for increased benefit packages. While civil rights leaders term their stance in favor of entitlement as "positive," the dissidents argue the opposite: Entitlement cleaved from obligation has transmogrified the inner city by subsidizing the dissolution of the black family.

Having supported welfare policies that weaken the black family, the civil rights establishment—by virtue of its unyielding opposition to private school vouchers—sends the children of these families off to "value neutral" public schools. Value neutrality, here, also applies to Sex Ed (another "positive" innovation), the instruction of which typically amounts to, in Loury's phrase, little more than a "how-to" endorsement. Loury's value-laden critique of contemporary trends in public education is echoed by Keyes:

> If we encourage our children to believe they can't control their sexual desire, what of their greed, their anger, their prejudice, and their hate? What condoms will we distribute to protect them from the consequences of these? Perhaps it's time we remembered that for a free people, the challenge of education is not to fill our children's heads with knowledge but to instill in their hearts the confidence they need to quell the storms and tempests of unruly passion.[170]

The dissidents' social *via negativa* continues: Rendered fatherless and value-free by such "positive" programs, inner-city children are now, for the sake of civil liberties, put at the mercy of armed classmates who, it has been determined, ought not be inconvenienced by weapons searches. (This, despite a recent *Time* magazine report that as many as 135,000 students bring guns to school each day![171]) Bob Teague, commenting on this "positive" affirmation of student rights, points out that in 1986, an average of one child every day was shot in Detroit.[172] In the courts of Detroit in 1986, the ACLU (part of the extended "civil rights establishment," by Bolick's definition) supported a landmark court decision that undid a public school policy of random searches for weapons.[173]

Though such unhelpful contributions by civil rights groups to the well-being of blacks could be multiplied ad nauseam, one more will suffice: The "positive" message of rap politicoes who preach "black consciousness" as the negation of all things white, assuring youth that their victimization is complete and their violent hate justified. Perversely, this nihilistic message is believed to inculcate a pride of racial heritage that produces self-esteem and then, somehow, self-sufficiency.

So it is emphatically true that the critique of the New Black Vanguard is, in part "negative," and their program disestablishmentarian. The dissidents would dismantle policies that tamper with the organic unity of the family, statutes that wedge parent from child, rhetoric that parts youth from practical aspirations. The dissidents, as we will see especially in Chapter 5, evince confidence in the ability of ordinary people, and families, to solve their own problems. For many dissidents, this confidence is based on the cross-cultural evidence of the family's natural effectiveness "as the center of social life, and correspondingly as the locus of formation of personal character," in Loury's words.[174] Though such an idea, says Loury, "would readily gain the assent of the common man or woman," it is an understanding that "conflicts with some expert thinking in the social sciences and allied professions."[175] Expert resistance to the idea of the family as the locus of socialization, or, in the thought of James V. Schall, S.J., as the locus of "charity,"[176] contributes to today's political climate, which affirms extrafamilial strategies as unerringly "positive." Meanwhile, this expert class denigrates any civic theory that recognizes the sui generis effectiveness of the family as a decision maker, belittling it as an anachronistic idea or as oversimplistically laissez faire.

Significantly, the dismissals of the dissident view as gratuitously negative reductively ignore many facets of New Black Vanguard social criticism, probably because the dissidents tend toward common sense analyses rather than the titillating "new ideas." The dissidents avoid stylish vogue neologisms and policy innovations for the sake of innovation. Sowell, for instance, having carefully surveyed what works in education and what does not, came to the unexciting conviction in *Education: Myths and Assumptions* that what works today in education is what has traditionally worked: discipline, an emphasis on the fundamentals, and strong, decisive administration. Underlying the whole of the dissidents' variegated social critiques is a sharp consciousness of the unintended consequences of social programs and "reforms."

Practically speaking, then, the first component of their social approach is to encourage black and white citizens to an unmasking of the ideological overlays that the knowledge-class cognoscenti and the media would slip over the events of the day, confounding personal experience. Black Americans have been particularly hurt by these overlays, says Sowell, especially as they have been appropriated by "a relative handful of the anointed [community activists] who have decided that they know what is truly good for us."[177]

Common sense and human experience, says Sowell, are the best antidotes to theory-induced social illusions, including the "racist under every bed" notion that the "experts," he argues, regularly purvey in social science classrooms and on the six o'clock news.[178] For example, commonsense would dictate that residents of poor neighborhoods take advantage of every opportunity open to them. It is commonly thought that impoverished black youth are excluded from higher education because of their poverty. Yet, as we have noted, college loans and grants are readily available. According to a financial aid counselor at one of

Los Angeles' nine community colleges, the following loans and grants are reserved for needy students who attend community colleges full time:

$1,530 Pell Grants
$1,196–$1,400 Cal Grants
$800 Perkins Loan
$2,600 Stafford Loan[179]

This comes to a maximum of $6,330 per year for all needy students. (In addition, students can qualify on a first-come basis for work-study on campus, for an additional $2,600). Yet, relatively speaking, only a small percentage of poor blacks in Los Angeles take advantage of this opportunity, and fewer still actually graduate. This is especially tragic given the practicality of such community college instruction. Such a social passivity is not surprising given the influential rhetoric of raptivists such as Chuck D, who recently opined:

> I can go to college and high school and get top grades, and when I go out into the job market, I don't know anything about business, which means business is a family thing, you understand what I am saying? If you ain't family, you're not going to get that fucking job![180]

What? In a manner a bit more precise than Chuck D's, recent statistics from the U.S. Department of Labor revealed the relationship between black educational attainment and black employment. For every significant level of increase in education realized by 25 to 34 year old blacks, the percent of black unemployment dropped by one-half. This means, in more concrete terms, that blacks with a four-year college degree are roughly six times as likely to be employed than those who have a high school diploma.[181] Chuck D's denial—common in the rhetoric of raptivists and even some civil rights leaders—of the financial value of higher educational attainment for blacks is blatantly counter-empirical. But such rebuke of opportunity is quite consistent with the dominant attitude among black youth and their disgruntled leaders: No part of "the System" can be hospitable to blacks.

At a local level, the New Black Vanguard's social *via negativa* would entail confronting and exposing such powerful community fictions. This would mean bucking the neighborhood party line and frankly discussing in public forums "the enemy within," as Loury describes it. Carolyn

Wallace, a Newark social worker, thinks that bold intracommunity debunking would lead, by degrees, to a rebirth of vital neighborhood values. She told journalist Bill Moyers, "If you say it on your corner, and I say it on my corner, and everybody's saying it, it's going to be like a drumbeat."[182] It is this sort of approach that Ogbu and Fordham recommend in battling the antiachievement ethic they found in predominately black schools, the ethic fostered by the belief that achievement is "white behavior."

In *The Flip Side of Soul,* Bob Teague also argues for intracommunity debunking. Too often, says Teague, community members look the other way as children are taught "the mind-set of despair that can only regard black folks as victims who have many rights in this society but few responsibilities."[183] Too often children are socialized to accept the reckless rhetoric of the Black Redneck Society (Teague's name for stridently antiwhite blacks), which, for instance, cried racism at the firing of eighteen black lawyers from the staff of the Legal Aid Society, as required by law, because they "flunked the state bar exam. Twice."[184] Teague finds that community standards have plummeted since his youth.

> Unlike black families today—isolated and full of pain—we recognized one another as wounded parts of ourselves. Being good neighbors meant looking out for one another's children. . . . In retrospect, we had a sprawling black conspiracy that really worked. . . . In many black neighborhoods today, to even suggest, *sotto voce*, that the anti-lifestyle of urban terrorists serves to reinforce unflattering stereotypes is a no-no, akin to treason.[185]

Teague urges dissenters to ignore convoluted charges of "treason" and press ahead with local debunking of false ideas and "anti-lifestyles," so to halt and reverse the deterioration of community values and strengthen the black family in poor communities. "Social engineers keep inventing substitutes for parental responsibility," writes Teague, "but nothing works."[186]

Woodson articulates a guiding principle here: The black poor ought not to wait for solutions to be "parachuted in by middle-class, professional service providers."[187] Woodson's promotion of self-help strategies, which emphasize the power of both personal initiative and voluntary associations, is characteristic of the New Black Vanguard approach. In general, the dissidents favor public policy that draws on "mediating structures," such as the family, the church, community schools, and other voluntary associations; these, they argue, have been the traditional backbone of black progress, not entitlement programs, which leave undeveloped their recipients' personal potential.[188]

For the dissidents, empowerment is achieved primarily through inner resources of personality. They do not regard as passé the traditional advice given by black elders to their children, as Clarence Thomas remembers his grandfather giving him: "Study hard, work to improve yourself, and always do what's right."[189] These values, say the Vanguard, have traditionally been invigorated by "intermediary institutions"—a third, salutary force between individual resources and government megastructures.[190] This contrasts sharply with a "civil rights ideology" of empowerment that focuses on group entitlement and wealth redistribution—strategies that have set in motion a debilitating "alms race," says Woodson, feverishly run by politicians, alliances of rights groups, and bureaucrats. The victories won through this style of advocacy are largely "symbolic," says Sowell, and largely Pyrrhic. Loury makes this specific:

> In central city ghettos across America, where far too many young black mothers struggle alone to raise the next generation of black youth, it is difficult to see the potential for fundamental change via these traditional [civil rights] methods. Even the election of black candidates to the highest municipal offices has so far failed to effect such change. Yet to the extent that we can foster institutions within the black community that encourage responsible male involvement in parenting, help prevent unplanned pregnancies, and support young unwed mothers in their efforts to return to school and become self-supporting, important changes in the lives of the black population can be made.[191]

The dissidents' philosophy of mediating institutions defies the "bootstrap" stereotype regularly imputed to them, "that all we have to do is open the doors of economic opportunity and let the winners and losers fight among themselves."[192] In terms of Sowell's concept of an "intergenerational relay race" mentioned earlier, the work of these mediating structures is to reclaim or reinforce social capital that has been sacked by a "poverty industry" that emphasizes, in Woodson's terms, incapacity over capacity and is silent on values traditional to black survival and flourishment.

The specific policy proposals of the New Black Vanguard focus on ways to help neighborhoods help themselves. School voucher plans may serve as a case in point. Contrary to criticisms of public education by conventional black advocacy, which allege racism, the dissidents' objection is characteristically practical: The schools—especially inner-city schools—have shown themselves incapable of adequately educating, protecting, and inspiring black youth.[193]

The Detroit school system serves as an example. In one gang-plagued neighborhood (where 80 percent of the children are being raised by single mothers), parents were outraged in 1991 by a series of horrors. The school janitor was killed in a drive-by shooting; a pre-schooler was shot in the back; and the mother of one third grader removed her son from school because he owed his employer, a neighborhood drug dealer, $300 and his life was in danger.[194] Responding to the terror that filled their neighborhood, parents tried to organize a school for black boys. But the plan was roundly denounced by the American Civil Liberties Union and the National Organization for Women, who successfully fought the creation of the all-boys school, arguing that it would promote sexism.[195] Significantly, at least one women's rights group in the area offered no opposition to the plan. Its director, a black woman who recognized the urgency of the situation, told us, on condition of anonymity: "Children are being killed. This school will give at least some children a chance."

Milwaukee schools experienced similar problems. In fact, there the teachers and administrators had such a low level of confidence in their own public education system that 62 percent of them were sending their own children to private schools.[196] But in Milwaukee, due to the efforts of Wisconsin state representative Polly Williams, a school voucher plan was created for low-income parents. The plan offered parents a voucher worth $2,500 (a small fraction of Wisconsin's public school per pupil expenditure), which they could use to enroll their children at any private, nonsectarian school. The program has faired well, despite the underpreparation of the voucher students who have transfered from public to private schools.[197]

Encouraged by the success of the Milwaukee plan, Clint Bolick has initiated efforts to duplicate the plan in post-riot Los Angeles, where he has encountered adamant opposition from local black politicians. Such opposition is not unexpected—William Bennett, the former Secretary of Education, attributes the black leadership's resistance to vouchers, in part, to traditional coalitions between the civil rights leadership and the powerful teachers' unions, who are hostile to voucher plans. (As an indication of the power of this special interest group, membership in the nation's teachers' unions is put at 2.3 million.)[198] Dissidents tend to see such resistance as antidemocratic, as the opposition of a handful of special interest groups to the will of individual citizens. With respect to the situation of inner-city schools, teachers' union opposition seems especially hypocritical. Middle-class teachers, who generally live outside the inner city and whose children generally do not attend school in the inner city, resist plans that would allow the poor, who live in the inner city, greater control over their children's educational curriculum and environment.

During a debate at the University of Tennessee on the merits of school voucher plans, Anne Wortham made this point about the value of vouchers in promoting self-governance:

> We need to do more than merely call for reforms in the public education system. We need a different system altogether—a system that fosters choice, competition, and efficiency. . . . [In public education] there is little systematic incentive for educators to provide the quality education that consumers want and that a democratic society and the high technology of the computer age require. We are not likely to improve the quality and efficiency of education under such conditions.[199]

Is a plan that endows the family (whatever its state) with the authority to make important decisions inconsistent with the dissidents' critique of "antieducational homes" in the inner-city? Absolutely not. By restoring self-determination to the family, a voucher plan functionally recognizes the intimate and responsive nature of the family unit, and so preserves the dignity and concern that inheres in familial ties. In addition, the experience in Milwaukee has shown that the responsibility a voucher plan confers on dysfunctional families works to bring healing and parental competence, where before there was resentment and negligence. A by-product of the program has been better parenting, says Representative Williams. "When you empower people and give them a sense of ownership, they become responsible, and they learn how to make decisions."[200] Such a voucher system has been cogently characterized as simple justice for citizens of a republic committed to liberty and self-governance.[201]

Woodson believes that such self-governance, when practiced in poor black neighborhoods, can unleash dormant social capital. His system for accomplishing this is to give "the poor access to information and share with them the success stories of their peers, enabling them to figure out what is their best option."[202] Voucher schools are but one example of the arena in which Woodson's self-help philosophy would flower. Too few success stories, insists Woodson, are shared with poor people, including children, by those black advocates who believe that accentuating the victimhood and "disenfranchisement" of blacks—not their potential for self-reliance—makes better political sense.

Nevertheless, Loury's point is worth remembering: "The self-help approach [is] . . . more a philosophy of life than a list of specific projects."[203] Steele, too, regards interior activism essentially as a disposition, rather than a paint-by-numbers formula. For him, true activism requires an existential commitment to personal identity, above and beyond racial association. This fostering of the person has the final effect of establishing a sense of dignity that garners the "freely conveyed respect" of other citizens.

Reflecting on the need for, and the meaning of, such a course-change in black advocacy, and its implications for our public life, Sleeper points out the mutual obligations that would inhere in such a revitalized American civic compact:

> It is long past time for the ordinary black people who are standing in job lines, ready to share society's burdens as well as its rewards, to demand of their leaders a change in course; for the politics of paroxysm, grievance, and conspiracy is clearly not working. Surely it is time for the rest of us to demand it too. But, for whites, fair warning: as we make such demands upon our black neighbors, the closest of strangers, we also obligate ourselves.[204]

Having made this brief overview of figures and themes, we shall now investigate in more detail four individuals shaping the challenge of the New Black Vanguard. When beholding the people and ideas that comprise this challenge to the revised agenda, it must always be remembered that their voice is not monotone and their thinking not homogeneous. In speaking of a "New Black Vanguard" we are not talking about a political party or a univocal, systematic worldview, but rather about the manifestation of a social and political dissent by a cross-section of African-American thinkers, who find a common ground in their valuation of personal responsibility and self-help.

NOTES

1. *Business Week*, 30 November 1981.
2. Recent remarks by Rowan indicate his rhetorical and propositional consistency in these matters over the years. On Clarence Thomas he has remarked, "With a little flour in his face, you'd have [former Klansman] David Duke."

William McDuran, "The Trials of Clarence Thomas," *National Review*, 12 August 1991, p. 38.

3. Robert D. McFadden et al., *Outrage: The Story Behind the Tawana Brawley Hoax* (New York: Bantam, 1990), p. 325.

4. Peter L. Berger, *Invitation to Sociology* (Garden City, N. Y.: Doubleday Anchor, 1963), p. 41.

5. Nat Hentoff, "The Magazine You Have to Fight Your Way Out of," *Village Voice*, 19 May 1992.

6. Julius Lester, *Falling Pieces of the Broken Sky* (New York: Little, Brown, 1992), pp. 181–82.

7. Ibid., p. 181.

8. "Academic Freedom and the Black Intellectual," *Black Scholar*, November/December 1988, p. 19.

9. Walter Williams, *All It Takes Is Guts* (Washington, D.C.: Regnery-Gateway, 1987), p. 31.

10. Ibid.

11. Orlando Patterson, "Race, Gender and Liberal Fallacies," *New York Times*, 20 October 1991.

12. Brad Stetson, interview with Clint Bolick, Washington, D.C., 20 May 1992.

13. Daniel P. Moynihan, *The Black Family: The Case for National Action*. (Washington, D.C.: Superintendent of Documents, 1965).

14. William Ryan, *Blaming the Victim* (New York: Vintage, 1976), p. 63.

15. Glenn Loury, "The Family, the Nation, and Senator Moynihan," *Commentary*, June 1986, pp. 21–26.

16. Glenn C. Loury, "The Need for Moral Leadership in the Black Community," *New Perspectives* 16, no. 1 (Summer 1984), p. 17.

17. William Julius Wilson, *The Truly Disadvantaged* (Chicago: University of Chicago Press, 1987), p. 173.

18. James Q. Wilson, "The Rediscovery of Character: Private Virtue and Public Policy," in *Private Virtue and Public Policy: Catholic Thought and National Life*, edited by James Finn (New Brunswick, N.J.: Transaction, 1990), p. 112.

19. Robert L. Woodson, *On the Road to Economic Freedom* (Washington, D.C.: Regnery-Gateway, 1987).

20. Shelby Steele, *The Content of Our Character* (New York, St. Martin's, 1990), p. 174.

21. Thomas Sowell, *Compassion versus Guilt* (New York: Morrow, 1987), p. 133.

22. Ibid., p. 83.

23. L. Brent Bozell and Brent H. Baker, eds., *And That's the Way It Is(n't)* (Alexandria, Va.: Media Research Center, 1990), p. 24.

24. Ibid., p. 27.

25. Brad Stetson, interview with Clint Bolick, 20 May 1992.

26. Joseph Conti, interview with Chris Blatchford, Los Angeles, 5 October 1992.

27. Oscar Lewis, "The Culture of Poverty," *Scientific American* 115, no. 16 (October 1966), pp. 19–25.

28. Ryan, *Blaming the Victim*, p. 123.

29. Ibid., pp. 103–123.

30. Leon Dash, *When Children Want Children* (New York: Morrow, 1989), p. 9.

31. Ibid., p. 11 (emphasis in original).

32. KABC Radio, Los Angeles, Calif., 3 May 1992.

33. Glenn C. Loury, "Responsibility and Race," delivered at the Center for Constructive Alternatives Seminar (Hillsdale College, Hillsdale Michigan, November 7, 1982) in *Vital Speeches*, April 13, 1983, p. 400.

34. Orlando Patterson, *Ethnic Chauvinism* (New York: Stein and Day, 1977), pp. 155–56.

35. Loury, "The Family," p. 25.

36. Ibid., p. 23.

37. Joseph Conti, interview with Jesse Peterson, Los Angeles, Calif., 10 January 1992.

38. Ibid.

39. Thomas Sowell, "The High Cost of Hoodlumism," *Destiny*, December/January 1991, p. 28.

40. Joseph Conti, interview with Jesse Peterson, Calif., 14 March 1992.

41. Sowell, "High Cost of Hoodlumism," p. 28.

42. Joseph Conti, interview with Dennis Prager, 12 March 1992.

43. Quoted in David Horowitz, "The Radical Left and the New Racism," *New Dimensions*, December 1990, p. 23.

44. Alphonso Pinkney, *The Myth of Black Progress* (Cambridge: Cambridge University Press, 1984), p. ix.

45. Thomas Sowell, *Civil Rights: Rhetoric or Reality?* (New York: Quill, 1984), p. 15.

46. "Gap Grows between Black Middle Class and Those Mired in Poverty, Study Finds," *Los Angeles Times*, 9 August 1991, p. A27.

47. Quoted in Ibid.

48. Ibid.

49. Ibid.

50. Thomas Sowell, *The Economics and Politics of Race* (New York: Quill, 1983), p. 194.

51. Quoted in William Bennet, *The De-Valuing of America* (New York: Summit, 1992), p. 197.

52. Joseph Conti, interview with Jesse Peterson, Los Angeles, Calif., 18 May 1992.

53. Joseph Conti, interview with Jeffrey Clayton, director of Upward Bound, at the University of Southern California, Los Angeles, 8 May 1992.

54. Ibid.

55. Jim Sleeper, *The Closest of Strangers* (New York: Norton, 1990), p. 312.

56. *Village Voice*, 22 October 1991, p. 16.

57. John Ogbu and Signithia Fordham, "Black Students' School Success: Coping with the "Burden of 'Acting White'," *Urban Review* 18, no. 3, pp. 176–206.

58. "The Hidden Hurdle," *Time*, 16 March 1992, p. 44.

59. Joseph Conti, interviews at a meeting, Brotherhood Organization of a New Destiny (BOND), Los Angeles, Calif., 17 May 1992.

60. Ibid.

61. Thomas Sowell, "The Racial Numbers Game Counts Out Young Blacks," *Orange County Register*, 14 April 1992.

62. Edith Efron, *The News Twisters* (Los Angeles: Nash, 1971), p. 74. See also Rothman and Lichter, *Watching America*.

63. Linda Lichter, S. Robert Lichter, Stanley Rothman, *Watching America* (New York: Prentice Hall Press, 1991), p. 198

64. Ethelbert W. Haskins, *The Crisis in Afro-American Leadership* (Buffalo, N.Y.: Prometheus, 1988), p. 19.

65. "The Lure of Excuses," *Newsweek*, 29 July 1991, p. 27.

66. Jonathan Kozol, *Savage Inequalities* (New York: Crown, 1991), p. 57.

67. Glenn C. Loury, "The Saliency of Race," in *Second Thoughts about Race in America*, edited by Peter Collier and David Horowitz (Lanham, Md.: Madison Books, 1991), p. 77.

68. William B. Allen, "The Civil Rights Revolution," *Imprimis*, April 1989, p. 2.

69. Stanley Crouch, "Role Models," in Collier and Horowitz, eds., *Second Thoughts about Race*, p. 61.

70. Bob Teague, *The Flip Side of Soul* (New York: Morrow, 1989), p. 103.

71. Loury, "Need for Moral Leadership," p. 19.

72. Steele, *Content of Our Character*, p. 88.

73. Ibid., p. 87.

74. Walter Williams, "We Hold Black Rioters to a Lesser Standard," *Orange Country Register*, 20 May 1992.

75. Joseph Conti, interview with Dennis Prager, 12 March 1992.

76. For the record, Sister Souljah says her remarks in the 13 May 1992 *Washington Post* were reported out of context, that she was speaking from the mindset of a gang member. Should she not have condemned gang members, then?

77. *USA Today*, 15 June 1992, p. 2a.

78. Peter L. Berger, *Invitation to Sociology* (Garden City, N.Y.: Doubleday, 1963), p. 81.

79. William B. Allen, C-SPAN interview with Peter Kaye of the *San Diego Tribune*, aired 23 May 1992.

80. "Lee Gets By with a Little Help from Friends," *Los Angeles Times*, 21 May 1992, p. F1.

81. Anne Wortham, "I'm Not Supposed to Exist," *Reason*, August 1984, p. 51.

82. William Julius Wilson, *The Declining Significance of Race* (Chicago: University of Chicago Press, 1980).

83. William Julius Wilson, "The Black Underclass," *Wilson Quarterly*, Spring 1984, p. 98.

84. Ibid., p. 97.

85. Lawrence Mead, *The New Politics of Poverty: The Nonworking Poor in America* (New York: Basic Books, 1992), p. 12; for a discussion of Wilson's mismatch theory, see pp. 99–105.

86. Ibid., pp. 145–47.

87. Walter Williams, *The State against Blacks* (New York: McGraw-Hill, 1982), p. 75.

88. Clint Bolick, *Changing Course* (New Brunswick, N.J.: Transaction, 1988), p. 100.

89. Ibid., pp. 107–8.

90. For a discussion of work availability for African-Americans in the inner cities and the standard of living available through the minimum wage, see, respectively, Chapter 5, "Are Jobs Available?" and Chapter 4, "Low Wages and Hard Times," in Lawrence Mead, *The New Politics of Poverty* (New York: Basic Books, 1992).

91. Ibid., p. 107.

92. Cited in Mead, *New Politics of Poverty*, p. 142. For a discussion of pay expectations, see Harry J. Holzer, "Black Youth Nonemployment: Duration and Job Search," and Linda Datcher-Loury and Glenn C. Loury, "The Effects of Attitudes and Aspirations on the Labor Supply of Young Men," in *Black Youth Employment Crisis*, pp. 386–89.

93. Mead, *The New Politics of Poverty*, pp. 69–72. This is a point made by Mead. He also notes that the poverty rate for workers paid at or below $3.35 was only 8 percent in 1984 if there were other workers in the family (usually the case, according to Mead) but 45 percent if there were not. Despite frequent characterizations of the minimum-wage earner as a household head working to support a family on his or her income alone, relatively few minimum-wage earners are actually in that position. So the fact that a minimum-wage earner is frequently dependent on another family member's income accounts for the surprisingly low percentage of minimum-wage earners below the poverty line. See Mead, *New Politics of Poverty*, p. 70.

94. See Mead's discussion in *New Politics of Poverty*, pp. 71–72; also see Robert Rector and Peter T. Butterfield, "Reforming Welfare: The Promises and Limits of Workfare," *Backgrounder* (Heritage Foundation, Washington, D.C.), 11 June 1987, and Robert Rector, "Strategies for Welfare Reform," Heritage Lecture no. 378, Heritage Foundation, Washington, D.C., 1992.

95. Ibid., p. 123.

96. Ibid.

97. Ibid.

98. Andrew Hacker, *Two Nations: Black and White, Separate, Hostile, Unequal* (New York: Scribner's, 1992), exhaustively documents the multiracial social dysfunction in the United States.

99. James Smith and Finis Welsch, *Closing the Gap: Forty Years of Economic Progress for Blacks* (Santa Monica, Calif: Rand Corporation, 1986), p. 19.

100. Mead, *New Politics of Poverty*, p. 28.

101. *Time*, 25 May 1992, p. 45.

102. Robert L. Woodson, "Poverty: Why Politics Can't Cure It," *Imprimis* 17, no. 7 (July 1988): 1.

103. Thomas Sowell, "Politics and Opportunity: Background," in Institute for Contemporary Studies, *The Fairmont Papers: Black Alternatives Conference* (San Francisco: Institute for Contemporary Studies Press, 1980), p. 7.

104. Smith and Welsch, *Closing the Gap*, p. 103.

105. Sowell, *Economics and Politics of Race*, p. 248.

106. Thomas Sowell, *Pink and Brown People* (Stanford, Calif.: Hoover Institution Press, 1981), p. 15.

107. Thomas Sowell, "Throwing Money and Intercepting It," *Washington Times*, 19 February 1991.

108. Teague, *Flip Side of Soul*, p. 164.

109. Robert Woodson, appearing on "This Week with David Brinkley," ABC News, 3 May 1992.

110. For a discussion of the "enabling" of unwed pregnancy, see Charles Murray, "No, Welfare Isn't the Problem," *Public Interest*, Summer 1986, pp. 3–11.

111. Robert Rector, "Strategies for Welfare Reform," p. 4. Rector explains that the "payment" sums cited equal the value of welfare benefits from different programs for the average mother on AFDC. He adds, "Technically the mother can be married to a husband who works part-time at very low wages and still be eligible for some aid under the AFDC-UP program. However, if the husband works a significant number of hours a month even at a low hourly rate, his earnings will be sufficient to eliminate the family's eligibility to AFDC-UP and most other welfare."

112. Robert Rector, interviewed by Phil Reed, "Live From LA," KKLA radio, 21 May 1992.

113. Richard Vedder, "Welfare Spending and the Poverty Rate," in *Welfare Reform: Consensus or Conflict?* edited by James S. Denton (Lanham, Md.: University Press of America, 1988), p. 72.

114. Rector interview. Statistics cited by Rector are from *Strategies for Welfare Reform*, (Washington, D.C.: Heritage Foundation, 1992).

115. Ibid.

116. "Why the Poor Stay Poor," *National Review*, 8 June 1992, p. 16.

117. Constance Williams, *Black Teenage Mothers: Pregnancy and Child Rearing from Their Perspective* (Lexington, Mass.: Lexington Books, 1991), p. 86.

118. Maya Angelou, "Save the Mothers," *Ebony*, August 1986, p. 39.

119. Thomas Sowell, "Playing Moral One-Upmanship," *Washington Times*, 3 April 1991.

120. Marian Wright Edelman, "Dreams Shattered for America's Young Families," *Tri-County Bulletin* (Orange County, Calif.), 21 May 1992, p. 4.

121. Mead, *New Politics of Poverty*, p. 54.

122. Rector interview.

123. John Leo, "A Pox on Dan and Murphy," *U.S. News & World Report*, 1 June 1992.

124. Quoted by Daniel Patrick Moynihan in his foreword to Denton, ed., *Welfare Reform*, p. xi.

125. Joseph Conti, interview with Lawrence Picus, Los Angeles, 5 October 1992. Emphasis ours. For a discussion of Picus's analysis of educational funding, see A. R. Odden and Lawrence Picus, *School Finance: A Policy Perspective* (New York: McGraw Hill, 1992). (Emphasis added.)

126. Joseph Conti, interview with Norma Anders, Los Angeles, 5 October 1992.

127. Emily Sachar, *Shut Up and Let the Lady Teach!*, New York: Poseidon Press, 1991, p. 221.

128. *New York Times*, 14 August 1991, p. A11.

129. Joe Clark, *Laying Down the Law* (Washington, D.C.: Regnery-Gateway, 1989), p. 24.

130. This figure is for the 1992–1993 academic year.

131. Sowell, *Economics and Politics of Race*, p. 195.

132. *Annual Information Digest of Los Angeles Community Colleges 1989–1990*, published by the Educational Services Division of the Los Angeles Community College District, reveals that the typical Los Angeles–Southwest student was likely to be a black female in her mid-twenties with no definite educational goal. This profile is consistent with the contention that educational opportunities in South Central Los Angeles are going largely unrealized. This is especially tragic, since community college fees are rising; indeed, they have gone up to $10 since the riots, and may rise further.

133. James Cashing, Jr., "You Bet Your Life! (And Mine Too!)," *Los Angeles Sentinel*, 28 May 1992, p. A7.

134. Brad Stetson, interview with Clint Bolick, 29 May, 1992.

135. Ibid.

136. Thomas Sowell, "Society Lets Barbarians off the Hook," *Newsday*, 5 May, 1989.

137. Indeed, Loury resists a simple equation of single-parent families and criminality in youth. See Glenn C. Loury, "The Family as Context for Delinquency Prevention: Demographic Trends and Political Realities," in *From Children to Citizens*, edited by James Q. Wilson and Glenn C. Loury, vol. 3 (New York: Springer-Verlag, 1987), pp. 3–26.

138. Rector interview.

139. Ernest Harris, "Selling Dependency," *National Review*, June 1992.

140. Joe Klein, "Whose Values?" *Newsweek*, 8 June 1992, p. 21.

141. *Newsweek*, 6 April 1992, p. 20

142. Ibid.

143. This according to Los Angeles County, District Attorney's Office report, "Gangs, Crime and Violence in Los Angeles," May 1992, reported in the *Los Angeles Daily News*, 22 May 1992, p. 18.

144. Cited in Glenn C. Loury, "Black Dignity and the Common Good," *First Things*, June/July 1990, p. 13.

145. "Plan to End Oakland Bloodshed Met with Skepticism," *Los Angeles Times*, 30 March 1992, p. A9.

146. *Newsweek*, 18 May 1992, p. 37.

147. See Sowell, "High Cost of Hoodlumism," p. 28.

148. Of course, they also routinely demean or overlook the role of the male parent, but here we are only discussing the economic question.

149. *New York Times*, 20 May 1992, p. A11.

150. "Single Mothers Tell of Varied Reasons for Their Situation," *New York Times*, 26 May p. A1; Pat Friedmann, *The Exact Image of Motherhood*.

151. *New York Times*, 14 August 1991.

152. Rector interview.

153. Ellen Snortland, " 'Values' Is Code for 'Dad is the Boss'." *Los Angeles Times*, 22 May 1992, p. B11.

154. Thomas Sowell, "What Price Circuses?" *Orange County Register*, 22 October 1989.

155. Robert Detlefsen, *Civil Rights under Reagan* (San Francisco: Institute for Contemporary Studies Press, 1991), pp. 172–73.

156. Walter Williams, "After Civil Rights," in Collier and Horowitz, eds., *Second Thoughts about Race*, p. 30.

157. Anne Wortham, "Individualism: For Whites Only?" *Reason*, February 1979, p. 31.

158. Walter Williams, "Will Blacks Recapture Their Neighborhoods from Criminals?" *Orange County Register*, 27 May 1992, p. B9.

159. Thomas Sowell, *Economics and Politics of Race*, p. 140.

160. For discussion see ibid., pp. 135–82.

161. "The Quotas Issue," *National Review*, 15 April 1991, p. 15.

162. Thomas Sowell, "Election Year Spawns Reckless Rhetoric," *Los Angeles Daily News*, 5 June 1992.

163. "White Firefighters, Hank Aaron, and Affirmative Action," *First Things*, no. 15 (August/September 1991), pp. 14–15.

164. Bolick, *Changing Course*, p. 57.

165. Nathan Glazer, *Affirmative Discrimination: Ethnic Inequality and Public Policy* (New York: Basic Books, 1975), p. 18.

166. "Does Affirmative Action Help or Hurt?" *Time*, 27 May 1992, p. 119.

167. Michael Sandel, *Liberalism and the Limits of Justice* (Cambridge: Cambridge University Press, 1982), pp. 141–42. Truth is stranger than fiction. Oblivious to the perversity of its understanding of merit, William B. Allen reports that the University of California, Berkeley, "proudly announces to the [minority] candidate it deigns to accept, 'You are an affirmative action admit!' " William B. Allen, "The Civil Rights Revolution," *Imprimis*, April 1989, p. 3.

168. Nat Hentoff, "Affirmative Action: What of Those Left Behind?" *Village Voice*, 8 October 1991.

169. Joseph Conti, interview with Glenn C. Loury, 5 June 1992.

170. *Orange County Register*, 8 May 1992, p. B14.

171. *Time*, 8 October 1990, p. 42.

172. Ibid.

173. Teague, *Flip Side of Soul*, p. 128.

174. Loury, "Family as Context for Delinquency Prevention," p. 3.

175. Ibid.

176. James V. Schall, S.J., *The Distinctiveness of Christianity* (San Francisco: Ignatius Press, 1982), pp. 138–39.

177. Sowell, *Pink and Brown People*, p. 21.

178. Sowell, *Compassion versus Guilt*, p. 133.

179. *The Student Guide: Financial Aid from the U.S. Department of Education 1992–1993*, Washington, D.C., U.S. Department of Education, 1991.

180. Chuck D., interviewed by Vivien Goldman, *Spin*, October 1992, p. 46.

181. "Unemployment Rate of Persons 16 Years Old and Over, by Age, Sex, Race/Ethnicity, and Years of School Completed: March 1988," *Digest of Education Statistics*, 1989, p. 363. Primary Source: U.S. Department of Labor, Bureau of Labor Statistics, Office of Employment and Unemployment Statistics, "Educational Attainment of Workers, March 1988."

182. Quoted in Michael Novak, "The Neglected Cultural Frontier in Public Policy," in Denton, ed., *Welfare Reform*, p. 7.

183. Teague, *Flip Side of Soul*, p. 139.

184. Ibid., p. 184.

185. Ibid., pp. 48–53.

186. Ibid., p. 163.

187. Robert L. Woodson, *On the Road to Economic Freedom* (Washington, D.C.: Regnery-Gateway, 1987), p. 23.

188. See Peter L. Berger and Richard John Neuhaus, *To Empower People* (Washington, D.C.: American Enterprise Institute, 1977).

189. *Los Angeles Times*, 15 July 1991, p. A16.

190. Woodson, "Poverty: Why Politics Can't Cure It," p. 3.

191. Glenn C. Loury, "The Moral Quandary of the Black Community," *Public Interest*, no. 79 (Spring 1985): 14.

192. Ibid., p. 4.

193. Williams, "After Civil Rights," p. 30.

194. "Detroit Hopes to Save Its Young Men," *New York Times*, 14 August 1991, p. A11.

195. Ibid.

196. Polly Williams, "Inner-City Kids: Why Choice Is Their Only Hope," *Imprimis*, March 1992, p. 3.

197. "Tough Choice," *Time*, 16 September 1991, p. 54.

198. Ibid., p. 56.

199. "The Case for Educational Vouchers," a debate between Charles Hyder and Anne Wortham (Chattanooga, Tenn.: Center for Economic Education, 1986), pp. 3–4.

200. Williams, "Inner-City Kids," p. 3.

201. John E. Coons, "School Choice as Simple Justice," *First Things*, April 1992, pp. 15–28.

202. Woodson, "Poverty: Why Politics Can't Cure It," p. 3.

203. Glenn C. Loury, "A Prescription for Black Progress," *Christian Century*, 30 April 1986, p. 437.

204. Sleeper, *Closest of Strangers*, p. 316.

THOMAS SOWELL: THE FOUR
TARGETS OF A MAVERICK THINKER

I want to tell you of the story of a black community: its birth in the
country at the end of the Civil War, its move from county to city, its
disintegration during the war on poverty.

Scott C. Davis, *The World of Patience Gromes*

Dear Comrade: Serious charges have been brought against you by Party
comrades because of the nature of certain of your recent contributions
to the *Courier* and *American Spectator*. You are requested to appear
before the next meeting of the Membership Committee of the New
York Branch to answer these charges.

My Dear Friends: I shall have to disappoint you by refusing to be the guest
of honor at your inquisition. . . . I have always said and written just
what I thought without apologies to anyone, and I continue doing
so. Whatever I think is wrong, I shall continue to attack. Whatever I
think is right, I shall continue to laud, whether it be left, right, or
center. In doing so, of course, I incur the enmity of some people from
time to time, but I have always been more concerned with being true
to myself than to any group or groups.[1]

This treatment accorded George S. Schuyler's dissent from the Communist Party in the 1930s parallels the treatment given to the rogue
perspective of Thomas Sowell by today's civil rights leaders. A disaf-
fected Communist, Schuyler suspected that the Party was using blacks
as a stalking horse for political ends, and he incurred the Party's wrath
for rebuking it in *Black and Conservative* (1966). Similarly, much of Sowell's
social criticism has been rejected as woefully unorthodox by the civil

rights establishment—he, too, has been taken to task by the arbiters of orthodox thinking.

Sowell's discontent is manifested in bracing and iconoclastic animadversions against all manner of pretension, whether by academics, bureaucrats, crusading politicians, or the civil rights establishment. It would be an understatement to say that his politics are not the politics of today's civil rights movement. To Sowell, that movement and its liberal political heritage have lost the grounding in rationality and justice that they once had. "In retrospect," wrote even conservative firebrand Patrick Buchanan, in *Right from the Beginning*, "the civil-rights movement was liberalism's finest hour." Buchanan continues:

> The liberals paid a heavy price for having championed civil rights in the '50's and early '60's, for preaching and advancing the ideal of equality and justice under the law. If they have stumbled and blundered terribly since, they knew what they were doing then, and what they were doing was right.[2]

An ironic and tragic reversal of moral justification appears to have taken place in the decades that followed. A sadly perverse illustration of this sea change in the racial outlook of civil rights practitioners is the case of James Meredith. In 1962 Meredith gained national attention for his efforts to attend the University of Mississippi as its first black student. Demonstrating for equal rights, Meredith was nearly killed by a blast from a 12-gauge shotgun. Years later in 1988, Meredith was invited to speak at Hollins College in Virginia, by its Black Student Alliance (BSA). But before he could deliver his message to the students, the BSA caught wind of the content of an address Meredith had delivered at nearby William and Mary College, in which he had supported traditional family values and hard work. For doing this, Meredith was barred from speaking on campus and censured as a sellout by black students two generations his junior, who apparently didn't like the purport of his self-help message. It seems that the bullet Meredith had taken three decades earlier, quite literally on their behalf, meant little to these morally outraged students.

In the decades since the Civil Rights Act, the consolidation of liberal ideology as *the* ideology of black progress cognitively isolated those who disagreed with its presuppositions and methods. Walter Williams, during those years, quipped that he and Sowell once made a pact never to fly together on the same airplane: a crash, they agreed, would mean the end of black conservatism in America! In the early 1980s, when Williams made that remark, it was certainly closer to the truth than today.

It was largely through the writings of Sowell and Williams that the recent surge in black conservatism (since 1988, by our reckoning) was spawned and nurtured. We focus here on Sowell's work, though in full recognition of Williams's foundational contribution.

ELEMENTS OF ICONOCLASM

In H. L. Mencken's ever-new astonishment at the reformer's belief "that since a rose looks good and smells good, it will make good soup," we have something of the palpable amazement of Sowell at the "wonderful world of solutions," as he terms the array of government answers to social problems. And just as the acerbic Mencken, at political conventions earlier this century, would peer out from his perch, beholding the hoopla of placarded humanity, marveling at the gaudy rhetoric with glee and disgust, so it is easy to imagine Sowell through his prose, walking today's campuses bemused by the social solutions confronting him at every kiosk.

Thomas Sowell is a unique figure in American scholarship. From humble beginnings in North Carolina and then Harlem, Sowell has risen to become one of the preeminent economists and social commentators in this country. Having had to drop out of high school in the tenth grade due to his family's economic hardship, and following military service, Sowell enrolled in night school at Howard University. There a lasting impression was made on him when a professor he admired, Sterling Brown, whose writings, in Sowell's words, were "a bitter and eloquent indictment of racism," warned Sowell on the eve of his departure to Harvard University, "Don't come back here and tell me you didn't make it 'cause white folks were mean." Of these words, Sowell wrote years later that it was the best advice he could have gotten. It is too bad, he added, that young black men and women today do not get "that kind of advice, instead of being fed the paranoid party line."[3]

In 1958 he graduated from Harvard *magna cum laude* with a degree in economics. The promising young scholar continued his study of economics, earning his masters at Columbia University and his 1968 doctorate at the University of Chicago, where he served an intellectual apprenticeship under economists Milton Friedman and George Stigler.

A fiercely independent academic, Sowell worked in the private sector for a short time following his graduation. After an unpleasant teaching experience at Cornell University, where his conservatism was alien to both the black militants and the white liberals enthroned in the late 1960s, Sowell began writing prolifically. His *Black Education: Myths and Tragedies* (1972), which foreshadowed Dinesh D'Souza's later bestselling *Illiberal Education* (1991), caused quite a commotion due to its unconventionality and established him as a bold iconoclast.[4]

Following an especially intense period of writing in the 1970s, in 1980 Sowell became a senior fellow at the prestigious Hoover Institution on War, Revolution and Peace. Later that same year, Sowell helped organize the groundbreaking Black Alternatives Conference, which represented to his mind a "historic opportunity."[5] It effectively announced the presence of an intellectually sophisticated and politically unique cognitive minority that, as black and conservative, constituted a new voice of social and cultural analysis. After a stint on President Reagan's Economic Policy Advisory Board, Sowell returned to his research and writing at the Hoover Institution.

It certainly bears pointing out that the considerable influence of Sowell rides beyond the scope of his books and articles. Justice Thomas, during his confirmation process, was unabashed regarding his intellectual debt to Sowell, freely acknowledging that Sowell's social and political criticisms informed his understanding of society and the individual's place in it.[6] Given Thomas's relative youth, his tenure on the U.S. Supreme Court, and therefore Sowell's ideological impact, is likely to continue far into the future.

Inasmuch as the scope of Sowell's scholarly work is unusually broad, our consideration of his thinking will be confined only to those areas that bear a direct relevance to his dissent from the usual course of civil rights discussions. Our analysis is framed by what we consider to be Sowell's four primary foci—or as we call them, his four targets. But before we engage these targets, we will deal with the most common objection raised against Sowell.

BOOTSTRAPS

Sowell's relentless critique of what he sees as counterproductive welfare policy has regularly inspired charges of naive "bootstrapism." Typical is this conceptualization of Sowell's project by Benjamin Hooks: "It's a bankrupt, hackneyed, and unrealistic idea, that we should go back to the nineteenth-century idea of everyone pulling [himself up] by his own bootstraps without any help.'"[7] Hooks's viewpoint is shared by many others, including Carl T. Rowan. "In a passage so phrased that a reader could easily think that it was a direct quote from me," commented Sowell on Rowan's caricature of him, "syndicated columnist Carl Rowan expressed what was supposedly my position on my own career: 'I did it on my own, with hard work, so I don't want government to give any lazy bastard anything.' "[8] Echoing Rowan's criticism, CBS correspondent Lem Tucker told millions of viewers of the "CBS Morning News" that Sowell believed "that he alone, almost without bootstraps, pulled himself out of the ghetto through Harvard and the University of Chicago."[9] Still another attack, though more generalized, came from a columnist, Julianne Malveaux. "These people, such as [Clarence] Thomas, who claim to have pulled themselves up by the bootstraps, are very likely to use the bootstraps to strangle people. They are sleeping with the enemy."[10]

How accurate are these pictures of Sowell's self-understanding, and by extension, of his general analysis of the sources of individual achievement in a social context? Here is what Sowell has actually written of his own life:

> It would be premature at best and presumptuous at worst to attempt to draw sweeping or definitive conclusions from my personal experiences. It would be especially unwarranted to draw Horatio Alger conclusions, that perseverance and/or ability "win out" despite obstacles. The fact is, I was losing in every way until my life was changed by the Korean War, the draft, and the G.I. Bill—none of which I can take credit for. I have no false modesty about having seized the opportunity and worked to make it pay off, but there is no way to avoid the fact that there first had to be an opportunity to seize.[11]

Sowell's own self-assessment appears starkly dissonant with the "self-made man" pretensions imputed to him by his critics. Indeed, so pronounced is this dissonance that it raises questions about the general nature of the "bootstrap" charge commonly lodged against the social philosophies of black dissidents, as well as satellite criticisms, such as that of the dangerous "atomism" that supposedly inheres in their calls for self-help and self-reliance. As such calls are, unquestionably, common in the writings of Sowell and other dissidents, we might reflect on them here.

To begin with, while Sowell freely credits the G.I. Bill for providing him an *opportunity* to go to college and begin a career, the simple availability of the chance to study and develop by no means meant that he

would study and develop. It was his personal effort and personal commitment—informed and supported by insights and habits developed
under many mentors, formal and informal—that helped him take advantage of the opportunity. In this sense, Sowell does indeed look to
individual men and women to initiate and sustain their own progress,
a position that is not so counterintuitive as the incredulous criticisms
offered by Hooks and Malveaux would suggest.

He also recognizes the viability for black Americans of self-effort in
the context of America's democratic capitalism. He would agree with
Loury, who makes the following point:

> No, we have not suddenly all become Horatio Alger, but one does not
> have to pull oneself by the bootstraps into great wealth in order to rec-
> ognize the objective relationship which exists in this society between effort
> and reward. There is much greater scope for change at the level of the
> individual than is often recognized in the political discourse on this ques-
> tion.[12]

For Sowell, while the presence of a strong family, other intermediate
structures, and government assistance certainly places one in a position
to flourish, they by no means guarantee achievement. One one hand,
then, Sowell acknowledges the contribution of outside help (e.g., familial
nurturing, apprenticeship, and government-provided aid and opportunity) to individual advancement. On the other hand, he does not view
these as sufficient conditions for achievement.

But Sowell's tempered recognition of the role of the individual in his
or her own achievement is certainly not the herculean individualism
denoted by the pejorative "bootstrap" label. Certainly Sowell's critics
would not themselves deny the individual this modest role in achievement. The label becomes even less instructive when applied to a social
philosophy such as Sowell's, which explicitly articulates a broad vision
of "social processes"—a vision that recognizes the vital roles that supra-
individual structures or "mediating institutions" (e.g., the family,
church, schools, and clubs) have played in history—especially their role
as foils to social atomism and incivility. In terms of Sowell's human-
capital theory, the mediating structure of the family is typically the key
"relay" institution, passing on, in a unique way, the deposit of values
and traditions deemed important to a people. Understood this way, the
"self" in such phrases as "self-reliance" and "self-help" has a deep
communal residence, and as such, is far from the 'bootstrap' atomism
its critics often make it out to be. The "self-help" strategies recognized

as useful by Sowell and others hardly posit a Hobbesian self, detached from societal moorings and "looking out for number one," but rather one equipped by organic and voluntary relationships with a repertoire of skills, values, and habits that incline the self toward community. That is why the dissidents place such a high premium on "little platoons" (in Edmund Burke's phrase) and the policies that strengthen them, for such associations have a proven track record in equipping individuals for success in the community. Writes Sowell in the final paragraph of *Race and Economics* (1975):

> If the history of American ethnic groups shows anything, it is how large a role has been played by attitudes of self-reliance. The success of the antebellum "free persons of color" compared to the later black migrants to the North, the advancement of the Italian-Americans beyond the Irish-Americans who had many other advantages, the resilience of the Japanese-Americans despite numerous campaigns of persecution, all emphasize the importance of this factor, however mundane and unfashionable it may be.[13]

In the above passage, Sowell is counterposing the success of groups that have embraced the path of self-reliance to ones that have leaned less successfully (as a matter of historical record, he contends) on political and juridical paths to empowerment. But to characterize the "self-reliance" that Sowell addresses here as "bootstrapism" is obviously to distort it. The habit of "self-reliance"—along with other components of human capital—is likely to come to the individual as a "windfall" inheritance of family or community, and so, paradoxically, is not self-generated, as the term "bootstrapism" would caricature it. Writes Sowell in *The Economics and Politics and Race*:

> The need to form more human capital if prosperity is to be increased is not based on any belief that those who currently possess larger amounts of human capital do so as a matter of personal merit. There is no question that many—perhaps most—of the more fortunate people are recipients of windfall gains they derive from the accident of where they were, if not to immediate affluence, then to families, communities, or nations where the values and patterns of life were a human capital that made economic success more readily obtainable.[14]

The "self-reliance" of successful groups is often communal and cooperative, with group members supporting each other both through material aid and shared traditions. Sowell's recognition of the superior practical value of the self-reliance *of groups* reveals the "bootstrap" charge of Sowell's critics to be a kind of false dichotomization. That is, while the anti-"bootstrap" position typically recognizes both the public and private sides of citizenship, it tends to inflate the governmental aspect of "public" and shrink the significance of those intermediate institutions that are most able to manifest and foster individual and group self-reliance—the highroad to social mobility, in Sowell's analysis of history.

As noted above, Sowell identifies the family as the principal relay station of human capital. The importance of the family in particular—and the assault on the family by centralized policies that presuppose an omnicompetent government—are themes constantly recapitulated in Sowell's work. For Sowell, institutions like families, churches, neighborhoods, and schools are "the way to make the best of the tragic human condition. These very same institutions are often viewed as obstacles to the 'solutions' prescribed in the vision of the annointed" [i.e., the academic and governmental elite].[15]

Following this line of reasoning, it could be argued that critics who protest Sowell's so-called "bootstrapism" on the grounds that it is atomistic, are themselves promoters of atomism, insofar as they regularly support legislative and judicial measures that tend to unhinge the individual from communal moorings in family and other mediating institutions. It is these mediating institutions that have proven, through time, most effective at shielding individuals from anomie and infusing their lives with meaning, as well as imparting skills and practical behavioral standards. Sowell's critique of sex education in the public schools addresses this point. "One of the great, tragic frauds of our time has been the name 'sex education' for courses that indoctrinate fad thinking on sex, behind the backs of the parents. These courses are not about biology but about ideology."[16]

The irony, then, is that those who would accuse Sowell of atomistic bootstrapism may themselves be engaged in a project of atomism, given their support for policies that shift power and decisionmaking away from family and voluntary institutions and toward government, thus distancing both children and adults from their most natural communal bases. This breed of statist atomism, as it were, ignores the time-tested value of the "little platoons" that have so well invited individual flourishment and fostered the project of democratic capitalism. Distrusting these organic and voluntary associations as parochial and atavistic, such statist atomism drives toward expanding the relationship between the individual and government, subsuming all the other relationships the individual has. It tends to seek the creation of more institutions and policies which direct to government an ever-increasing supervisory role. This latter idea—to reconstruct, as it were, the old "little platoons" along new lines—is valuable only if the new institutions strictly respect the importance of individual autonomy and the need for self-governing communitarian institutions.

As noted, Sowell goes so far as to find an active and principled animus toward traditional institutions in the "vision of the annointed." This vision conceives of these institutions as obstacles to government-sanctioned social justice and an aggressive personal liberation, even at the cost of common neighborhood values. This animus is made especially explicit in the work of gender feminists, with their pronounced hostility toward the traditional nuclear family, and their persistent attempt to deconstruct it into merely one option, among many, of organizing intimate relationships. Beyond that, more committed radicals disdainfully dismiss marriage and the family as pernicious tools of patriarchal manipulation, as when one attendee at the 1992 National Women's Studies Association Conference complained about the sacrilege of weddings being held at the same hotel hosting the conference: "Why have they put us in a setting where *that* sort of thing is going on?"[17] Framing this idea academically, Alison Jaggar of the University of Cincinnati claims that the nuclear family is "a cornerstone of oppression," guilty of an unreasonable bias that "enforces heterosexuality" and "imposes the prevailing masculine and feminine character structures on the next generation."[18]

And yet many critics of Sowell's alleged "bootstrap" philosophy certainly do not regard themselves, or the policies they advocate, as anti-family and hostile toward the traditional voluntary associations. On the contrary, in the political arena they habitually speak of the urgency of adopting a national "family policy." In light of this ostensible commonality between Sowell and his critics, it is tempting to dismiss their differences as mere semantical or "perceptual" confusion; after all, they both see value in "family" and "community." But here we must agree with Sowell on a methodological point: Too often, real differences are belittled as "perceptual" difficulties. That certainly is not the case here. Sowell and his critics are indeed offering sharply different philosophies of the relationship of individuals to community and government, leading to very different policies and outcomes.

FIRST TARGET: "THE SCHOLARSHIP OF ADVOCACY"

A hallmark of Sowell's methodology is his cool empiricism—his avowedly "factual" approach to issues. So it is that the first of Sowell's targets is politically tilted social science, or what has become known as the "scholarship of advocacy." In column after column, book after book, this emerges as Sowell's academic bête noir. The biased subjectivism and political jockeying of agenda-bent social analysis renders it both methodologically unsound and ultimately counterproductive, according to Sowell. He notes, for instance, that university courses priding themselves on manifesting "diversity" and accenting "non-Western cultures" are commonly imbued with a hatred of all things Western. In this logic, white racism in America is just the tip of the fathomless iceberg of Western evil. Vague references to the "legacy of Western evil," then, come to be used as a kind of analogous evidence that "exposes" instances of current American racism. In this style of non sequitor argument, references to Columbus's seizure of Indian slaves precede by milliseconds assertions that opposition to busing is typical of white racism.

So typical is this anti-Western agenda in "diversity" lectures that exceptions to it really stand out, says Sowell. He notes, with clear appreciation, that when Bernard Lewis of Princeton University spoke at Stanford in 1991, on the topic of the Islamic world and the West, he avoided a habitual "one-sided glorification of a foreign culture in order to denigrate the culture of Western Civilization," and even answered critics who castigated the West as the breeding ground of slavery, imperialism, and sexism.[19] Acknowledging Western evils, Lewis broke with the anti-Western bias by insisting that the same evils egregiously marred non-Western civilizations as well. Indeed, the worldwide battle to end slavery was almost entirely the work of the West, over the resistance of Islamic, Asian, and African rulers.

Sowell also purposely eschews "right" history and sociology, privileging empirical arguments instead. He sees this methodological disposition as an earmark of black dissident thought. "Most of today's black dissenters—the so-called 'black conservatives'—are scholars whose skills are analytical," he writes. "Wheeling and dealing is not their thing. What they want to know is how the deals have turned out."[20]

So it is that the dissenters regularly question what others assume as *fait accompli*. For instance, while mainstream academic and media analysts assume that affirmative action has helped inner-city blacks, and only ask if these benefits are *just* entitlements, Sowell scratches his head and asks whether the people in the ghetto have *actually* benefitted from the affirmative action policies that have helped better-off blacks, or have they "stagnated during the same era when the elite have prospered?"[21]

Characteristically, Sowell begins his examination at an earlier point, looking first to empirical data for indications of programmatic success or failure. This "deal," according to Sowell's empirical analysis, turns out exactly opposite from its habitual representation in the media and by academia; affirmative action has *not* benefitted the neediest blacks, reports Sowell—nor, the statistics suggest, can it. In this way, Sowell habitually looks beyond the commonly accepted presuppositions of liberalism and subjects policy to detached statistical analysis and unsentimental questioning. He consistently refuses to automatically draw the usual inferences, such as that hiring preferences create job opportunities, and that employers can meet their quality requirements drawing from any population.

Sowell's discontent with the "scholarship of advocacy" stems from his insistence that ideas, if they are to be deemed true and acceptable, must conform to fact—statistical, social, and historical. When Sowell subjects the "solutions" of civil rights strategists to the crucible of history, he is treading a road seldom walked by his colleagues. For instance, in *Civil Rights: Rhetoric and Reality* (1984) Sowell notes that the mainstream black leadership regularly advertises black political clout as necessary to racial progress. And the public has responded; the number of black elected officials has soared over the past twenty years, from two thousand in 1970 to seven thousand in 1989.[22] But is this approach appropriate in the light of historical precedent? Sowell does not think so; his research into the economic development of ethnic groups finds a general *negative* correlation between ethnic political clout and economic progress. The turn-of-the-century Irish, for instance, were the most politically well connected ethnic group of their time, and yet were surpassed in economic and social progress by nearly every other immigrant group. It is counter historical and limiting, then, insists Sowell, to make political clout the motor force of any group-uplift movement. Emphasis on the political and the social, at the expense of the economic, puts group progress on a slow track at best, and at worst insulates the racial-ethnic group behind a wall of political solipsism, sealed off from the dynamics of a market economy. This lesson has obviously been lost, holds Sowell, on the mainstream black leadership, who continually call for more blacks in public office. Their strategy has had predictably dismal results.

Sowell points out that black-run cities (e.g., New York, Washington, and Los Angeles) have not solved the socioeconomic exigencies facing them any more effectively than white-run cities. Yet confidence in political messiahs persists, as evidenced in comments made to television reporters in the midst of the 1992 riots in Los Angeles. "I have only four words to say to you," one black man told a reporter with passionate conviction: "Wait 'til Willy Williams." This reference to the black successor to Los Angeles police chief Daryl Gates evinces a confidence in political answers to the problems of the black poor. Ironically, news clips of the Watts riots of 1965 show Los Angeles residents of the previous generation expressing the same confidence in the coming of a black mayor. But Mayor Tom Bradley, the fruit of their hopes, hardly showed himself to be the "answer." Says Jesse Peterson, "Black people in LA don't need a mayor of a certain color. What we in this city need is to turn to *ourselves*, and restore family values and personal responsibility. Only this kind of foundation will support black educational and business achievement."[23] At this writing, Peterson's plea for a truly internal strategy for blacks in post-riot Los Angeles is practically inaudible, amid the din of protestations issuing daily from that city's "community spokespersons"—drowned out from one side by yells for more aid from Washington, D.C., and from the other by freedom cries for the "LA Four," who "protested" the King verdict by yanking a white stranger from his truck and beating him nearly to death.

Other black dissidents, while appreciating Sowell's point that African-American progress has been retarded by the black leadership's penchant for political solutions, stress that politics as such has not been the problem, only the liberal hegemony and the exclusive reliance of the black community on political means. William B. Allen, a former director of the U.S. Civil Rights Commission and currently a dean of James Madison College at Michigan State University, comments:

> I disagree with my friend Tom Sowell on this point. While Sowell has done a magnificent job laying the foundation for a rethinking of strategies for black progress, I cannot agree with his downplaying of the importance of political measures. Political campaigns confront people with new ideas on a large scale, and there is real value in this.[24]

In fact, Professor Allen thinks that the present political scene provides a unique opportunity for black conservatives to confront the public with the reality that some African-Americans disagree with the civil rights establishment. Allen would have politicians, black and white, undo the "damage" caused by overweening government.

Addressing a large gathering on the anniversary of Martin Luther King's birthday in 1991, Coretta King declared, "Hope is becoming the most endangered commodity [in America]." Noting that a quarter of America's children under the age of six live in poverty, and citing high rates of infant mortality among the poor, Coretta King affirmed, "There are only two words that can adequately describe such conditions for so many children in the wealthiest country on Earth, and those two words are, 'national disgrace'."[25]

In a column written nearly a year before Coretta King's anniversary oration, Sowell once again plied his trade of questioning prevailing assumptions—in this case, what some take to be the necessary connection between infant mortality rates and poverty. Strangely, no one seems interested in the fact, he says, that the infant mortality rate of Mexican-Americans, who are generally a low-income group, is lower than that of whites, who generally make considerably more money. With typical Sowellian bluntness, he comments:

> No one wants to face the fact that parental negligence, not low income, is what is crucial in high infant mortality rates. But once you start talking about personal responsibility, you jeopardize the whole poverty industry, which thrives by turning collective guilt into dollars and cents.[26]

Obviously, this is not the only explanation for the deaths of black infants, nor does Sowell so posit it.[27] But by considering more than just a black-white race dynamic, Sowell is able to illumine here, as elsewhere, the actual complexity of that dynamic and of the issue as a whole, while at the same time supplying insight into the nature of political allergies to certain issues. Fully aware that many of his comments may be termed "grossly insensitive," Sowell is not dissuaded, believing that half-truths produce only dangerous results, and that policy built on such quicksand invariably sinks under the feet of its "beneficiaries." He would have leadership replace the emotional rhetoric, which cries, "racism!" "national disgrace!" or "Do something!" with rational and evidential evaluation, issuing in policies formulated with a sharp awareness of unintended consequences. Effective policies will also soberly and realistically take into account the painful "trade-offs" that he says few "moral crusaders" acknowledge, insisting that there are no shadows in the "wonderful world of solutions."[28]

Something of this world of solutions was seen in the graphics of a *Time* magazine story, "Shameful Bequests to the Next Generation." The insert, titled "Pay Now . . . or Pay Later," counterposed the cost of a variety of "intervention programs" against the cost of *not* using them. For instance, a price tag of $125 was placed on the intervention, "school-based sex education." Should this "solution" not be adopted, taxpayers could expect to pay, according to the other price-tag, $50,000 in "public assistance for a child born of a teenage parent, for twenty years."[29] In light of much of the material presented here in our earlier chapters, including evidence that sexual ignorance is not responsible for many teenage pregnancies, the postulation of a straight $48,875 savings should this "solution" be adopted is, to put it mildly, untenable. The neat "solution" represented by this graphic, Sowell would point out, brooks no unintended consequences; it fails to take seriously the very real chance that a pregnancy or two might result from adolescents' exposure to the "science of sexuality" in a value-free, coeducational group setting. An example of the folly of such naiveté is seen in Adams City High School in Commerce City, Colorado, which has had a condom distribution program for three years and an in-school nursery since 1979. Yet this hardly proved a panacea. One in eight of its female students is expected to have a baby in the 1992–1993 school year. The school's pregnancy rate is a full 31 percent above the national average for high school students.[30]

This brings us to a cardinal methodological practice of Sowell's. Enveloping the whole of his social critique is a bifurcated conception of competing worldviews. Sowell, here, has made an original and powerful contribution to social hermeneutics. His model of competing visions, which he terms "constrained" and "unconstrained," constitutes an attempt to interpret and understand society and the whole range of its constituent phenomena. Put another way, the competing visions represent opposite and competing conceptions of what policies and institutions can accomplish.

To speak descriptively, the unconstrained vision is always optimistic—it is the potential plenum of the "wonderful world of solutions,"—while the constrained vision is realistic. The unconstrained has a high view of man's capacity to order and change his world; the constrained is more tempered in its confidence in human potential. The unconstrained vision parallels Age of Enlightenment optimism about human destiny; the constrained is a conceptual brother to the theological realism emphatically articulated by Reinhold Niebuhr earlier in this century.[31] Though these are highly generalized and abstract ideas, in these visions lie the roots of practical and tangible clashes on issues common to everyday life.

Sowell carefully stresses the practical import and concrete reality these models hold for daily living. Though the terms "constrained" and "unconstrained" rarely appear in his columns, they are present as the conceptual backdrop ordering his evaluations of policies and problems. Though an explicit expression of Sowell's espousal of one of these visions is difficult to find in his work, there is no doubt that he favors the "constrained vision" of politics and the human condition. It is this understanding that drives his suspicion of government "elites" and their programs. Institutional competence, in Sowell's eyes, is influenced by the self-interest inherent in bureaucratic structures and affecting service professionals. The realism of the preferred "constrained" vision controls Sowell's evaluation of the proper means for social change. His bias in favor of market forces and individual decision making causes him to shy away from the constant calls for political and juridical redress coming from many black leaders.

SECOND TARGET: THE RHETORIC OF PERCEPTION

Recently, a Minority Cultures class at the University of Southern California was asked by a teaching assistant to break up into small groups and "brainstorm for stereotypes." After a period of embarrassed silence, the group members started awkwardly recounting *gender* stereotypes— ironically, not one ethnic or racial stereotype emerged. When the teaching assistant chalked on the board the stereotypes from each group, it became clear that not one student in the class of twenty-five had dared describe an ethno-racial stereotype. But this section of Minority Cultures was not, it seems, atypical in its reluctance to give voice to stereotypes. In all three class sections of Minority Cultures, not one of the seventy-five students expressed knowledge of an ethnic or racial stereotype.

Some may construe their silence as a sign of enhanced student "sensitivity," and so a heartening index to progress in tolerance on campus. And yet, in the context of this exercise, their silence makes little sense— it was, after all, clear to the students that they were engaged in a sociological exercise, not a donnybrook of ethno-racial acrimony. An alternative explanation appears more plausible: the silence of these students was enforced by fears of being thought personally bigoted. In other words, even in the context of sociological brainstorming, the pointing out of cultural differences had been transmogrified into a kind of conversational pornography, beyond the pale of civil discourse.

The reaction of these students pictures in cameo a trend that Sowell deplores. "Peoples are different," writes Sowell, "and these differences have consequences. Much of our fashionable deep thinking on social issues—in the media and academia alike—consists of elaborate denials or evasions of this basic reality."[32] Sowell's remark highlights what appears to be a certain contradiction in the media and in academia today. On one hand, the zeitgeist of multiculturalism electrifies the airwaves and enscribes course syllabi, with the increasing tendency to recognize the uniqueness of ethnic cultures; on the other hand, *it is practically anathema to speculate on the economic consequences of these differences*, especially if they are used to buttress anything resembling a "culture of poverty" argument. It would seem that the USC students in Minority Cultures are heir to this double-mindedness. Problematic differences between cultures are often downplayed as subjective "perceptions."

Sowell's empiricism is in direct tension with such thinking—with contemporary social scientists' *rhetoric of perception*.[33] In particular, Sowell is skeptical about their heavy emphasis on the observer's perceptual filter and all the encumbrances it is said to entail. Objective analysis is assumed, from the outset, to be an impossibility. All that can be offered are interpretations of varying plausibility, each of which is, to one degree or another, polluted by the perceptual framework of the observer. This emphasis on individual perception, while not intellectually foolhardy, is, Sowell would say, disingenuous.

His criticism of these perceptual nonrealists, if you will, is not theoretical as much as it is psychological. He accuses them of mixing self-interest with scholarship. For them to acknowledge that group differences in "human capital" are real and lead to actual economic consequences (and are not merely *perceptions*) is to imperil their preferred theories and visions of (usually) "unconstrained" human accomplishment.

Sowell argues that substantial cultural differences between ethnic groups—many originating in the "Old Country"—*have* historically affected income differences. In *The Economics and Politics of Race*, Sowell offers many provocative examples of the effect of this "trans-generational relay race," referred to earlier, upon the occupation choices of immigrants. For instance he finds "human capital" finally decisive in the "relay race" between Irish and Jewish immigrants in America. Despite the political, economic, and educational advantages of the earlier-arriving Irish over the Jews (and higher Irish scores on mental tests administered to masses of soldiers in World War I), Jewish attitudes and values proved decisive, and Jews surpassed the Irish by all the standard economic, and educational, indices.[34]

Perhaps anticipating that critics would be disposed to dismiss such a human-capital theory as pernicious cultural stereotyping, Sowell offers this definition of "stereotypes," in a tongue-in-cheek article titled "A Political Glossary." Stereotypes, he writes, are "behavior patterns you don't want to think about."[35] With less irony, but just as plainly "politically incorrect," Sowell writes in *Civil Rights, Rhetoric or Reality?* "Cultural differences are real, and cannot be talked away by using pejorative terms such as "stereotypes" or "racism."[36]

At a certain level, the privileging of personal perception over objective, social understanding is especially disheartening to scholars such as Sowell, who recognize that such an epistemology is tailor-made for demagoguery. The puppet of the demagogue is the man or woman who believes that his or her "rage," because it is a personal feeling, must be justified. "I feel rage," goes the operative logic, "therefore the object of my rage must be guilty of the offense that has given rise to my rage." The demagogue counts on this supplanting of cognitivity with affectivity. In this way, those who "feel" are also convinced, by virtue of that feeling, that they "know." In this state of suspended criticism, they are ripe for self-deception and primed for the demogogue's manipulations.

Such a sanctification of personal perception is popular at various levels of society, as is well illustrated by a remark made by a minister on the KABC radio program "Religion on the Line," broadcast from Los Angeles the weekend after the 1992 riots. Minorities in Los Angeles, the minister said in essence, had felt that their situation was hopeless before the riots. He then added gravely, "And I don't argue with people's perceptions."[37] This is a remarkable statement coming from the clergy, whose special vocation traditionally has been the reverse, namely, to urge their fellows to a depth of insight that transcends habitual and surface perceptions—including the "perception" that the physical world is the final reality. But beyond the peek it offers into the climate of theological reflection today, the minister's remark is provocative because of the kind of social leadership its solipsism would seem to ratify—a leadership that accepts pure subjectivity as the basis of social programs. It is this kind of leadership, says Sowell, that, in exchange for political power, has pandered to and fed self-deception in the inner-city en masse, and so stalled the advance of a people. In sum, the "rhetoric of perception" works to obscure not only self-criticism, but also what Sowell sees as the concrete reality of group differences, both intergroup and intragroup.

An example of intragroup differences is the case of West Indian blacks. Sowell has challenged the belief that discrimination is the cause of today's black-white differences in occupations and incomes. His doubts about the soundness of the discrimination hypothesis as the universal explanation of social and racial problems were sharpened when he reviewed surprising statistics on the incomes of black West Indian immigrants to the United States.[38]

So puzzled was Sowell by his first look at these statistics that he sent them back to the computer room to be run again. But they came back the same: The incomes of the West Indians, it turned out, were 94 percent of the U.S. national average, while the incomes of American-born blacks as a group were only 62 percent of the national average. Sowell discovered that West Indian "representation" in professional occupations was twice that of American-born blacks.[39] What to make of this data? As black West Indians and American-born blacks are physically indistinguishable, the statistics seem to indicate a nonracial answer. Sowell suggests a hypothesis that stresses the role of human capital in economic empowerment. The human capital that has benefitted West Indians so well, he says, has been their skills, frugality, and entrepreneurial spirit.[40]

In an interesting passage discussing this same point, Lawrence Mead in *The New Politics of Poverty* writes:

Many immigrants come to America because they want to live an achieving, American-style life, leading to the paradox of immigrants preaching self-reliance to poorer native-born Americans. West Indians typically outstrip native-born blacks, taking jobs that native-born black youths decline due to low pay. In Miami, American-born blacks accuse Cubans and Haitians of truckling to the white man, while the immigrants accuse the natives of lacking the pride to get ahead on their own. "The Haitians," confessed a local black psychologist, "have a sense that we complain too much, that our children are out of control, that we don't do enough for ourselves."

Dawit Wolde Giorgis is an Ethiopian now working with the homeless in New Jersey. He says that his clients often lack the "skills" and "motivation" to "become self-sufficient in this competitive society." He preaches to them the possibility of controlling their lives: "I say, 'Look, where I come from there is nothing you can do about what happens to you. Nature, God, the government, these are beyond your control. But here, you can work and fight to change things.' Still it is hard for them. . . . They are not aggressive."[41]

Clearly, the implications of the reality of intergroup differences are troubling for the black political leadership. The presence of concrete differences would seem to attenuate the victimization hypothesis, and thereby transfer the onus of responsibility from the "oppressing class" to the individuals of the "victimized" class. This is problematic for a political leadership that thrives by advertising the illusion that the growth of the black middle class is due essentially to the *leadership's* push for affirmative action rather than to the efforts of individual blacks who have acquired the human capital that disposes individuals to success in the free market.

Given, then, the cardinal role that human capital has played in the advancement of African-Americans, the black dissidents contend that the goal of black Americans, on the eve of the twenty-first century, must be to acquire and sustain the human capital needed for their further integration into the American political economy. They are ill-served, Sowell believes, by political leaders who claim responsibility for the lion's share of their success. Such a strategy plays down the role of self-effort and plays up the role of victimization, throwing a bright spotlight on political leadership as paladins, riding to the rescue. From Sowell's *Knowledge and Decisions*:

> The victimhood approach. . . . requires ignoring, suppressing, or deemphasizing successful initiatives already undertaken by the disadvantaged group or portions thereof—thereby sacrificing accumulated human capital in terms of know-how, morale, and a favorable public image.[42]

Here, black political leaders walk a threadbare tightrope. On one hand, they have been reluctant to emphasize the role of individual human capital in black success, for it undercuts their role as indispensible saviors. On the other hand, they have drawn what Martin Kilson has called "an ethnic *cordon sanitaire*" around areas of black social life, including certain particulars of black underclass behavior. For just as the importance of the black political leadership is diminished if black achievement is recognized as mostly a matter of personal human capital, it is also diminished if black failure is understood as a matter of a deficit of human capital rather than one of racial discrimination.

So it is that the rhetoric of the civil rights establishment casts criminality among blacks as less a matter requiring remediation than one of biased "perceptions" by other groups. This would appear to be the very message that Larry Aubry of the *Los Angeles Sentinel* sent readers of his "Urban Perspective" column. "The stereotype of young black males as a criminal menace has become a mainstay. The fact is, three of every four young adult Black males is [sic] not involved in criminal behavior.[43]

We cannot stress vigorously enough our dismay at Aubry's bizarre acquittal of a 25 percent crime rate among young black males! By all standards, he offers a rather feeble debunking of a severe problem. One wonders if the readership of the *Sentinel* would not be better served by an honest assessment of criminality in black communities and its myriad ill-effects on neighborhoods, rather than a dismissal that dresses up a destructive and shameful social fact in the popular garb of a "perception" problem.

THIRD TARGET: THE CIVIL RIGHTS STRATEGY

In 1969, partisans of an Italian-American anti-defamation league rallied by the tens of thousands in Brooklyn to cheer their flamboyant leader, Joseph Gambino, who had led the organization in a drive to dispel the myth of an active Mafia. It was, he argued, a figment of the FBI and other persons who wished to use Italians as scapegoats. But unfortunately for Gambino, before he could address this theme in front of the thousands of cheering *paisons*, he was executed—Mafia style. As is so often the case, the hard realities of social life asserted themselves against the fictions of untempered ethnic pride. The inability to be self-critical, no matter the ethnic context, is a danger to which any group is vulnerable.

This idea brings us to the "civil rights strategy," Sowell's third target. Fundamentally, this strategy—a corollary of Sowell's concept of the "civil rights vision," discussed earlier—accents group rights and reliance on political power and capital, rather than individual performance and the values of traditional mores. Sowell's dissatisfaction with this outlook centers around its emphasis on the political rather than the personal and its failure to foster intragroup criticism.

Sowell's impatience with antipoverty blueprints dispatched from academic ivory towers and campaign headquarters is legendary. This manifests itself in his biting impatience with knowledgeable policy architects. Sowell's facetious advice for solving poverty is to invite one hundred of the country's top antipoverty experts to a remote island conference and leave them there.

Among those Sowell would invite on this permanent vacation from social tinkering would be those who masterminded the Great Society's expansion of welfare eligibility. Black Americans were especially hard hit by this policy. "The black family—which survived slavery, discrimination, poverty, wars and depressions—began to come apart as the federal government moved in with its well-financed programs to 'help'."[44]

It is on these same empirical grounds that Sowell would have "self-help" strategies evaluated—but in their case, he says, the verdict of history is quite different. Rooted in organic and voluntary associations and interacting with the dynamics of a market economy, self-help approaches have proven to be remarkably effective catalysts for social mobility in democratic capitalist polities. Apart from any sentimental or philosophical appreciation of the forces that operate in self-help approaches, Sowell finds evidence that such approaches usually "deliver the goods." "I do not have faith in the market," he says; "I have evidence about the market."[45] He writes:

> The "self-help" approach simply recognizes that blacks do not have unlimited time or resources to put into political crusades, nor are these crusades likely to produce as much net benefit as putting time and resources into developing yourself or your community.[46]

In a first-principle objection to the foundations of Sowell's self-help approach, Alphonso Pinkney wrote in *The Myth of Black Progress*, "Sowell's conservative bias is so strong that he sometimes shows a lack of understanding. . . . What meaningful choice have black people ever had in the United States?"[47] Flatly disagreeing, Sowell affirms that blacks today have plenty of meaningful choices. Even in the past, when obstacles were more patent, blacks were not without options. "An earlier generation of black college students understood that they were going to encounter obstacles," he writes, "but there was no pervasive paranoia that these obstacles were going to stop them."[48] Demonstrating a measure of economic autonomy obtained even before the civil rights gains of the 1960s, individual blacks (in the years 1963–65) earned 23 percent higher wages, than the average amount for blacks, for each year of schooling.

Further arguing for the reality of choice as an economically significant concept, Sowell points out that entry-level jobs, so frequently disparaged by the black leadership as "dead-end" work, serve as useful instructors in the "instrumental," or bourgeois, values (e.g., diligence, discipline, punctuality), which as components of larger social processes equip the

young person for social mobility. While Douglas C. Glassgow, a professor of social work at Howard University, is dismayed by the fact that
young blacks "have had at best only limited low level or part-time experience,"[49] Sowell understands such realities, at least in part, as the
effect of pejorative descriptions of entry-level work as "menial" or
"dead-end" jobs. Such descriptions he sees as misleading and unnecessarily demoralizing, since such jobs teach important habits. The "real
culprits," he says, are not dead-end jobs but "those who created a system
that makes it dangerous to work and safe to loaf, those who have turned
honest work into a shame and made being a parasite respectable."[50]

The larger point here is Sowell's concern at what he sees as the black
leadership's unnecessarily severe devaluation of self-driven activity.
While references to "self-help" are occuring with increasing frequency
in public statements from mainstream black leaders, they still privilege
the political and the juridical over the individual. In other words, self-
help is a secondary component in their total programme of black advocacy. Here is Sowell's unflattering speculation about their motives:
"The self-help message is anathema to minority elites who owe their
position to their influence—at least their visibility—within the Washington Beltway, where the welfare goodies are handed out."[51]

Sowell's impatience with the primacy of the political is also informed
by his conviction that it can at best secure only short-term benefits.
Apart from what he sees as the dismal track record of political remedies
for the problems facing African-Americans, Sowell disfavors them on
the basis of their ephemerality:

> Whatever the merits or demerits of a particular political policy, it is almost
> certain to change, perhaps drastically, and often unpredictably. A shift of
> 10 percentage points in the voting can bring a new administration that
> changes policy 180 degrees. This volatility reduces the reliability of politics
> as a factor in long-run progress.[52]

This concern is supplemented by a further apprehension that misguided racial solidarity for the sake of political viability muffles valuable
intragroup criticism. The following kind of hyperbole, from Pinkney in
The Myth of Black Progress, is bound to reinforce the *de facto* ban on self-
criticism:

> Black social scientists, as well as white, appear to be supporting the grow-
> ing conservative movement in the United States. That white social sci-
> entists should engage in these activities is not surprising. However, black

sociologists who support the conservative movement are not unlike government officials in (formerly) South Vietnam who supported American aggression against their own people.[53]

Sowell comments on the consequence of a group reluctance to enter into the interior conversation of self-criticism:

> Dissenting views are common in every group of people and in every society. A more balanced judgment often emerges out of these clashes of ideas. There is no reason why black Americans must be the only people on this planet who have to skip this process and hit the nail on the head with the first try.[54]

In line with this, Sowell regards as particularly vapid the out-of-hand dismissal of controversial political stances merely because the epithet "divisive" is attached to them. He sees this as dangerously limiting and as impeding discussion in the public square.[55] Although a clearly anti-democratic tendency inheres in this use of the term "divisive," it nevertheless has slipped into our political and journalistic nomenclature with strange ease, joining other recent entries in the lexicon of political correctness, including "insensitivity," "polarizing," and "bashing."

A mainstay of politicized civil rights strategy, says Sowell, is affirmative action. Sowell's critique of affirmative action policies is voluminous; for our purposes, the most significant element is that these policies, despite their larger pretensions, fail to assist the neediest African-Americans. Indeed, the neediest, according to Sowell, are victimized by such policies. Although he offers a number of reasons in support of this point, we will focus on two of the most telling.

Sowell's investigation of the effects of preferential treatment policies in the workplace, has led him to believe that middle-and upper-class blacks are its actual beneficiaries, while lower-class blacks, and those with little education and work experience, actually suffer from such policies. But while this effect is contrary to the avowed purpose of the laws and guidelines, it is nonetheless, in Sowell's estimation, their inevitable consequence. He finds instructive the story of a female academic who hires only "promotable females" as professors because she has "no time to waste at [Equal Employment Opportunity Commission] hearings and in the courtroom." Sowell explains that this phenomenon, certainly not unique to this one professor, has the effect of shutting out those with little hireability, "making the less educated, the less skilled, and the less experienced members of the group a more risky gamble for an employer than they would otherwise be."[56]

The inefficacy of affirmative action for the very poor, says Sowell, is not unique to the American scene. Commenting on global testimony to the built-in impotence of affirmative action as social philosophy, Sowell holds that preferences toward minorities paradoxically damage the occupational chances for members of the group most in need. "The gains have gone to those already more fortunate. . . . The actual retrogression of less fortunate blacks is also in keeping with what happened among the untouchables in India or the Malays in Malaysia."[57] Viewed in this light, preferential treatment policies are not just "stunningly irrelevant" to the black poor, as asserted by Stephen Carter, the author of *Notes of an Affirmative Action Baby* (1991), but a definite stumbling block.

Turning from the workplace to higher education, Sowell finds equally perverse unintended consequences generated by preferential treatment. Very concerned by the tragic waste of talent often produced by these policies, Sowell wrote *Choosing a College* partly to help black students sidestep snares layed by administrators who are more concerned about meeting quasi-official racial quotas than about seeing that students attend the university best suited to their needs and interests. The result of this pursuit of "racial fairness" by university administrators is a "mismatch," in Sowell's key phrase, of students with institutions, some of which have lowered entrance standards to admit them. In this way, poorly prepared black students are admitted into fine universities, and moderately well prepared black students are admitted into the toughest schools. Both cohorts suffer an unusually high dropout rate. Sowell points to a 70 percent dropout rate of black students at the University of California at Berkeley, even though their performance is above the national average.[58] "A student does not get a better education," says Sowell, "in a class that is moving at a faster pace than he is able to keep up with."[59] Viewing this determined administrative "search for a body count" as unconscionably unconcerned with its ultimate effect on individuals, Sowell recognizes in it the typical reformer's admixture of "moral crusading" and blunt self-interest.

A strong point of interest here is Sowell's pragmatism. Though he is not uninterested in matters of fairness and equity, defined judicially and otherwise, his briefs against preferential treatment policies are not typically conducted along these lines. Instead, Sowell points to the punishing practical effects of these policies on the ones who, according to conventional wisdom, profit from them. Here again we see Sowell working upstream of his colleagues. While they are asking, "Are the benefits blacks getting fair?" Sowell is asking, "Where are the benefits?" There is in his work a tenacious concern for overall effects. This concern controls his social science. Such pragmatism is perhaps the most distinct earmark of Sowell's social philosophy.

FOURTH TARGET: THE MOTIVES AND LEGACY OF THE REFORMERS

On public-access cable television in Los Angeles, a recent episode of a program devoted to uncovering racist plots against African-Americans featured a guest who announced that the HIV virus was a concoction by white conspirators hoping to destroy blacks the world over. The virus was first loosed in Africa, and it subsequently spread all over the globe. What we see in the world today are the effects of this scheme.

But the network of conspiracy did not stop there. The next week's program brought news of a local gun show attended by the investigator. He reported back that of the thousand-plus gun enthusiasts in attendance, he was one of only a handful of blacks present. Our guide revealed the true character of this assemblage when he coyly insinuated that the conventioneers seemed to have more on their minds than hunting and home protection. The show's co-host quickly understood the racist menace that had been uncovered. Fascinated and horrified, she wondered, "It makes you wonder how they all knew to go there." Having discovered yet another weave in the tapestry of national racial conspiracy, the concerned hosts courageously resolved to attend more gun shows, and recommended that their viewers purchase firearms to defend themselves. "Racial paranoia," writes Sowell, "pictures white people as both all-wicked and all-powerful."[60]

This brings us to Sowell's fourth target vis à vis black advocacy: those reformers, renovators, and social critics who, in Sowell's eyes, are unhelpful, to put it mildly. Sowell would include in this group intellectuals who, though not intoxicated solely by self-interest, operate under the constraints of intellectuals and are given to the belief that they have special knowledge that common people lack.

Sowell routinely inveighs against ideologues who believe that social salvation lies in more utilization of the services of intellectuals. These true believers are unswayed by empirical evidence demonstrating the profound ineffectuality of their pet programs. Similarly, Sowell lays bare those who make pretense to community service but actually are in pursuit of their own aggrandizement: the college professor who uses his podium for the dissemination of attention-grabbing theories about race, spending more time at news conferences than in research libraries; the reverend who is seen at the right hand of victims of racist attacks, establishing himself as their moral guardian; the bureaucrat who expands his administration of community programs, and thereby his sphere of influence.

An example of bureaucratic self-aggrandizement in the name of "community service" is seen in the $1,000 bonus paid to the Milwaukee school district for every new bus route it is able to devise. The proliferation of bus routes is somehow understood to improve education, while conveniently earning revenue for the school district. Over the last fifteen years, forced busing in Milwaukee has cost the taxpayers $335 million, even though among those bused, currently only 40 percent of ninth graders eventually graduate.[61]

In this way, Sowell goes after the "compassionate" ideology of the left and the contemporary phenomenon of regional racial power brokers. The political-legal measures instituted and maintained by liberal Democrats to facilitate African-American progress are hardly pristinely altruistic, he argues. In fact, he makes the case that the existence of these measures is a response to personal and impersonal factors having little to do with actual "compassion." The personal factor is a sincere but unreflective impulse to "do something" for the poor. The impersonal element fostering and preserving the "black-interest" juggernaut is a palpable social inertia that forbids the abolition of longstanding social service programs, since such dismantling could easily be seen as the proximate cause of disenfranchising the poor and oppressed, and this is a main odium of the "compassion" brokers. At the same time, Sowell does not see this as a monolithic conspiracy, but as more the product of a fragmentary composite of decision makers.

Thus, both in motivation and practice, the "assistance industry" functions not only as a safety net for the needy, but also as a self-serving and self-justifying bureaucracy. It could be seen to exist as much to satisfy the visions of idealogues, palliate the consciences of policy makers, and pad the power bases of bureaucratic administrators, as to secure a floor of well-being for the impoverished.

The Example of Reform in Education

Sowell offers the same manner of critique in the area of education. One example of the way Sowell's social analysis sharply penetrates the illusion of rationality is in his debunking critique of educational reform. His frustration with ideologues, activists, and bureaucrats on this point stems from their habit of devising and advocating ever-new proposals without regard for the results of previous attempts along the same lines. Sowell's discontent is mirrored by Walter Williams's remark:

> If the Grand Dragon of the Ku Klux Klan wanted to deny blacks upward mobility, reinforce racial stereotypes of black mental incompetence, and foster racial conflict, he couldn't find a better tool than our public educational system.[62]

With Williams, Sowell believes that popular assumptions hold sway over evidence in the thinking of educational reformers. "We cannot educate on the basis of assumptions," he insists, "but must test even our most cherished beliefs against the facts of the past and the present."[63]

Typical of Sowell's radical dissent from mainstream black attitudes toward education is his displeasure with the famous, and nearly sacred, *Brown v. Board of Education* decision of 1954. Sowell points out the irony that though the decision held that racially separate schools were inherently inferior, only blocks away from the Supreme Court there was an all-black public school that had for more than 80 years, equaled or surpassed the academic performance of the white schools in the District of Columbia. Such excellence in all-black schools, Sowell continues, was not the rarity that various experts alleged. Indeed, the NAACP lawyer who argued the Brown case before the Court, Thurgood Marshall, had come from such a school in Baltimore. Sowell says, "Most of the things that social reformers promote as 'prerequisites' for good education today seldom existed in these or other outstanding black schools—nor outstanding schools for Jews, Chinese, or Japanese youngsters."[64]

Sowell's usual contrariness, evidentially based, is again seen in this quote, and his suggestion that all-black schools are not inherently inferior to integrated schools. This evidence is basic to Sowell's evaluation of busing as a profoundly wrongheaded policy, typical of the procrustean policies of the "unconstrained vision" in its reliance for justification on malleable psychosocial research, even when such research contradicts the data of common experience. Common experience did not show that black students were automatically harmed by lack of proximity to white students, but psychologists insisted otherwise, and judges were convinced—perhaps none more so than a Los Angeles judge, Paul V. Egly, who fretted that minority students would be "irreparably damaged" unless busing was quickly implemented. He intended to make the most effective use of scarce white students by sprinkling them around for the benefit of the nonwhite children who were the majority in Los Angeles schools.[65] Sowell comments, "Kipling's doctrine of 'the white man's burden' was now transformed into a judicial doctrine of the 'white child's burden'—a doctrine that came very close to fighting racism with racism."[66]

Given Sowell's emphasis on the importance of human capital for social mobility and the key role that formal schooling—a schooling stressing the basics—can play in its transmission, his contempt for the flashy reformism of liberal educrats is understandable. Over the years this reform agenda has included advocacy of "Black English," recalcitrant opposition to school voucher plans, promotion of sex education, a propagandist deprecation of Western civilization, promotion of school nurseries for children of teens, militant calls for increased "student rights," a deprecation of standardized testing, and promotion of busing—all policies that Sowell sees as demonstrated duds. It is the very ordinariness of Sowell's proposals—his common sense and his Franklinesque emphasis on a work ethic for students, which insists on a relationship between personal effort and personal reward—that galls his critics so, and leads them to dismiss out of hand his classic American perspective on education.

The Mystique of the Civil Rights Establishment

How is it, then, that reformist measures that do not deliver on the promises made, continue to be entrusted with at least implicit public support, and how is it that the black leadership escapes responsibility for political failures? In both cases, we believe, a kind of mystique is operative.

We see an instructive parallel between Sowell's critique of the liberal black leadership's shield from culpability and British economist Digby Anderson's analysis of the social armor that protects the welfare state from criticism. In *Breaking the Spell of the Welfare State*, Anderson writes:

> I think it more appropriate to call this complex thing [the welfare state] a "spell" than a proposition and I argue that to analyze the welfare state involves breaking that spell. . . . Breaking the spell depends on recognizing it as such.[67]

Anderson finds the word "spell" appropriate because the real nature of the welfare state, its true inner workings, and its actual long-term effects are masked by a pleasing film of self-congratulating phrases, such as "assistance," "fairness," and "service." With compassion and social fairness as its averred goals, "being an employee of the welfare state is more honourable than being a critic," says Anderson.[68] Those in its employ are at least "doing something" for others, unlike the purely self-interested workers in the private sector—or worse, those who cavalierly carp at the welfare state. By definition, goes the logic, social workers are active contributors to the common good.

In many respects, Anderson's critique of the welfare spell is analogous to Sowell's the-emperor-has-no-clothes approach to the program of the ambitious civil rights leadership. Their "spell," as we find it in Sowell, consists of the public perception that their work is untainted by self-interest and that their policies are unambiguously effective. Sowell's project, here, has an affinity to what Peter L. Berger, in another context, has called "the penetration of verbal smokescreens to the unadmitted and often unpleasant mainsprings of actions."[69]

Just as apologists for the welfare state, in Anderson's "spell" model, defend it on the grounds that "social service" employees are at least "part of the solution, rather than part of the problem," mutatis mutandis, the civil rights leadership habitually parries the thrusts of its "carping" critics by insisting that civil rights theorists, politicoes, and activists are at least "doing something." This idea informs the following rebuke from *Los Angeles Sentinel* publisher Kenneth R. Thomas: "Make no mistake, racism is alive and well and is being increasingly practiced and sanctioned by the power structure. . . . So long as we are so prone to criticize and castigate (with our $^{20}\!/_{20}$ vision) those who are at least trying to do something . . . we shall surely fail."

Though Kenneth Thomas's frustration with those who offer exclusively negative criticisms is understandable, his approach to policy formulation is the very antithesis of Sowell's. This is the case insofar as Thomas implies that we ought not criticize programs that fail, or the "visions" of their architects. But how then, Sowell would ask, are we to evaluate the effectiveness of programs and hold their designers accountable for success or failure?

Sowell contends that those who design and promote failed social programs should be criticized, complaining that they "pay no price whatsoever for being wrong, no matter how high a price is paid by the public, both in money and in blood."[70] At the very least, Sowell would have them pay the price of public accountability. Along with Digby Anderson, Sowell rejects the notion that moral credibility should be automatically conferred upon policy proposals simply because their authors are "trying to do something," or because the banners fluttering over their organizations lay claim, by virtue of their slogans, to the moral high ground. Just as Anderson shows how the welfare state's self-descriptive nomenclature (e.g., "assistance," "fairness," and "service") serves its spell, Sowell demonstrates how the lexicon of rights groups serves their mystique. For example, surely only a scrooge would murmur against something called the Children's Defense Fund, however obscurantist its tracts on "young black families."

It does seem, then, that this perceptual "spell" we are postulating has a definite moral element, as seen in the title of Spike Lee's popular movie *Do the Right Thing*. This phrase embodies an appeal to the self-evidently immoral nature of racism. There is no elaborate ethical deduction of the moral properties of certain behaviors, but rather the simple confidence that individuals' consciences will attest to the violation of natural rights that racial prejudice constitutes. This claim to a priori ethical authority takes on the nimbus of moral legitimacy, which works to empower the advocates' program in the minds of the general public.

This is not to gainsay the possibility of directly perceiving the moral qualities of human actions—it was this very process that undergirded the social philosophy of Martin Luther King.[71] Rather, it is simply to point out that today's civil rights leadership offers many policies and practices, some of which are far from morally unambiguous, under the canopy of a priori moral truths.

But beyond this moral component, the power of self-interest masquerading as *disinterest* also contributes to the persistence of this "spell," projected by both the welfare state and the civil rights establishment. In *Knowledge and Decisions*, Sowell shows how self-interest, rather than avowed motives such as "community improvement" or "the cause of rights," commonly motors and steers the work of the intellectual theorist, the bureaucrat, and the political activist.

Intellectuals as a class, writes Sowell, stand to benefit both personally and professionally from the sustained cycle of policy proposal-forecasted effectiveness, implementation, and assessment. Sowell's point here is a rather simple one: despite the mystification of their role in society, intellectuals, being human, are driven by the same motivations as everyone else, including the "psychic and financial" ones.[72] One way that this plays out, contends Sowell, is that intellectuals have a stake in preventing nonintellectuals from understanding their own knowledge as self-sufficient. The intellectual tries to insure that

> the meaning of knowledge [is] narrowed only to those particular kinds of formal generalities peculiar to intellectuals. Assertions of gross inadequacy of existing institutions and ideas likewise increase the demand for intellectuals by discrediting alternatives."[73]

Prohibitively simple "alternatives" suggested by average women and men are unacceptable to trained intellectuals:

> Where the public differs from intellectuals, it is often taken as axiomatic that that demonstrates the misguided ignorance of the public and their need to be "educated." However, the supposed "alienation of workers," "black rage" . . . are subjects on which these respective groups are *themselves* the experts.[74]

In sum, the force of intellectual opinion on black issues and policy proposals is substantially founded on this mystique of professorial knowledge and disinterest. Both are illusions, according to Sowell, as the project of the intellectual and of the professional service provider is bent with self-interest. "Poverty used to be a condition," Sowell writes, "but now it's an industry. Grants, careers, turf, movements and bureaucratic empires all depend on poverty. With so many vested interests at work, the truth is often buried under a blizzard of rhetoric and myth."[75] Berger's comments on the New Class (i.e., intellectual elites and social service experts) are pertinent here:

> The greater part of the New Class derives its livelihood from public-sector employment; it has the most tangible interest in expanding this type of employment. Thus the vested interest in this group in replacing market forces with government intervention is, at the very least, as important in explaining the statist inclinations of the New Class as more idealistic aspirations. . . . Because government interventions have to be legitimated in terms of social ills, the New Class has a vested interest in portraying American society as a whole, and specific aspects of that society, in negative terms. Bad news about America is *ipso facto* good news for New Class aspirations. This ideological function serves to explain the consistently "critical" orientation of New Class interpretations (such as facts of *income distribution, poverty, the state of civil rights, or the changes in the racial situation*). The same ideological function helps to account for the consistent sympathy of the New Class for foreign movements and regimes, provided these can plausibly be pictured as some sort of antithesis to American society.[76]

Yet another reason for the abiding "spell" surrounding the welfare industry and, we are suggesting, the civil rights establishment, is the political principle that "privately admitted truths about the welfare state are denied in public."[77] Anderson writes:

> There is no problem finding teachers who will reveal abuses and extravagancies in schools. At the drop of a gin they will go further than any outside critic in their tales of futility and extravagance. But there is a world of difference between what individual employees of the welfare state will say in private and what their association secretaries will say at the Blackpool Annual Conference.[78]

Similar "tales of futility and extravagance" are privately admitted by bureaucrats and other professionals involved in projects ostensibly devoted to the betterment of African-American communities. Many are intimidated into silence by the "spell" of the alleged inherent righteousness and practicality associated with mainstream black advocacy. Fearing public criticisms would elicit career-ruining charges of insensitivity, betrayal, or even racism, many confine their voicing of controversial stances to private conversations. Nonconformists in matters of racialist ideology often pay a heavy price for their dissent.

Such was the experience of a black journalist, Leon Dash, author of *When Children Want Children*, which, you will recall from Chapter 2, demythologized certain aspects of black teenage pregnancy. When a black friend of many years heard that Dash was writing a candid study of teen pregnancy, he angrily told Dash, "But you can't! You are doing damage to us." The friend went on to explain that Dash's frank examination would only entrench whites in their animosity toward blacks, especially unwed mothers. Despite Dash's passionate insistence that a true picture of black teen pregnancy would ultimately benefit young black mothers, his friend was unrelenting in his objection to the project and finally broke his relationship with Dash.[79]

Dash's investigation cost him a friendship, but for others, expected to reflect an untainted social liberalism, that is, to represent the official "black viewpoint," opposition to the "official story" could cost them their jobs or future advancement. Some admit their apostasy only in private. Visiting a largely black Catholic school—at the time in decline, though at this writing returned to much of its former glory—Sowell recalls meeting the school's new principal. "When the door was closed and the two of us were alone," writes Sowell, he "whispered to me that he wanted to restore some of the spirit of Father Grant," a former principal who had set high standards for the students. These standards had been undone by the "politically aware types" who replaced him says Sowell. Sowell reflects, "I think this is a commentary on our times that he felt it necessary to express himself in this conspiratorial way about restoring values."[80]

Finally, added to these other components of the "mystique" of liberal black advocacy is religion, an especially potent legitimating influence. Though this is not an idea explicitly considered by Sowell, we believe that such a component does inhere in the presence and maintenance of the civil rights mystique we have been explicating. The religious pathos that first imbued the civil rights movement has remained in it, even though the movement has metamorphosed since the 1960s. The formative role of religion here has been to provide strong, convincing, and—eventually—*unexamined* assurance of the righteousness of the cause for black participants and white sympathizers.

The power of this symbolism is demonstrated by the fact that despite the current predominance of secular themes in the movement, and the generally diminished influence of the churches on racial matters, the religious mystique continues, in many ways, to sanctify the civil rights establishment, its rhetoric, and the legislation it supports. An obvious reason for this is that the civil rights movement of thirty years ago drew much of its inspiration and power from the religious proposition that "all men are created equal." The children of God are of many colors and ethnicities, and dignity rests upon them equally.

From its religious beginnings and early nurturing in the black churches to the watershed moment of Dr. King's "I Have a Dream" speech, wherein he affirmed the transracial fatherhood of God, the movement has been heir to a rich deposit of religious imagery, captured in personal memory and documentary film: phalanxes of nonviolent protesters braving racial taunts, billyclubs, and policedogs with Christian stoicism and trust; fiery orations in church halls, with antiphonal "amens" answering the preachers' calls for equality and fairness. The ultimate religious symbol is the martyred Dr. King, assassinated shortly after predicting, "I may not make it there with you" to the promised land of racial equality. Religion is still a big force within the movement, and it still serves as a pipeline supplying leadership. This is not surprising, as a reliance on clergy for social leadership is a longstanding tradition among African-Americans. Booker T. Washington remarked a century ago, "The minister in the Negro church has an influence for good or evil, is looked to for advice on many subjects, to an extent that is not true of any other class of ministers in this country."[81]

But while religious ethics and principles have been employed by the civil rights establishment as a potent force for moral renewal and social change in American society, religious symbolism has also been manipulated to legitimize some questionable practices. An instance of this would seem to be the vigil held in the "people's prayer tent" set up outside the courtroom during Marion Barry's drug trial:

> Barry joined a handful of preachers and supporters in singing, "I Shall Not Be Moved" (to the tune of "We Shall Overcome"), then bowed his head. The Reverend Willie Wilson prayed for a man Wilson called "a prime example of what prayer can do."
> "We pray that You move on this system perpetuating all manner of evil and wrongdoing," Wilson implored.
> "Lord, we thank you for those who came along in the sixties," intoned [another supporter of Barry's]. . . . "People like Martin Luther King, Jr., and Marion Barry."[82]

Without impugning the religious sincerity of the former mayor or his clerical support team, it is instructive to note that the pairing demonstrated here of religious adjurations with the immorality of racism brings about a powerful association in the public psyche, again lending a numinous mist to any project carried out under the banner of civil rights. This is part of the "spell" enjoyed by certain strains of black advocacy today. Indeed, such is the power of this mystique that it is regularly coopted by other "rights" groups that seek to add wattage to their haloes by deploying its symbolism, including reworded versions of "We Shall Overcome," tailored to their projects. Jim Sleeper's comment in *The Closest of Strangers* is right on target. The "ability to fuse the spiritual and the political which has been the blacks' greatest strength may now have become their greatest weakness."[83]

So it is that the religious mystique works to authorize a priori acceptance of virtually any notion introduced under the rubric of civil rights. Though this psychological interpretation is not subject to empirical validation in the Sowellian sense, it is a reasonable inference to make, based on the religious underpinnings of the movement, its symbolism and iconography, and the prominence of religious figures in its ranks—as well as the fact that in matters that are deeply important to people and are thought to shape their lives, *homo religiosus* naturally moves toward religious associations. Thus the mere mention of "the Dream," or of the injustice of oppression, evokes, vaguely yet persistently, the mystique of divine approval.

CONCLUSION

In light of the remarkable body of scholarship Sowell has amassed during his long career, it is ironic that he is so commonly dismissed, especially by black politicians, civil rights leaders, and liberal academics—with little more than a nod to his eccentricity. Perhaps the greatest compliment that can be paid to Thomas Sowell is that despite this decades-long intellectual banishment, his own work continues, and as the theme of this book indicates, his social outlook is gathering support. It remains to be seen how much of Sowell's thought will be vindicated by the oracle of time, but his foundational role in the New Black Vanguard is beyond question. Whatever success and political hegemony this movement may achieve, it will be profoundly and uniquely indebted to the acerbic pen and rapier mind of Thomas Sowell.

NOTES

1. George S. Schuyler, *Black and Conservative: The Autobiography of George S. Schuyler* (New Rochelle, N.Y.: Arlington House, 1966), pp. 222–23.

2. Patrick Buchanan, *Right from the Beginning* (Boston: Little, Brown, 1988), p. 306.

3. Thomas Sowell, "Blind Alley of Racial Paranoia," *Washington Times*, 22 January 1991.

4. Thomas Sowell, *Black Education: Myths and Tragedies* (New York: McKay Publishers, 1972); Dinesh D'Souza, *Illiberal Education* (New York: Macmillan, 1991).

5. See Institute for Contemporary Studies, *The Fairmont Papers: Black Alternatives Conference, December 1980* (San Francisco, the Institute, 1980).

6. *Newsweek*, September 10, 1991, p. 27.

7. "Thomas Sowell," in *Current Biography*, edited by Charles Moritz (New York: H. W. Wilson, 1981), p. 393.

8. Thomas Sowell, *Civil Rights: Rhetoric or Reality?* (New York: Quill, 1984), p. 124, note 5.

9. Quoted in ibid., p. 125.

10. Julianne Malveaux, "Black Conservatives in the Spotlight," *San Francisco Chronicle*, 6 July 1991.

11. Sowell, *Civil Rights, Rhetoric or Reality?* p. 125, note 6.

12. Glenn C. Loury, "Responsibility and Race" *Vital Speeches*, 13 April 1983, p. 400.

13. Thomas Sowell, *Race and Economics* (New York: Longmans, 1975), p. 238.

14. Thomas Sowell, *The Economics and Politics of Race* (New York: Quill, 1983), p. 255.

15. Thomas Sowell, *Pink and Brown People* (Stanford, Calif.: Hoover Institution Press, 1981), p. viii.

16. Thomas Sowell, *Compassion versus Guilt* (New York: Morrow, 1987), p. 133.

17. Christina Sommers, "Sister Soldiers," *The New Republic*, 5 October 1992, p. 29.

18. Christina Sommers, "Feminism and the College Curriculum," *Imprimis*, June 1990, p. 2.

19. Thomas Sowell, "West Holds Up Well in Cultural Comparisons," *Rocky Mountain News*, 28 May 1990.

20. Thomas Sowell, "Burying Black Differences under Labels, Myths," *Orange County Register*, 6 September 1991.

21. Ibid.

22. *Destiny*, December 1990, p. 28.

23. Joseph Conti, interview with Jesse Peterson, 17 May 1992.

24. Joseph Conti, interview with William B. Allen, 9 March 1992.

25. "Nation Honors King," *Los Angeles Daily News*, 21 January 1992, p. 16.

26. Thomas Sowell, *Washington Times*, 23 April 1991.

27. The complexity of this issue is highlighted by a June 1992 report in the *New England Journal of Medicine* that found that black babies are almost twice as likely to die in their first year of life as white babies, even babies of black college-educated parents.

28. Sowell, *Compassion versus Guilt*, pp. 21–24.

29. "Shameful Bequests to the Next Generation," *Time*, 8 October 1990, p. 45.

30. "Do-Good Plans and Unintended Consequences," *Los Angeles Daily News*, 15 June 1992, p. 11.

31. This is not to imply that Sowell's project is a theological one: just that its realism and tempered anthropology have affinities with Niebuhr's Christian Realism.

32. Sowell, *Compassion versus Guilt*, p. 16.

33. See Kenneth Minogue, *Alien Powers: The Pure Theory of Ideology* (New York: St. Martin's, 1985).

34. Sowell, *Economics and Politics of Race*, pp. 167–72.

35. Sowell, *Compassion versus Guilt*, p. 126.

36. Sowell, *Civil Rights: Rhetoric or Reality?* p. 45.

37. "Religion on the Line," Dennis Prager, host, KABC radio, Los Angeles, Calif., 3 May 1992.

38. Sowell, *Civil Rights: Rhetoric or Reality?* p. 139.

39. Ibid.

40. Sowell, *Economics and Politics of Race*, p. 107.

41. Lawrence Mead, *The New Politics of Poverty: The Nonworking Poor in America* (New York: Basic Books, 1992), p. 153.

42. Thomas Sowell, *Knowledge and Decisions* (New York: Basic Books, 1981), p. 356.

43. Larry Aubry, "Are Black Males the Nation's Throw-Aways?" *Los Angeles Sentinel*, 16 January 1992.

44. Thomas Sowell, "Throwing Money and Intercepting It," *Washington Times*, 19 February 1991.

45. Thomas Sowell, quoted in William F. Buckley, Jr., ed., *On the Firing Line* (New York: Random House, 1989), p. 321.

46. Thomas Sowell, *Washington Times*, 21 August 1991.

47. Alphonso Pinkney, *The Myth of Black Progress* (Cambridge: Cambridge University Press, 1984), p. 12.

48. Sowell, "Blind Alley of Racial Paranoia."

49. Douglas G. Glassgow, *The Black Underclass* (San Francisco: Jossey-Bass, 1980), p. 85.

50. Sowell, *Compassion versus Guilt*, p. 36.

51. Sowell, *The Washington Times*, August 21, 1991.

52. Sowell, *Economics and Politics of Race*, p. 172.

53. Pinkney, *Myth of Black Progress*, p. 17.

54. Sowell, "Burying Black Differences."

55. Thomas Sowell, "Election Year Spawns Reckless Rhetoric," *Los Angeles Daily News*, 5 June 1992.

56. *Insight*, 25 June 1990.

57. Thomas Sowell as quoted in Diane C. Weber, "When Favorites Are Picked by Policies," *Washington Times*, 12 September 1990. For detailed discussions of Sowell's evaluation of the effects of affirmative action in an international context, see Sowell, pp. 135–257 *Economics and Politics of Race*, part 2.

58. Sowell, *Washington Times*, 26 June 1990, p. 125.

59. *New York City Tribune*, 15 September 1989, p. 37.

60. Sowell, "Blind Alley of Racial Paranoia."

61. Polly Williams, "Inner-City Kids: Why Choice Is Their Only Hope." *Imprimis*, March 1992.

62. Walter Williams, *All It Takes Is Guts* (Washington, D.C.: Regnery-Gateway, 1987), p. 116.

63. Thomas Sowell, *Education, Assumptions versus History*, preface, p.x.

64. Sowell, *Civil Rights: Rhetoric or Reality?* p. 83.

65. Ibid., p. 69.

66. Ibid.

67. Digby Anderson, June Lait, and David Marsland, *Breaking the Spell of the Welfare State: Strategies for Reducing Public Expenditures* (Cambridge: Social Affairs Unit, 1981), p. 12.

68. Anderson et al., *Breaking the Spell*, p. 27.

69. Peter L. Berger, *An Invitation to Sociology* (Garden City, N.Y.: Doubleday Anchor, 1963), pp. 41–42.

70. Thomas Sowell, *San Francisco Examiner*, 5 August 1991.

71. For a classic discussion of the justification of this type of ethical reasoning, see A. P. D'Entreves, *Natural Law: An Introduction to Legal Philosophy* (New York: Hutchinson's University Library, 1951).

72. Sowell, *Knowledge and Decisions*, p. 340.

73. Ibid.

74. Ibid., p. 355 (emphasis ours).

75. Sowell, *The Washington Times*, April 23, 1991.

76. Peter Berger, "Ethics and the Present Class Struggle," *Worldview* 21, no. 4 (April 1978): 7 (emphasis ours).

77. Anderson et al., *Breaking the Spell*, p. 25.

78. Ibid.

79. Leon Dash, *When Children Want Children* (New York: Morrow, 1989), pp. 61–62.

80. Thomas Sowell, "False Assumptions about Black Education," in Institute for Contemporary Studies, *Fairmont Papers*, p. 80.

81. Victoria Matthews, ed., *Black-Belt Diamonds* (New York, Negro University Press, 1969), p. 106.

82. Jonathan I. Z. Agronsky, *Marion Barry: The Politics of Race* (Lantham, N.Y.: British American Publishing, 1991), p. 300.

83. Jim Sleeper, *The Closest of Strangers* (New York: Norton, 1990), p. 313.

——— 4 ———

SHELBY STEELE: BEYOND "COMIC-STRIP RACISM"

For every white I have met who is a racist, I have met twenty more
who have seen me as an equal.
> Shelby Steele, *The Content of Our Character*

Earlier we noted Edith Efron's characterization of media presentations
of American racial discourse as simplistically bifurcated: "comic strip
racist bad guys" versus heroic black advocates.[1] The picture of American
race relations limned by Shelby Steele is intended to serve as a corrective
to this.

In addressing this theme, Steele's overall aim is the "right *fit* of idea
to reality."[2] He is frankly exasperated by the current state of race discussions, which he sees as dominated by ill-fitting theories, reckless *ad
populum* appeals, and political interests. Steele is very familiar, for instance, with the media truism that traces the paucity of black college
graduates in the United States to discrimination, economic and social,
by college admissions departments. But to Steele this explanation simply
does not fit the facts. Many black students are admitted to San Jose State
University, where Steele teaches English, but 72 percent drop out before
graduation. It is, says Steele, "a flight from opportunity that racism
cannot explain."[3]

Then there's the "lack of support" theory. Again, Steele finds no
convincing fit of theory to reality, and an obvious weariness with textbook explanations colors his reply. The dropout rate is what it is at San
Jose State, he says, despite many academic support programs, a black

studies department, black administrators, a multicultural curriculum, and other special programs designed to aid and assist black students.

Certainly, these two explanations for the dropout rates do not exhaust the list of standard explanations. Steele knows this, and naturally recognizes a combination of factors at work. But what he finds starkly missing from conventional discourse about the phenomenon, and what he believes must be factored into the equation if we are after the "right fit," is something so repugnant to what Steele sees as the "liberal orthodoxy" that to murmur it in academia, he reports, is to receive the noumenal equivalent of a tomato-and-rotten-egg pelting.

But before we consider Steele's general theory of race relations and his specific views on high dropout rates, we should first note his role as gadfly. By every standard of civil discourse, Steele's questioning of what conservative social critics have termed "knowledge class" truisms—the common criticisms of liberal intellectuals, such as that justice demands proportionate representation of minorities on college campuses—is hardly gratuitous carping, a play for media attention by presenting an unorthodox viewpoint. *The Content of Our Character* cannot be described as an obsequious appeal to the racial insecurities of whites for the purposes of filthy lucre, despite the regular insinuations by Steele's critics that he is more interested in attracting the limelight to himself than in shedding light on these sensitive matters. (Typically, one article on Steele is titled "Up from Obscurity," to contrast, we suppose, Booker T. Washington's *Up from Slavery* with the product of what is seen as Steele's silly yuppie ambition for fame.[4]) Whether or not the reader finally finds Steele's argument persuasive, his desire for equality and his fairness cannot be convincingly impugned.

STEELE'S HERESY

Though Steele's writings are comparatively few in number, they nonetheless constitute a comprehensive discussion of many pivotal racial issues. With the publication of his compendium of essays, the best-selling *The Content of Our Character*, in 1990, Steele attracted widespread attention and controversy.

The "heresy" of *Content* is clear from the first. Steele begins with a personal anecdote. He is at a dinner party in Silicon Valley that is stopped cold when a black engineer, with what Steele calls "a coloring of accusation," remarks on a racial issue. Averted glances and an awkward silence ensue. Steele's memory is jogged back to his college days in the

1960s and what he now calls the "cheap thrills" of youthful race-baiting. He speaks of his zeal for, and perverse delight in, pinioning white liberals with descriptions of their racism and of their denials of it.

For Steele, to admit such dissembling is simply to admit the obvious, namely that black persons, as human beings, are capable of venality and gratuitous meanness—yes, even for "cheap thrills"—in discussing matters as serious as racial victimization. Yet, while "white" hypocrisy and self-deception in racial matters appears as a fait accompli in textbooks on the psychology of black-white relations, a complementary proposition about dissembling, ulterior motivation, and self-deception on the part of blacks in racial discussions is hardly a truism in the literature. But it is a capital proposition in Steele's work, and its honesty has been appreciated by many reviewers as adding a realism and even-handedness to discussions of race that had become ritualistic and imperious, "catechismal rather than give-and-take."[5]

Although Steele's work has been criticized as nothing more than an extended black mea culpa, his thesis in no manner exculpates whites from racial pathology. But here the approach he takes is also not conventional. Against the neo-Marxist view that racist beliefs are for the most part "culturally sanctioned, rational responses to struggles over scarce resources,"[6] Steele advances an existential view, arguing that what he sees as the natural human impulse to innocence paradoxically drives individuals to flaunt viewpoints that would seem to constitute a moral sin.

And against the trend to redefine white racism so broadly as to make a denial of racism merely a more subtle form of racism—a favorite Catch–22 of the left—Steele finds more apposite to the present debate the varied and indirect ways that white persons escape from moral responsibility.[7] For instance, rather than risk *appearing* to take the moral low ground in debates over special minority entitlements, many whites simply capitulate to demands that go beyond fairness.[8] Steele is disappointed by the silence of whites who share his views and those of other black dissenters, but do not speak their minds publicly. There is real cowardice and hypocrisy in their private nods, which belie the gravity of these issues. Steele is convinced that politicians, activists, and "knowledge class" intelligentsia who insinuate a "victim identity" into blacks are setting them up to fail. Because of this, he is especially disappointed by those who realize the corrosive effects of this rhetoric but remain publicly silent. They are not innocent bystanders at all—they are complicit in what Steele sees as an irresponsible silence. As we will discuss in Chapter

6, Glenn C. Loury also sees irresponsibility in those who assent to his message but fail to act in line with that support.

This brings us to a cardinal irony of contemporary race relations as discerned by Steele: Today the moral mettle of liberal whites would be best proved, he insists, by a willingness to take a stand against what he calls "escapist racialist policies" (e.g., preferential treatment) and so risk being branded with the same nasty epithets they have readily applied to America's rednecks and Archie Bunkers. He appears to doubt, though, that many will rise to this challenge. He told a *Time* reporter:

> The one thing a white liberal can never do with a black is be honest and tell him what he tells his own children. . . . Which is that you have to work hard and your life in many ways will reflect the amount of effort you put in. They teach that every day to their own children, but they come out in public and talk about blacks just as victims who need redress. This is racial exploitation by white liberals, who transform this into their own form of power. We're being had by them, and we really need to know it.[9]

"GROUP EGOISM" AND THE IMPERATIVES OF INDIVIDUAL CONSCIENCE

As a matter of record, mainstream civil rights leaders roundly denounced Steele and his thesis. Steele, they argued, had written "a feel-good manual for whites"—that from Ronald Walters of Howard University, a former Jesse Jackson campaign advisor. Roger Wilkens, of the Washington Institute for Policy Studies, feared that Steele's book provided "comfort to whites." According to Benjamin Hooks, former director of the NAACP, Steele was simply the "latest black conservative discovered by the white media."[10]

As has become something of standard practice in books by dissident black thinkers, Steele's introduction anticipates this line of criticism, maintaining that all racial groups have an "official" view of their own social status. Blacks, he believes, have striven to maintain their victim identity.

Steele's point here recalls theologian Reinhold Niebuhr's discussion of "collective egoism" in *Moral Man and Immoral Society* (1932). While Niebuhr recognized the need for group solidarity as a sine qua non of effective political power, he cautioned about its tendency to regiment thought and curb self-criticism within its ranks as "dangerous forms of inner conflict."[11] The saddest consequence of this, according to Niebuhr, is a decline in the moral posture of the group, as ethically sensitive individuals are ostracized from its ranks as misfits. In a classic passage, he argued:

> In every human group there is less reason to check impulse, less capacity for self-transcendence, less ability to comprehend the needs of others and therefore more unrestrained egoism than the individuals, who compose the group, reveal in their personal relations.[12]

Similarly, Steele abjures the "rigid racial protocol" he sees operating in the black community—a protocol that confers the nimbus of "authentic blackness" only on those blacks whose opinions and life-styles follow a definite, though unwritten, code.

> The effect of this censoring is to disallow authentic critical voices and, therefore, to stifle healthy debate within the black community. The few critical voices we have—Thomas Sowell, William Julius Wilson, Glenn Loury—are too often disregarded rather than debated.[13]

Against this "collective egoism" of groups, Steele counterposes free-thinkers who risk ostracism to argue for group course-corrections. He quotes from Ralph Ellison's *Invisible Man*: "Our task is that of making ourselves individuals. The conscience of a race is the gift of its individuals."

STEELE'S EXISTENTIALISM

This brings us to a key point in the debate over Shelby Steele's work—the matter of "the individual." Since criticisms of Steele regularly turn on his conception of the individual, an early note about it is in order.

David M. Potter has argued, influentially, that the American experience of individualism has stood for two things: self-reliance and nonconformity. Paul Sniderman and Michael Gray Hagen briefly explicate Potter's famous thesis:

> The first is the individualism of Frederick Jackson Turner; self-reliance is the theme of the frontier, with its premium on hardiness and physical adaptiveness, and an ability to do with little and get along without others to fall back on. The second is the individualism of Alexis de Tocqueville. Not the pioneer, but the dissenter, the nonconformist, the gifted or exceptional or eccentric heads up this version of individualism. Its concern is individuality itself, under the leveling pressure to uniformity, to mediocrity.[14]

Steele's thought partakes of both types of individualism, though each in a modified form. But his thinking is particularly qualified by deep communitarian concerns. Therefore, to understand his thought as driving at narcissism or as a so-called "bootstrap" philosophy, as have some of his critics, is certainly to misunderstand it. As we saw in Chapter 3, Sowell fell victim to this same misunderstanding. Steele's thought is not a crudely driven "ethical egoism"; rather, it could be accurately described as an existentialist individualism.

For such an individualist, to refuse the inexorable and painful demands of conscience is tantamount to a refusal of self; clearly, such a position is incompatible with ethical egoism.[15] On this point, Steele quotes Soren Kierkegaard's indicting maxim, "Innocence is ignorance." Steele creatively integrates this insight into his psychology of race relations, reformulating it as the principle of "seeing for innocence." The place of this principle in Steele's work is indicative of the universalism of his psychology. For although Steele has worked out something of a race-specific typology of psychological escapes, he doesn't conceive of "white failings" or "black failings" as somehow separate from the powerful, transracial *human* temptation to "double-mindedness" (Kierkegaard).[16]

It is in this vein that Steele does not hesitate to discuss hypocrisy, bad faith, prejudice, and self-deception in blacks as well as in whites; "innocence is ignorance" even in members of historically victimized groups. Steele finds no warrant for believing that historical group victimization somehow uniquely inoculates individual members against rationalization, racism, or double-mindedness. And yet, this is the subtext of much black advocacy, Steele contends, one that creates the impression of two moral orders, one for white people and one for black people, with white the color of destruction and vice and black the color of innocence and moral virtue. Steele sees this as a denial of the individual, whose moral agency, for better or worse, is his own, not the particular expression of an angelic or demonic generalized ethnic psyche. This "ethnic chauvinism," argued Orlando Patterson in a 1977 book by the same title, obviates self-criticism among group members and so encourages self-delusions inimical to individuality.[17]

To make this concrete, journalist-teacher Emily Sachar recounts the story of a black youngster in her junior high school classroom—a classroom comprised mainly of black students. Reacting with revulsion at the nomination of two Asians to be class leaders, this young man stood up and said, "No way I'm staying here if two slanty-eyed kids is running things." Sachar told him that he was free to run for the position, too, but that he would have to refrain from racist remarks. He seemed truly shocked and replied softly, "That was a racist remark?"[18] The boy's incredulity is indicative of a particular ethnic psychology that engenders and maintains the "seeing for innocence" mentality that Steele describes. In the case of the boy, it is his elders who have framed a cognitive environment wherein the holding of racist attitudes is beyond possibility for blacks. The resultant "innocence" conditions the behavior and thinking of those who are privileged to it.

"Seeing for innocence" can also cleave community leaders from the sentiments of those they purport to lead. In a remarkable display of lack of insight into the mood of their constituency, an "impressive array" of black community leaders, reported the *Los Angeles Sentinel* a few days before the 1992 riots, assembled in Los Angeles to

> express concern at what many of the leaders termed as irresponsible statements from among others, Police Chief Daryl Gates. The chief seemed to imply that a violent response was expected from members of the African-American community if an "adverse" verdict is reached in the Rodney King case."[19]

Announced the spokesman for the group, Los Angeles city councilman Mark Ridley-Thomas:

> We soundly reject any implication that we expect any organized or spontaneous display of violence from the members of our community in response to the Rodney King verdict, regardless of when it comes out and regardless of how it comes out. We strongly resent any suggestion to the contrary.[20]

Unfortunately, the councilman—who has a doctorate in social ethics—was unable to return to his office after the riots and rue his miscalculation, as it had been burned to the ground. In the wake of his Himalayan misgauging of community sentiment, the councilman was asked to chair the city council's Ad Hoc Committee on Recovery and Revitalization.

STEELE AGAINST "SELF-ENCLOSED INDIVIDUALISM"

To move from a broad overview of Steele's individualism to a closer look at two strands of it, self-reliance and nonconformity: Steele's critics are certainly correct in pointing out a definite strain of meritocracy in his appreciation of self-reliance. Steele affirms a causal relationship between effort and success. He opposes a treadmill theory of black social immobility. (No matter how much effort you expend, you will make no progress.) Steele recounted to a *Time* interviewer some advice that his brother had received from a Jewish woman: " 'Don't wait for people to love you,' [she said]. We are too preoccupied with whether white people love us or not, whether they are racist or not, what they think about the color of our skin or the texture of our hair."[21]

"Don't wait for people to love you." This traditionalistic aphorism succinctly captures Steele's work ethic. Nevertheless, while generally sanguine about economic opportunity in America, Steele does not offer a carte blanche endorsement of the American economic system. To the dismay of critics on the Left, however, neither does he endorse the view that a ubiquitous "structural racism" blocks black progress at every turn. Sounding themes featured prominently in the work of William Julius Wilson, Steele says:

> At this point, class, poverty, and isolation are far more difficult variables for blacks than racism. That does not mean racism is gone; I think you meet it wherever you go. But it does not have the power to contain your life as it used to have.[22]

Whether the critics of Steele's position on "structural racism" are on target or not, their disagreements with him are fair insofar as they accurately describe his views. Nevertheless, there is a tendency to ignore Steele's actual propositions and ascribe to his thought an ideological character that is alien to it.

For instance, Steele does not see self-reliance and collective action as antagonistic positions; nor does he think self-reliance and civil rights efforts to promote the common good are necessarily at odds.[23] Neither does he target "black culture" as a necessary casualty of his vision of radical selfhood.[24] And yet these propositions are regularly imputed to Steele by his detractors. For example, Harvard sociologist Martin Kilson contends that Steele's position calls for the "veritable depoliticization of black Americans" in favor of an "individualistic imperative."[25] But this, says Kilson, is to put the cart before the horse. Certainly the concern of Steele's critics, including Kilson, that he not devalue associations that tend to solidarity and political empowerment is understandable and laudable, especially in light of black civil rights gains of the last thirty years, which were in no small part realized through group solidarity.

But as these criticisms simply misunderstand or caricature his views, they engage straw men and miss the substance of his arguments. Steele, indeed, believes that Kilson has quite misunderstood his argument. Kilson, says Steele,

> mischaracterizes my arguments and then attacks the mischaracterizations. ... Kilson fails to understand my point: both racism, and a lack of development are problems for blacks. We don't have one problem; we have two, and the two are not mutually exclusive. We must struggle on both fronts, individually and collectively. ... Groups don't learn to read well or open businesses; individuals do. Individuals don't get civil rights legislation passed; groups do.[26]

Steele's use of the term "individual" in the above passage and throughout his work is comparable to Jacques Maritain's special philosophical use of the term "person," as "a locus of insight and choice."[27] What makes this parallel particularly apt is the antideterminism of Steele's psychology. Whatever obstacles may impinge on the individual (including group opposition), or whatever prejudices he may experience, the individual himself or herself is the final gatekeeper for self-understanding and volition. This individual affirms, "Emotively and psychologically, 'the buck stops here,' with my own consciousness and will." Considering these features, Steele's radical questioning of the identity-statement "I am a victim" is most natural. Unlike psychological determinists, who understand decisions as necessarily conditioned by experience, Steele offers the possibility of an autonomous "leap," à la Kierkegaard, the freedom of which is a necessary condition of virtue. This statement, of course, has implications beyond the individual—it has manifest importance for the group, too. (Here we may recall Steele's citation of Ellison: "The conscience of a race is the gift of its individuals.")

This brings us to the second strand of individualism in Steele's thought: nonconformity. We broached the subject in finding affinities between Steele's protests against "a certain totalitarianism," exerted by ethnic groups on their own members, and Niebuhr's warnings against the shortcomings of "group egoism." Steele's nonconformist revolt, then, is ethically purposed; it is not a "self-enclosed individualism," to borrow a phrase from Michael Novak. "Neither a self-enclosed individualism," writes Novak in *Free Persons and the Common Good*, "nor an unfree collectivism adequately liberates human persons."[28]

On one hand, then, personal liberation can be looked at as a means to an ethical good, as when the liberation of individual conscience vitalizes the moral life of the group and acts as a hedge against "group egoism." On the other hand, personal liberation is a good in itself. To eschew "double-mindedness" and act according to insight is an intrinsic good, as it reveals to the self its own spiritual dignity.

Steele's defense of the individual, both as an instrumental good and an intrinsic one, appeals to Stanley Crouch, author of *Notes of a Hanging Judge*. "One of the most important things he is doing," writes Crouch, "is questioning Pavlovian racial responses. What's important is not that other people agree with what he says. It's that serious discussion is brought to the discourse dominated by slogans and cliches."[29]

ANTECEDENTS TO STEELE'S THOUGHT

Certainly Steele's analysis of black and white "power-moves" breaks much new ground, but a number of its key themes were at least partially developed by authors earlier. Anne Wortham's astute and complex *The Other Side of Racism* (1981) is notable here, as is Orlando Patterson's *Ethnic Chauvinism* (1977).[30]

Preceding Steele's book by nearly a decade, Wortham's book achieved limited fame in academic circles, but unlike Steele's work, it has had little popular audience. A sociologist, Wortham essayed to expose and debunk what she regarded as hazardous pressures exerted on black Americans to subordinate their individuality to "ethno-race consciousness." She writes of her book:

> This study aims to lift the shroud of social sanctity from racial "victimization" to reveal the other side of the coin of American racism—the side which few are courageous enough to admit is there and has always been there.[31]

Wortham disputes claims by advocates of "black consciousness" who insist that "the content of a Negro's consciousness is to be analyzed and understood not on the basis of his identity as man *qua* human being, but as man *qua* racial being."[32] For Wortham, one of the most disturbing implications of such "reverse racism" is the limitation on understanding, appreciation, and empathy among ethnic groups that it implies. Discussing James Baldwin's self-description as "a bastard of the West"— whose African lineage, he believed, precluded any empathy with the art of Shakespeare, Bach, Rembrandt, and so on—Wortham questions the "ethno-race consciousness" behind such anguish and sees in it a self-imposed isolation. The individual who is overcome by race-consciousness becomes, in effect, a racial robot thinking what people "like him" should think, doing what people "like him" should do.

Crouch finds in such racialism a new brand of provincialism. Placed side by side with the kind of horizonless cultural appreciation his "blues collar mother" insisted on and the open-mindedness he found so characteristic of the elders of his community, this new provincialism disturbs him as shriveled and inauthentic.[33]

Steele, too, notes a fallacy in seeing "black consciousness" as definitive of the essence of any black man or woman. He argues for a more cosmopolitan view of human nature. To Steele, as with Martin Luther King, it is simple but true that virtue is not race-specific. Human beings, whatever their color, are faced with the same moral challenges and are all heir to innate selfishness. Psychological processes, for Steele, are essentially unaffected by race.

Although Steele recognizes the life experience of each person as unique, he does posit the collective conditioning of entire peoples in history. One particularly pernicious method of conditioning is oppression, owing to the longevity of its effects. Steele notes that oppression leaves a "residue of doubt" in the victim. The residue of doubt has the ability to influence victims' understanding of themselves and their social roles.

Certainly there is nothing innovative in Steele's pointing out that the effects of black oppression are enduring. Others have focused on the political, economic, and judicial legacy of this oppression. However, while not discounting the seriousness of these, Steele trains his attention on the psychological legacy of oppression, and does so uniquely. For Steele, the current political, economic, and judicial status of black Americans cannot be understood apart from complex psychological factors that he sees as a legacy of oppression. The old oppression of the wretched slave ship and the brutal plantation has given way, he believes, to a new, insidious oppression. Herein we have the linchpin of Steele's thesis, and one of his most controversy-stirring claims: "I think black Americans are today more oppressed by doubt than by racism."[34] Steele says that this doubt is a natural consequence of the systematic *de jure* and *de facto* discrimination of the past.

This doubt has led to "racial inversion"—a preoccupation with racial identity and racial ideology, as a means of quashing self-doubt and vulnerability. Though natural and not without authentic compensations, the pendulum swing from doubt to ardent racial pride, insists Steele, is ultimately a postponement of individual self-reckoning. Harvard sociologist Orlando Patterson argued similarly in *Ethnic Chauvinism*.

> Sanity and self-respect demanded the celebration of things black, and solidarity demanded the homogenization and loyalty of all. Thus blacks had to believe first that all blacks are beautiful; black culture and "soul" had to be declared superior; and all blacks, no matter what the objective differences, had to become alike, or else be condemned as "Toms."[35]

While Patterson warned against the self-delusion and political mischief that comports with ethnic cheerleading, others hailed the pendulum swing to black racial consciousness as perfectly right and fitting. Prominent among them is James H. Cone, the foremost spokesman for black theology.

> In order for the oppressed blacks to regain their identity, they must affirm the very characteristic which the oppressor ridicules—*blackness*. Until white America is able to accept the beauty of blackness ("Black is beautiful, baby"), there can be no peace, no integration in the higher sense. Black people must withdraw and form their own culture, their own way of life.[36]

Anne Wortham would disagree and side with Steele and Patterson on this point. In her view the pendulum has missed the mark—the mark being "psychointellectual freedom"[37] for black Americans—and has swung over to a new form of repression.

> Some refer to this movement as a transition from being "Negro" to being "Black"—from being preoccupied with "whiteness" to accepting only those values and attitudes that can be called "black." But, as much as the rhetoric and analysis of the black-identity movement indicates, the transition from "Negro" ("whiteness") to "Black" ("blackness") was merely the substitution of one authority for another. It was not self-reliance that was the goal but *group* reliance.[38]

If effective political action were offered as a rationale for "group reliance," Steele would, as noted above, concede the wisdom and the need for concerted action among blacks—but he would also add the Niebuhrian caveat that group egoism is prone to shortsightedness and political error. In this regard, Steele points to the sorry effects of fantastic anti-black conspiracy theories—red herrings that regularly obscure insight into the actual (and much more quotidian) nature of community problems, and so forestall remedy. Steele is seconded in this wariness

by black syndicated columnist Clarence Page, who wrote of the conspiracy defense of Marion Barry, former mayor of Washington, D.C.,
"Charging the FBI with luring Marion Barry into a cocaine trap, for
example, makes about as much sense as blaming banks for tempting
John Dillinger to rob them."[39] Looking at the broader picture, Steele
writes, "The price blacks pay for inversion, for placing too much blame
for our problems on society, is helplessness before those problems."[40]
Patterson in *Ethnic Chauvinism* anticipates this view:

> Indeed, as always, ethnicity has turned out to be a two-edged sword, for
> one of the major obstacles to black economic progress is the group's intense
> ethnicity. Ethnic allegiance works against the interest of the group. . . . It
> has become a kind of mystification, diverting attention from the correct
> kinds of solutions to the terrible economic condition of the group.[41]

Steele is not only wary of the retrogressive effects of "racial inversion"
on black advocacy, but distrustful of its practice by other ethnic groups.
It threatens to unravel the very fabric of democracy, he believes, as it
undoes the warp and woof of civic discourse, empathy, and commonality. Steele is wary of calls for "diversity" and "pluralism" on university
campuses and elsewhere; they betoken, he believes, a destructive politics
of difference. He does not doubt the puissance of such politics, but its
morality. Race, as a naturally predetermined physical characteristic, can
never serve as a justification for moral or social power.

We have already noted Wortham's similar fear: that civil discourse is
being dangerously subverted by "ethno-race consciousness," which re-
moves the possibility of radical empathy among ethnic groups on the
basis of common humanity. There is danger, she writes, in any ethnic
group "declaring itself beyond the majority's comprehension."[42] It
would seem that such a sentiment is being telegraphed by a T-shirt
motto popular with black college students in the early 1990s: "It's a black
thing, you wouldn't understand."

What Orlando Patterson finds so odd about "ethnic revivals" of this
kind is that their boosters often warrant them on the claim that pluralism
bodes well for individuality. Patterson argues that this claim is both
unreasonable and ahistorical. Ethnic revivalism, he states,

> celebrates diversity, not however of individuals but of the groups to which
> they belong. It is a sociological truism that the more cohesive an ethnic
> group, the more conformist or anti-individualistic are its members. Thus
> the call for a diversity of cohesive, tightly knit groups actually amounts
> to an assault on the deeply entrenched principle of individualism.[43]

THE MORAL FORCE OF MARTIN LUTHER KING'S LEGACY

Though the expositions by Steele, Wortham, and Patterson differ definitively on a number of points, the thought of these authors commonly drives toward the primacy of individual moral responsibility—this, over any ethical imperatives or exemptions that some would derive from racial heritage. They find repugnant any claims to moral impugnity or moral superiority based on race. In their writings, such special pleading on racial grounds takes on the aspect of a latter-day Ring of Gyges—the magic band that, in Platonic lore, effectively freed its wearers from moral law by cloaking the wrongdoer. They point out that politicians who slip on the Ring, expecting their invocation of racism to render invisible their own offenses, only impugn the credibility of black leadership. Such is Steele's perspective on the spirit of Marion Barry's defense.

In sum, the dissenters' arguments turn on the indispensability of individual moral agency over racial heritage. Steele's title, *The Content of Our Character*, harkens back to the moral power and relentless passion of the civil rights movement of the early '60s. In his "I Have a Dream" speech, King eloquently gave voice to what many believe is a natural desire, to "not be judged by the color of their skin but by the content of their character." Why, asks Steele, are there no Martin Luther Kings around today? One reason is the tremendously attractive seduction of racial power, open to those who exploit white guilt on the one hand, and black resentment on the other. As Steele remarks, King saw past this temptation:

> King understood that racial power subverts moral power, and he pushed the principles of fairness and equality rather than black power because he believed those principles would bring blacks their most complete liberation.... What made King the most powerful and extraordinary black leader of this century was not his race but his morality.[44]

To the chagrin of much of today's civil rights establishment, the title of Steele's book and the emphasis of his thought would lay claim, perhaps unintentionally, to the moral force of King's legacy. By criticizing the "revised agenda" of the civil rights establishment, Steele and kindred thinkers may have themselves become charismatic figures, in the manner of Max Weber's model.[45]

THE LANGUAGE OF SHELBY STEELE

A hallmark of Steele's approach to race issues is his development of the distinctive terminology that orders his analysis. Among Steele's coinages: *victimology, racial inversion, race-holding, seeing for innocence, race fatigue, integration shock, anti-self, race bargaining, self-preoccupied white guilt, contained guilt*. Indeed, many of his essays appear as elucidations of these terms. As no warrant for this practice is found explicitly in his work, we might speculate as to its overall meaning. Such a rhetorical tack may be understood in the context of what Steele has seen as the virtual nondebate in academia and the popular media over these issues. Of course there have been skirmishes. The Moynihan affair; Murray's thesis; the renegade polemics of Sowell, Loury, Patterson, and Wortham—all these have occasioned some discussion in the media. But in the main, these were voided as insidious variations of the "blaming the victim" syndrome. The rhetorical approach Steele takes, then, appears to be an attempt to enable his ideas to penetrate the popular mindset and amplify his own minority voice. In other words, in an important way, Steele's work is an exercise in "nominization," to use Berger's language.[46]

Steele perceives his task as one of making ideas socially real, so to speak, that have been implicitly falsified in the last two decades by their linguistic absence in the virtual nondebate over these matters. His implicit point is that the naming of problems must precede worthwhile discussion of them.

But Steele's critics argue that what black Americans really need are material opportunities, not psychological analyses. Kilson, for one, sees Steele's emphasis on black psychology as misbegotten, and regards Steele's theory as another, though perhaps subtler, version of the standard "blaming the victim" mentality.[47] But for Steele it is critical to examine the deeply rooted network of viewpoints and other psychological intangibles that invisibly pilot racial discussions and necessarily affect the evaluation of proposed solutions.

RACIAL DEFENSIVENESS

In our chapter on Sowell, we introduced his hypothesis that the multifarious conflicts natural to civic debate can be traced back to two archetypal social visions, and these to opposite views of human nature. The first, the "unconstrained vision," has at its nucleus a self that is innocent, plastic, and eminently teachable. Contradistinctly, the "constrained vision" recognizes in human nature certain inherent and abiding dispositions, especially a stubborn egocentricity and an intermittent irrationality.[48] Analyzed under this rubric, Steele presents a "constrained vision" of human nature, inasmuch as he features an irrational "anti-self" as an inevitable component of human consciousness. (We have already met another feature of irrationality in Steele's thesis, "seeing for innocence," which prefers soothing self-fictions to painful truths.)

The "anti-self" is a coalescence of the many wounds inflicted on self in childhood. It is a self-saboteur, emerged from the hurtful acts perpetrated against us in our youth. It embraces the negative vision of ourselves shown to us by those antagonistic toward us. It remains with us as a voice of doubt and accusation, a sort of internal Satan.

Although the relative force of the irrational "anti-self" in each person's life depends on the character of individual experience, it is inseparable from the larger mosaic of history and culture, and the collective experience of ethnic groups and classes. Applying this principle to the experience of blacks in America, Steele notes that today's *legal* equality does not protect blacks from the invisible stigma of doubt inflicted on them in personal encounters with prejudice; nor does it protect from stigmatization en masse by a centuries-old American mythology of black inferiority—a mythology as nearby as any schoolchild's history textbook. That is not to say that the textbooks in use inculcate an antiblack mythology; on the contrary, they uniformly debunk it as cruel pseudoscience.[49] Nevertheless, it would appear axiomatic that at the very moment a history textbook is endeavoring to inoculate a student against racist mythology, it perforce perpetuates this mythology to one degree or another by its repetition, despite the accompanying negations in the text. One wonders, then, if there is not a curious naiveté in the assumption that a black youngster in a fifth-grade history class, after a lesson on the antebellum South or on Sheriff Bull Conner's Birmingham, would not search the eyes of white schoolmates for an ember of old Dixie. Should he see it, or even imagine it, it is bread for the "anti-self," in Steele's view. Add to these oblique encounters with white racism, overt ones during tender years ("My first awareness of race was when I was about three," writes one woman, "and a little white kid called me 'nigger' "),[50] and we have the raw experience Steele is trying to make sense of with his concept of the "anti-self." For Steele, it is a sad reality that black Americans do endure more wounds to their self-esteem than other Americans. They are thus saddled with the extra burden of having

to succeed, economically and personally, in spite of the inevitable resistance offered by a victimized self. Theirs is quite literally an uphill
fight.

Steele now offers a specific example of this, one that returns us to an
earlier topic—the high rates of attrition among black college students.
Against the conventional wisdom, which attributes these high dropout
rates primarily to institutional discrimination and poor academic preparation, Steele affirms a psychological component: The abiding myth of
racial inferiority causes young blacks, in many cases, to withhold effort
rather than risk failing on their own merits, and thereby confirming the
myth of inferiority.

Interestingly, a former UN ambassador and the current (1992) candidate for a U.S. Senate seat in Maryland, Allan Keyes, has also articulated a different view of the anti-self that, in his eyes, was the root
cause of the Los Angeles riots of 1992:

> For several days citizens in the afflicted area looted, trashed, and burned
> the businesses that provide jobs for their community. It's too easy to
> assume that the rioters acted irrationally, destroying the businesses that
> symbolized what they wanted most. It makes more sense to assume that
> what the rioters destroyed, and what they rioted about, symbolized what
> they hated most—outside influences, outside powers, and the fact that
> outsiders dominate every aspect of their lives.
>
> Because they have power over nothing, nothing in their environment
> reflects their own image. Because they see themselves in nothing, it is not
> long before they see nothing in themselves. And it is not long again until
> this emptiness itself becomes their identity. The self becomes the anti-self,
> a moral vacuum that sucks all meaning from the things and people around
> it.[51]

In a review of Steele's book, a *Washington Post* columnist, Juan Williams, commented in the *New Republic* on why Steele's thoughts on self-
doubt (which are parallel to Keyes's articulation of the role of self-doubt)
might strike readers as somehow strange—readers who had, over the
decades, passionately participated in America's ongoing struggle over
race:

> The cardinal rule of black political etiquette—enforced by advocates of
> Black Power in the 1960's and by racial separatists like the Nation of Islam
> today—is to keep the doubts, the alienation, the diabolical questions about
> self-worth far away from the public debate over race. Instead, what is
> intentionally revealed is a single-minded focus on one emotion only, the
> rage that black people feel about discrimination by white people.[52]

But Williams is only partly right. Steele's thoughts on self-worth strike us as both strange and *familiar*. They appear strange insofar as Black Power discourse has not, as Williams points out, typically featured references to self-doubt, but has regularly concentrated on black rage. A variation on this image is that of black men and women who have endured, souls unscathed, the indignities of Jim Crow and later slights—persons whose lives are object lessons in the survival of human dignity in poisonous circumstances. Clarence Thomas's grandfather Myers Anderson would seem to be an apt example of this, in his indomitable work ethic and quiet pride.[53] On the other hand, self-doubt is a *familiar* theme of black advocacy and a familiar feature of "black consciousness," inasmuch as mainstream civil rights advocacy has, *sotte voce*, regularly emphasized the stigma of self-doubt wrought by racism and discrimination. A conflict of images and a tension, then, clearly obtains in the popular culture of racial discourse.

Especially noteworthy are the implications of this tension for strategies of black advocacy. Think about the horns of this dilemma. On one hand, for black advocates to point to self-doubt in explanation of "performance gaps" is to risk legitimating images that may invite further discrimination—hence their reluctance to go beyond a certain point in discussing the effects of stigmatization on achievement. On the other hand, to accent the indomitability of the African-American will to succeed would be to risk downplaying the ill-consequences of self-doubt and low expectations, and thereby to lose a major warrant for programs premised on this social dynamic.

Such is the dizzying tightrope black advocates have been walking for years. Enter Shelby Steele with a jarring theory of race relations that spotlights self-doubt. With this theory he brings a discomfiting attention to the delicate balancing-act of black advocacy—one explanation for the heavy fire Steele has drawn from many civil rights leaders. How do they reply to him? Once again they are on the horns of a dilemma. In one sense, Steele has simply taken a truism of conventional black advocacy, the sorry effects of stigmatization, and advanced it to a logical conclusion, namely, that it has a part in black failure. But he has done so without hedging its implications for political purposes. To dismiss wholesale Steele's theory of stigmatization would be to repudiate a powerful rationale for various policies that black advocates have supported for years. But to agree with Steele on this point would seem to place other advocacy arguments on a slippery slope.

Perhaps feeling the critical void that Steele and others have claimed to feel, social psychologist Jeff Howard and physician Ray Hammond have, in a vein similar to Steele's, written on the origin and effects of self-doubt. In a widely-discussed *New Republic* article titled, "Rumors of Inferiority," Howard and Hammond inquired into "performance gaps" between blacks and the population as a whole, on standardized and professional tests, and examined the larger matter of black attitudes towards competition with whites. As for the performance gaps, they are obliquely reflected, say Howard and Hammond, in the phenomenon of "race-norming"—compensatory adjustment of scores according to race—which has become part of the testing practice of various institutions. In 1985, for instance, Florida "race-normed" test scores for teaching candidates, requiring a passing score of 80 percent for white applicants, and 35 to 40 percent for black applicants.[54]

With Steele, Howard and Hammond are unpersuaded by standard explanations of performance gap origins. "The traditional explanations—laziness and inferiority on the one hand; racism, discrimination, and biased testing on the other—are inaccurate and unhelpful."[55] Instead, they take a risky dissident viewpoint and attribute the gap, in large measure, to a tendency among blacks to avoid intellectual competition, fearing personal failure as embarrassing confirmation of "rumors of inferiority."

> Our hypothesis, in short, is this: (1) Black performance problems are caused in large part by a tendency to avoid intellectual competition. (2) This tendency is a psychological phenomenon that arises when the larger society projects an image of black intellectual inferiority and when that image is internalized by black people. (3) Imputing intellectual inferiority to genetic causes, especially in the face of data confirming poor performance, intensifies the fears and doubts that surround the issue.[56]

This hypothesis coheres with much in Steele's thought. Steele views this avoidance of intellectual competition as one tendency of "integration shock," that is, of those shocks of racial doubt that tend to afflict blacks in integrated situations. As noted, Steele sees black students' experience of "integration shock" as a missing piece to the puzzle of the extraordinarily high dropout rates among black college students. Yet it is a factor that few civil rights leaders have been willing to acknowledge, as it muddies a pure theory of structural victimization with an unavoidable component of personal volition, and thereby devalues the "exterior activism" that characterizes their brand of advocacy.

But Steele, Howard, and Hammond do not see the balance between exterior and interior activism as a zero-sum game that cannot withstand bold acknowledgments of the "enemy within"—in this case, the fear-of-competition factor. Just the opposite: For "exterior activism" to be most effective and not offer mere sound and fury, it must work in tandem with the facts as they are, including the disturbing realities of the "enemy within." To do otherwise is to invite absurdity, as when "gains" achieved by reformers exacerbate the very problems they are intended to remedy. Steele is clearly outraged by one such "gain" at Penn State, where a program has been implemented that pays black students to improve their grades. An improvement from a C to C+ average earns $580, and a sharper increase $1,100. Steele remarks that this Pavlovian system does nothing more than prepare blacks for dependency and teach them to hustle their victimization as a means to success.

In "Rumors of Inferiority" Howard and Hammond do not go as far as Steele, to suggest that blacks "hustle" their victimization, consciously or unconsciously. Nevertheless, the views of these men clearly cohere on the calamitous effects of self-doubt and the need for radical "interior activism." Howard and Hammond urge, "Teachers, parents, and other authority figures must encourage young blacks to attribute their intellectual successes to ability (thereby boosting confidence) and their failures to lack of effort."[57] They continue:

> It is time blacks recognize our own responsibility. When we react to the rumor of inferiority by avoiding intellectual engagement, and when we allow our children to do so, black people forfeit the opportunity for intellectual development which could extinguish the debate about our capacities, and set the stage for group progress.[58]

These comments on achievement dovetail into the Steelean concept of the "believing self." Contrary to connotations conjured by its name, the "believing self" in Steele's thought is not the product of some brand of Couesque positive thinking, but indicates the very ground of character and conscience. As such, it is hooked in constant tension to the "anti-self," which weirdly prefers fearful fantasy. Just as our experience of the "anti-self" is quite palpable, so is our experience of the "believing self." We intuitively feel it as the best part of ourselves; we experience it as the inner demand (one strong with absurd and hilarious conviction) that we squarely face our existential condition—face it with what existentialist theologian Paul Tillich called the "courage to be."[59] The "anti-self" habitually and perversely whispers of self-defeat (and is easily duped by "rumors of inferiority"), but while the "believing self" is critical of one's personal aspirations, this is but only on the basis of their merits. There is also a hint in Steele's thought that through the "believing self" we come upon the sacred.[60] From the vantage of Steele's thought, Martin Luther King's axiom, "It is not a sign of weakness, but a sign of high maturity to rise to a level of self-criticism," is an affirmation only the "believing self" can make.[61]

But the lure to "escape from freedom" is an ever-present seduction. One particularly seductive escape, argues Tillich in *The Dynamics of Faith*, is the flight into "nationalistic ecstasy," a submersion of the personality in the collective identity of the nation. Some have called this "political mysticism," in that it offers, in Susan Sontag's phrasing, "the dissolution of alienation in ecstatic feelings of community."[62] A Steelean coinage we've met, "racial inversion," offers an enlightening corollary to Tillich's "nationalistic ecstasy."

Steele sees "racial inversion" as having whirlpooled into the Black Power movement of the 1960s; it also explains in part the magnetic attraction of today's less strident, but no less influential, invocations of "black consciousness" and Afrocentrism.[63]

> Blackness itself was transformed [in the 1960s] into a grandiose quality that suggested a pervasive superiority and allowed us to win the competition with "white superiority." . . . White was the color of alienation and black the color of harmony and moral truth.[64]

Steele rightly points out that aficionados of "black consciousness" typically argue for the inherent inferiority of "white morality" obliquely and through "connotation," rather than by direct polemic. Atypical is Leonard Jefferies's public teaching at the City College of New York that the skin pigment melanin makes blacks, the Sun People, morally superior to whites, the Ice People.[65] This idea of two moral orders, one black and one white, is an intriguing one, and not as alien to public discourse as one might think.

Steele broaches the subject of two moral orders in his discussion of the burgeoning number of collegiate programs exclusively intended for blacks, including black "theme" dorms, black student unions, black yearbooks, and black homecoming dances. These special entitlements, he argues, go beyond fairness and encourage the separation of races on campus. They are "escapist racial policies," inasmuch as black students advocate them to escape the uneasiness of integration, and administrators agree to enact them to escape costly charges of racism. Anne Wortham terms these administrators "unprejudiced discriminators," people who have adopted these ways "to save their faces or ease their consciences."[66]

THE TWO MORAL ORDERS

Steele is fascinated by the psychopolitical winds blowing behind such concessionary policies. While not racist, these *racialist* policies have the effect of differentiating blacks into an interest group for whom the common standards and usual values do not apply. Steele's idea here is a provocative one: that self-preoccupied white guilt effectively consigns blacks to a different moral order. The credibility of Steele's idea here is enhanced by the insight it provides into a number of peculiarities of contemporary racial discourse, including the curious truism that black racism is an impossibility, that it is somehow a contradiction in terms.

Sometimes this proposition is stated outright, as in the following declaration on human psychology by film director Spike Lee:

Playboy: You've said that black people are incapable of racism. Do you really believe that?

Lee: Yeah, I do. . . . Blacks can't be racist. Racism is an institution. . . . But black people can be prejudiced. Everybody's prejudiced about something.[67]

This thought is not original with Lee, of course. He is repeating a new definition of racism that establishes separate moral categories for blacks and whites.[68] This bifurcation of responsibility hinges on the distinction between racism and prejudice. To Lee and those of the same opinion, the latter term denotes a personal idiosyncratic and irrational dislike, whereas the former encompasses an institutional affiliation, so that only one who is privileged to be part of the empowered class can participate in the racial oppression that institutionalized power fosters.

The thought expressed by Lee is problematic for two reasons. First, it ascribes to impersonal institutions a malice and intentionality that is more personal than structural; as such it is a kind of pathetic fallacy, an imputation of human feeling to a nonhuman thing. Second, the conceptual separation of racism and prejudice is a confusion. The two terms are not qualitatively different. Instead, their difference lies in their respective spheres of reference. Racism is a subset of prejudice. It is prejudice with specific reference to race, an irrational pejorative based on ethnicity. Prejudice is a more comprehensive word, referring, unless otherwise specified, to a general orientation toward discrimination of any sort, based on personal, self-justifying preference.

More commonly, however, the denial of black racism is present as an invisible presupposition in racial discourse. For instance, in a chapter on American attitudes toward race in *The Day America Told the Truth* (1991), pollsters James Patterson and Peter Kim, in discussing racial stereotypes, asked blacks for their opinions on white racism, but did not ask whites for their opinions about black racism. The differentiation of responsibility implicit in such a methodology would tend to confirm Steele's belief that assumptions of separate moral orders based on racial hegemony exist in middle America. Clearly, the title *The Day America Told the Truth* has reference to mainstream America.[69] A statement by Jesse Peterson provides complementary insight here:

> I am always surprised at what seems to me to be the hypocrisy that goes undetected in black conversations about "the man." I've heard blacks say to each other outright bigoted and racist things about white people they don't know without anyone objecting to it. We should hold ourselves to the same standards we hold other people to.[70]

Peterson's point, it seems, is that the notion of two moral orders is not only inherently fallacious, but immoral. Steele agrees, and is especially disturbed about the odious implications of this notion for ideological vitality among blacks. Such racial triumphalism, as it were, confers upon intraracial criticism the status of betrayal and hypocrisy, and thereby greatly reduces whatever effectiveness such criticism may otherwise have had.

...BUT STEELE IS NOT A SOCIAL SCIENTIST

Having considered Steele's concepts of *anti-self, believing self, racial inversion,* and *integration shock,* we come to something of a transition point in Steele's theory. So far we have examined his understanding of how a harsh legacy of political, legal, and economic oppression has intimately impinged on the consciousness of black Americans. Now the process turns around, as Steele considers how feelings of vulnerability are "recomposed" into a black identity focused on victimhood, and into a black political culture that is gripped by the illusion that deliverance only comes from reform in others.

But before starting this second part of our examination of Steele's thought, a general word is in order about the nature of his inquiry and his conclusions. Steele's approach to the subject of American race relations is existentialist, not only in its philosophical perspective, but at its source. Steele is not a "social scientist." His thinking on race is essentially based on self-understanding, individual experience, informal observation, discussion, and reflection both on the material of his experience and on that material in light of the work of Kierkegaard, Ellison, Jean Paul Sartre, and Franz Kafka.[71] "Steele is not a political scientist like myself, nor an economist," remarked William B. Allen, "but is coming at this from a humanities perspective. It's good that someone is tackling these questions from that perspective."[72]

While some see Steele's personalism as myopically limited, disposing to solipsism and distortion, others, like Allen, find in it the origin of his most daring and accurate insights. That he is not a social scientist by profession, it may be argued (though with some cynicism), redounds to the honesty of his work. As a professor of literature, Steele is under less pressure to conform his thinking on race relations to the artificial protocol that notoriously obtains in social science departments, where failure to arrive at politically safe conclusions can jeopardize a career. Professors of literature may be somewhat excused from these constraints; after all, they spend their days professing the untamed notions of the wild *literateur*. In light of Steele's nonconformism, it is likely that the import of a famous remark made by one of these, Hart Crane, would not be lost on him. During the heady years following the Bolshevik revolution, when the rage among American writers and expatriots was to undo Babbitry by cross-breeding their plot lines with dialectical materialism, Crane cautioned writers to resist pressures to political correctness. "Intellectual workers of the world unite!" cried Crane, in a twist on the *Communist Manifesto*. "You have nothing to lose but your brains."

Interestingly, some see Steele's paradigm as liable to the same calcification, and so obscurantism, as that of the civil rights ideologues he sharply challenges. One of his main methodological criticisms of civil rights ideology is that it is stuck in a kind of time warp—that it is viewing 1990s race relations through 1960s ideological overlays. Thus, Steele points to such incidents as the 1989 NAACP convention, where the myriad of problems facing black America (teen pregnancy, welfare proliferation, gang violence, incarceration rates, et al.) were taken as irrefutable evidence of the continuing victimization of blacks at the hands of the white establishment, and also the exoneration of the black leadership from any responsibility for repairing these problems.

And yet Steele's vision does appear more mutable than the paradigms of those he criticizes. He clearly does not view the economy of racial attitudes and behaviors in America as some fixed, Rube Goldberg-ish apparatus. His work is not the final exposure of the secret gears and flywheels that whirl below the bells, whistles, and shouts of American race relations. The situation, as Steele sees it, is fluid and will change. Who would have predicted, he asks, the amazing revolution of attitudes toward race that has taken place in the last quarter of a century? Therefore, to the extent that Steele does attempt to uncover the psychological subtext to the rhetoric of race relations, he would seem to understand his conclusions as strongly tied to prevailing currents of racial thought. Reflecting the protean nature of contemporary race relations, it is not difficult to imagine a book from Steele five years hence explicating a very different set of racial dynamics.

THE POLITICS OF RECOMPOSITION

We now return to Steele's theory of the "recomposition" of feelings of vulnerability into a victim-centered political culture.

The principle of "recomposition" is closely linked to that of "racial inversion" in Steele's psychology. "Racial inversion" relieves personal doubt through the pride of collective identity. Espoused to a collective identity, the individual "recomposes" his situation, tailoring reality to ideology. Those who engage in "recomposition" impose their race's historical status as victims onto a contemporary personal context, thus assuming the role of victim without reference to the manner in which they have actually been treated.

In this way, denied fears are translated into a caricatured white oppressor. This idea of recomposition would seem to be illustrated by the following experience in a race-relations course, recounted in a university faculty publication:

> A black woman, talking candidly in . . . class on race relations, describes how she was hurt and angered by a remark directed at her during a . . . sorority tea rush. One of the hostesses at the event, who was white, suggested [to the black woman] she might be more interested in the black sorority.
>
> Alarmed by this story, a white woman in . . . class, a sorority sister,

point[ed] out that not everyone would have made such a hurtful remark and that her house has been trying to increase its ethnic diversity.[73]

With campus kiosks layered with posters issued by various black campus groups inviting students to join black fraternities and black student unions, come out for black cultural events, attend black dances, be in the black student yearbook, and go to black graduation ceremonies, the hostess's remark that the woman might be interested in joining a black sorority hardly smacks of Willie Horton–ad tactics. But that is essentially what the black woman "recomposed" it into. Her "hurt and anger," rather than being an indication of some subtle ethical acumen, reveals moral immaturity—an inability or unwillingness to stand outside her role as "a black female" and observe the human elements of the situation. Did it occur to her that the hostess, even if her remark was a faux pas, was trying to be nice? But to make such a distinction would have required her to relax her grip on her role of "the black female" and see herself as just another human being among other flawed human beings, whose clumsy faux pas often contain genuinely positive sentiments.

Steele provides a similar example of recomposition. At Berkeley, a black student told him that he felt defensive every time he walked into a classroom filled with white students. Asked why, the student explained, "Because I know they're all racists. They think blacks are stupid." This line of thought is inevitably self-validating, with the student interpreting other students' behavior through the template of preassigned bigotry.

The effect of this student's "recomposition" of fears into a phalanx of enemies is an escape from personal responsibility for failure, and also a perverse way of disjoining achievement from effort, in a way that forbids the student to draw a healthy confidence from his successes. "I didn't fail," he can say to himself. "I never had a chance." The meaning of his successes is obscured, too.

Steele acknowledges that many black students enter the university handicapped by poor educational backgrounds, and are legitimately aggrieved to discover that their high school education was second rate, for one reason or another. But Steele is horrified to see black students encouraged by the black leadership, through rhetoric and general example, to handle poor grades by claiming victimization. Deficits in skills can be remedied through extra self-effort and mutual aid. Recourse to the reflexive rhetoric of "victimology" merely covers up deficits, and so in the long run sets black students up to fail.[74]

Though educators' responses to such "recomposition" vary, of course, two kinds of responses invite special consideration, as they represent emphases in Steele's work. The first response is fear. Tenure-conscious faculty are afraid, says Steele, to tell black students what they really think, fearing that the dreaded word "racist" will be uttered and work like a magic mantra, causing things to disappear, including their own chances of promotion. In *Education's Smoking Gun* (1985), Reginald G. Damerell documents the pervasiveness of this fear at his university during recent years. "Professors in the school feared being labeled racist or, in its less strident version, 'unsympathetic to minority students.' "[75] Allan Bloom, writing about this phenomenon at Cornell in *The Closing of the American Mind* (1987), found this fear manifest in "difficulty in giving blacks failing marks, and an organized system of grievance and feeling aggrieved."[76] Steele finds irony in black student responses to this capitulation; even as they "recompose" their failure into accusations of racism, hoping for concessions, the students are dispirited by the lowering of academic standards their activism achieves. This further engenders self-doubt. What especially disturbs Bloom, and Steele, about the whole affair is that it is glazed over with a shiny silence. This is especially revolting inasmuch as the charade is going on at *universities*, where paladins of free thought and honest, fearless inquiry are thought to be initiating the young into the trackless life of the mind. "And everywhere," says Bloom, is "hypocrisy, contempt-producing lies about what is going on and how the whole system is working."[77]

There is a second response to "recomposition": its radical encouragement by certain instructors. Steele and Howard and Hammond are making their plea to black parents, educators, and activists to encourage a vivifying "intellectual work ethic," but at the same time, "white intellectual provocateurs," in Orlando Patterson's phrase,[78] are blithely assuring black students that the "racist university system" won't give them an even break, that they will find no correlation between the quality of their work and their achievement. Exasperated by what appears to be a kind of glib ideological priming of black students, Stanley Crouch writes in another context, "I realized somebody was still using black students' heads as fish bowls in which they dropped penny slogans."[79]

Steele's theory of "recomposition" can also be applied, with some benefit, to modes of community activism. Case in point: the alleged antiblack character of Operation Cul De Sac, a special project of the Los

Angeles Police Department. In the summer of 1991, the LAPD erected concrete barriers across high crime streets in certain predominantly black neighborhoods. The idea was to turn two-way streets into cul-de-sacs to curb drive-by shootings and dope dealing from cars. But community activists complained that the police were using the cul-de-sacs to turn black neighborhoods into "concentration camps." In addition, a staff writer for the *Los Angeles Sentinel* characterized the program as a "Nazi-style ghetto plan."[80]

Several elements of Steele's theory are naturally applicable to this case. To begin with, the hyperbolic character of the charges ("concentration camp," "Nazi-style ghetto plan") is reminiscent of the credibility gap Steele sees as a feature of certain modes of black activism, especially those involving reckless and habitual wolf-crying. Legitimate complaints must be voiced and redressed. For instance, the public outcry against racism in the LAPD during the summer of 1991, brought to public light by the videotaped beating of Rodney King, summoned into being the Christopher Commission, which has recommended reforms. But unreflective suspicions and routinized accusations of harassment—as, it would appear, in the case of Operation Cul de Sac—have had the effect of impugning the credibility of those who made them, and at the same time diminishing the power of serious black advocacy.

Indeed, the protests against Operation Cul de Sac resemble the adversarial politics of "recomposition" more than they resemble a cool, objective assessment of community needs. By mechanically stamping the project "racist" and calling it yet another example of black victimization, activists tried to cordon it off from a serious, cost-benefit review by the black public. These activists appeared less interested in the empirical question, Will it make our community more livable for us and safer for our children? than in scoring ideological points, or perhaps laying up personal political capital. This would not surprise Sowell, who has wryly commented, in a different context, "Cost-benefit analysis is the last thing crusaders want to hear."[81]

As it turns out, Operation Cul-de-Sac has cut serious crime in the neighborhood dramatically, by about 17 percent, according to a study conducted by James R. Lassley, an assistant professor of criminal justice at California State University at Fullerton.[82] This included the almost total elimination of gang-related drive-by shootings. "People who used to literally sleep on the floor at night because they were afraid of being shot, feel a lot safer," said Lassley.[83] The increase in community pride that resulted, he added, was manifest in the restoration of derelict homes in the area. Impressed by these results, law enforcement officials in several other states instituted similar programs.

AFFIRMATIVE ACTION

Steele's analysis of affirmative action features a Sowellian distinction between symbolic victories and cost-benefit pragmatism. As might be expected from the psychological character of Steele's work, he does not measure the costs and benefits of affirmative action solely in raw economic terms, but instead he contemplates their noetic effects.

Central to Steele's analysis of black accomplishment and affirmative action is his description of the racial-psychological dynamic at work in the aggregate conscience of black and white America. This analysis, by its very nature, takes place on a general level and no doubt admits exceptions. Steele is making generalizations about all blacks and whites. Clearly he wishes to avoid any absolutistic interpretations of his analysis of racial psychology. Rather than making categorical statements about what all people (most of whom he does not know in any way) think and emotionally feel, Steele is speaking about a hidden psychological dialectic that takes place between two segments of the population, black and white.

This dialectic is really a cycle, a cycle that feeds off itself. We can enter this cycle by first recognizing the presence of white guilt. Steele is careful to point out that guilt is not necessarily unwarranted. As noted earlier, Steele nowhere says that white racism is nonexistent. His purpose in discussing white guilt, rather, is to show that it is this felt guilt on the part of whites that, in large measure, motivates them to sponsor and advocate special entitlement programs of all kinds.

Steele sees the discharging or atoning for this guilt as a fundamental cause of affirmative action and other political "reparations" programs. Indeed, inasmuch as many whites advert to the evils of slavery and the ill-effects of past racism in America as a justifying reason for present-day programs, these policies are clearly intended as atonements.

Now, while it is clear that advocates of such programs see them as a pragmatic necessity and an important device to create parity, the unarticulated effect, holds Steele, is to assuage the guilty consciences of whites who take responsibility for the injustices that preceded them. So in a very real sense, entitlement programs for blacks serve the personal interests of whites as well, indirectly clearing their consciences and leading them to believe that they have somehow righted a wrong, and corrected or undone the injustices of the past. In Sowellian terms, affirmative action offers whites a "symbolic victory" over guilt.

Steele sees white guilt as a sort of emotional capital laid up for blacks to use to enact various racial programs. His analysis is ultimately an account of a sort of psycho-emotional bartering game in which, piece by piece, the racial moral high ground historically reserved for blacks is gradually ceded to whites in return for political and economic power, or at least symbolic expressions of it. For Steele, preferential treatment policies are concrete expressions of this moral bartering. But moral bartering is not the same as efficacious social policy. Commenting on a University of Chicago study that indicated that segregation is as firmly entrenched today as it has been for decades, Steele said that it is the felt need of whites to expunge their guilt that has shaped a public policy to meet *that* need, rather than address the concrete problems restraining African-American advancement.

Steele sees preferential treatment as such a guilt-expunging policy, delivering "innocence," but to a relative few and at a great price. Part of this price is its bringing upon blacks "the stab of racial doubt" and tainting their accomplishments. To Steele, this entitlement-trap entrenches a black dependence on white kindness and inevitably obscures all real accomplishment under a pall of suspicion. This inadvertent effect of preferential policies (an inevitable one, says Steele) was manifest in the debate over Clarence Thomas's nomination to the Supreme Court. When a journalist reminded Steele that Thomas had been criticized for thinking "he made it all by himself," Steele adjured that Thomas had "made it himself"—through diligence, perseverance, and self-discipline. Affirmative action, as a public policy, did not secure Thomas's success. His own *personal* qualities predisposed him to success.[84]

Suspicion of black success, coupled with persistent cries of racism and black victimization, renews the cycle and once again draws on the emotional capital of white guilt. To Steele, this "victimized" mind-set stifles personal initiative and, in the long run, demoralizes and discourages blacks, especially the youngest. This has resulted in the tragic paradox sharply described by Ethelbert W. Haskins in *The Crisis in Afro-American Leadership*: "Afro-American youth in the decaying center-city ghetto represent the largest group in the history of the country to consider itself disadvantaged and at the same time remain uncommitted to self-betterment."[85]

Though Steele sees the politics of victimization and preferential treatment policies as ultimately backfiring for the reasons given above, he is not against other forms of political "affirmative action"—that is, policies, which proactively aid inner city residents in changing their own lives.[86] Against the media mythology of the black dissident as a heartless bootstrapist, Steele urges a role for government, but a role that supplements— not supplants—individual effort and the meeting of familial obligations. Sadly, the subtlety of this point is lost on media mavens eager to construct a comic strip version of the battle between ruthless, aloof conservatives and passionate, engaged liberals.

CONCLUSION

In concluding this look at the main currents of Steele's thought, we need note that its striking originality stems as much from the personal experience of its architect as it does from other factors. Steele is a black man, an African-American, steeped in the civil rights movement and its frustrated maturity. He is saying things that are rarely said by anyone, black or white.

He is raising his voice amid the cacophony of other civil rights voices. But his call is an altogether different one, striking a provocative and dissonant key, clearly distinguishable from what he sees as the intellectual monotone of what has become the civil rights establishment.

NOTES

1. Edith Efron, *The News Twisters* (Los Angeles: Nash, 1971), p. 66.
2. Shelby Steele, *The Content of Our Character* (New York: St. Martin's, 1990), p. xii (emphasis in original).
3. Ibid., p. 16.
4. "Up from Obscurity," *Time*, August 13, 1990, p. 45.
5. Ethelbert W. Haskins, *The Crisis in Afro-American Leadership* (Buffalo: Prometheus, 1988), p. 13.
6. David T. Wellman, *Portraits of White Racism* (Cambridge: Cambridge University Press, 1987), p. 4.
7. This trend is exemplified in Wellman, ibid.
8. Steele, *Content of Our Character*, p. 87.
9. Sylvester Monroe, interview with Shelby Steele, "Nothing Is Ever Simply Black and White," *Time*, 12 August 1991, p. 6.
10. "The Hidden Perils of Racial Conformity," *U.S. News and World Report*, 24 December 1990.
11. Reinhold Niebuhr, *Moral Man and Immoral Society* (New York: Scribner's, 1932), p. xi.
12. Ibid.
13. Steele, *Content of Our Character*, p. 74.

14. Paul Sniderman with Michael Gray Hagen, *Race and Inequality: A Study in American Values* (Chatham NJ: Chatham House, 1985), p. 99.

15. John Mullen, *Kierkegaard's Philosophy: Self-Deception and Cowardice in the Present Age* (New York: New American Library, 1981), pp. 59–77.

16. See ibid., pp. 66 and 141, for Mullen's discussion of "double-mindedness."

17. Orlando Patterson, *Ethnic Chauvinism* (New York: Stein and Day, 1977).

18. Emily Sachar, *Shut Up and Let the Lady Teach!* (New York: Simon and Schuster, 1991), p. 181.

19. *Los Angeles Sentinel*, 30 April 1992, p. 1.

20. Ibid.

21. *Time*, 12 August 1991, p. 8.

22. Ibid.

23. Ibid.

24. Steele, *Content of Our Character*, p. 63.

25. Martin Kilson, "Realism about the Black Experience: A Reply to Shelby Steele," *Dissent*, Fall 1990, p. 522.

26. Shelby Steele, "Shelby Steele Replies" (to Kilson, "Realism about the Black Experience"), *Dissent*, Fall 1990, p. 522.

27. As discussed in Michael Novak, *Free Persons and the Common Good*, (Lanham, Md.: Madison Books, 1985), p. 35.

28. Ibid., p. 35.

29. "Up from Obscurity," p. 45.

30. Anne Wortham, *The Other Side of Racism* (Columbus: Ohio State University Press, 1981); Orlando Patterson, *Ethnic Chauvinism* (New York: Stein and Day, 1977).

31. Ibid., p. 5.

32. Ibid., p. 41.

33. Stanley Crouch, "Role Models," in *Second Thoughts about Race in America*, edited by Peter Collier and David Horowitz, (Lanham: Madison Books, 1991), p. 61.

34. Wortham, *Other Side of Racism*, p. 54.

35. Patterson, *Ethnic Chauvinism*, p. 154.

36. James H. Cone, *Black Theology and Black Power* (New York: Seabury, 1969), p. 18.

37. Wortham, *Other Side of Racism*, p. 127.

38. Ibid., p. 110 (emphasis in the original).

39. *Los Angeles Times*, 17 September 1990, p. A14.

40. Steele, *Content of Our Character*, p. 163.

41. Patterson, *Ethnic Chauvinism*, p. 150.

42. Wortham, *Other Side of Racism*, p. 99.

43. Orlando Patterson, "Hidden Dangers in Ethnic Revival," *New York Times*, 20 February 1978.

44. Ibid., p. 19.

45. See *From Max Weber: Essays in Sociology*, translated and edited by H. H. Gerth and C. Wright Mills (New York: Oxford University, 1946), Chapter 9.

46. See Peter Berger and Thomas Luckmann, *The Social Construction of Reality*

(Garden City, N.Y.: Doubleday, 1967). Anne Wortham in *The Other Side of Racism* also offers a special nomenclature, perhaps to similar "nominizing" ends. Unlike Steele, whose special terminology emphasizes motivation and dynamics, e.g. "race holding," Wortham offers typological profiles that counterpose, for instance, the Power-Seeking Nationalist to the Ambivalent Appeaser.

47. Kilson, "Realism about the Black Experience," pp. 519–22.

48. Thomas Sowell, *A Conflict of Visions* (New York: Morrow, 1987), pp. 19–25.

49. See Anne Crutcher "Government as Social Worker," in *Values in an American Government Textbook*, edited by Ernest W. Lefever (Washington, DC: Ethics and Public Policy Center, 1978), pp. 33–34.

50. "Race: Can We Talk?" *Ms.*, July/August 1991, p. 36.

51. Allan Keyes, "Restoring Community," *National Review*, 8 June 1992.

52. Juan Williams, "The Fire This Time," *New Republic*, 10 December 1990, p. 33.

53. See "The Crowning Thomas Affair," *U.S. News and World Report*, 16 September 1991, p. 26, for a discussion of the personality of Myers Anderson.

54. Jeff Howard and Ray Hammond, "Rumors of Inferiority," *New Republic*, 9 September 1985, p. 18.

55. Ibid.

56. Ibid., p. 19.

57. Ibid., p. 21.

58. Ibid.

59. See Paul Tillich, *The Courage to Be* (New Haven, Conn.: Yale University Press, 1962).

60. *Time*, 12 August 1991, p. 6.

61. Martin Luther King, Jr., *Where Do We Go From Here: Chaos or Community?* (Boston: Beacon, 1968), p. 125.

62. Quoted in Stanley Crouch, *Notes from a Hanging Judge* (New York: Oxford University Press, 1990), p. 240.

63. In his University of Pennsylvania lectures, Huston Baker's references to American blacks as the "African body" and his likening their experience to the Roman Catholic Mass ("the materialization and engorgement of the body as a manifested covenant of a new order") illustrates this kind of quasi-religious paradigm. See Roger Kimball, *Tenured Radicals: How Politics Has Corrupted Our Higher Education* (New York: Harper and Row, 1990), p. 20.

64. Steele, *Content of Our Character*, p. 65.

65. "Black Professor Called a Racist," *USA Today*, 14 August 1991, p. 2A.

66. Wortham, *Other Side of Racism*, p. 39.

67. Quoted in, Clarence Page, "Spike Lee Flirts with Racism Even as He Decries It," *Orange County Register*, 11 June 1991.

68. See Wellman, *Portraits of White Racism*.

69. James Patterson and Peter Kim; *The Day America Told the Truth* (New York: Prentice-Hall, 1991).

70. Joseph Conti, interview with Jesse Peterson, Los Angeles, Calif., 10 January 1992.

71. Ibid.

72. Joseph Conti, interview with William B. Allen, 9 March 1992.

73. "Teaching about Race: An Old Topic Receives New Attention at USC," *Transcript*, 8 June 1992, p. 1.

74. See Steele's discussion of "victimology" in *Time*, 12 August 1991, p. 8.

75. Reginald G. Damerell, *Education's Smoking Gun* (New York: Freundlich, 1985), p. 4.

76. Allan Bloom, *The Closing of the American Mind* (New York: Simon and Schuster, 1987), p. 95.

77. Ibid.

78. Patterson, *Ethnic Chauvinism*, p. 154.

79. Crouch, *Notes from a Hanging Judge*, p. 22.

80. See *Los Angeles Sentinel*, "A Commentary: What is Operation Cul De Sac?" 20 June 1991, p. A3 and 8–14 August 1991, pp. A1, A5.

81. Thomas Sowell, *Pink and Brown People* (Stanford, Calif.: Hoover Institution Press, 1981), p. 45.

82. "LA Anti-Crime Plan Draws Praise," *Los Angeles Times*, 29 May 1991, p. B1.

83. Ibid.

84. Monroe, "Nothing Is Ever Simply Black and White," *Time*, 12 August 1991, p. 8.

85. Haskins, *Crisis in Afro-American Leadership*, p. 11.

86. Monroe, "Nothing Is Ever Simply Black and White," p. 6.

———5———

ROBERT L. WOODSON: PROTESTING THE "ALMS RACE"

The victimizer might knock you down, but the victim is the one who has to get himself up.

Robert L. Woodson

[The] first months of 1968 urban renewal put the houses of Fulton in jeopardy, and instantly the authority of the old ideals was lost. For the houses of Fulton had been proof that hard work and virtuous living—not political power or government money—bring success in the world. The houses were a statement of the essential morality of the universe, a statement which the housing authority bluntly and decisively rebutted.

Scott C. Davis, *The World of Patience Gromes*

Perhaps universities were never quite the intellectual speakeasies some now yearn for—places where the free and open exchange of ideas, any ideas, were commonplace. But even if such nostalgia is idealized, an unmistakable change has taken place, as noted in Dinesh D 'Souza's *Illiberal Education*[1] and alluded to in our earlier vignette about the silence in a Minority Cultures class at USC. It is ironic, but perhaps understandable, that the free exchange of ideas would move to a less institutionalized context.

It is an unpleasant reality that socially coercive forces are at work whenever one is in a position to publicly express a controversial belief. Personal criticisms of deviancy, insensitivity, and malevolence are the bullies that await one who challenges a dominant pattern of thinking. When the issues are highly emotional, the stakes are higher, and therefore the tendency to withhold expression of one's belief, to falsify one's true preferences, is greater. Timur Kuran, a professor of economics at the University of Southern California, has captured this concept in his theory of "preference falsification."[2] It seems to us that an objective correlate to the subjective notion of personal "preference falsification" is the idea of "public truth," supervising public conversations. While "public truth" is not necessarily "true," it is acceptable and functions, for the most part, as though it were rationally demonstrated truth.

The media shape this "truth" in a powerful way, by commission and omission. When CNN's Bernard Shaw informs tens of millions of television viewers that welfare is a "code word" and that political discussion of it is simply race baiting, he makes an addition—a dubious one—to the deposit of "public truth." In this way, "public truth" is developed by commission; on the other hand, when the scholarly and systematic presentations of social criticism by New Black Vanguard thinkers are given only token notice by the news media, "public truth" is shaped and conditioned by omission. Such omission and commission have a tremendous impact on the protocol of daily discussions of important public matters, including race relations and attendant issues. Informed from a seat of media authority that to criticize welfare policies is to engage in clever race baiting, many dissenting Americans, black and white, are inclined to conceal their personal opinions in public.

One such forum in which the force field of "public truth" is attenuated is the phone-in talk show. Obviously, the power of "public truth" that works to suppress politically incorrect views in public places is less controlling in the context of an anonymous phone comment. The following remarks were made on a "Donahue and Pozner" roundtable on the current state of African-American civil rights. Joining Phil Donahue and former Soviet mouthpiece Vladimir Pozner were Stanley Crouch and Amiri Baraka (LeRoi Jones). A particularly fascinating exchange was sparked by a call from a young white man who as a child had attended a nearly all-black inner city school. He suggested that there was no mystery to the post–high school failure of many of his fellow black classmates: many did not study, he said, and instead spent their time "strutting around."

Commenting on the young man's observation, Donahue was predictably sarcastic and Baraka intoned, "Racist," but Stanley Crouch broke through:

Wait a minute! What is wrong with someone observing that there is some kind of discontinuity in a number of people's households that mitigates against these kids best preparing themselves for what they are inevitably going to be faced with, which is their life in America. . . . Maybe this guy has some clumsy way of saying it—but this is not something that black teachers all over the country haven't noticed!

Co-host Pozner interrupted, and after reminding Crouch of the overwhelming power of racism in America, concluded, "There are two strikes against them [black youngsters] from the day they are born in the ghetto. And how you cannot admit that is beyond me." Crouch stopped him:

> Mr. Pozner, let me tell you something. My mother was a domestic worker—she worked six days a week, sometimes eleven hours a day, she raised three children, and was never on welfare, and encouraged us always to study. There were *plenty* of people like that! The world you're born in . . . is the world you've got to deal with. Now the thing is, we can either prepare people to fight for their lives in society by being best prepared, or we can let them sit up and bitch like a bunch of crybabies. Or let them take on self-destructive habits that don't take them anywhere.[3]

Crouch's dissent from the "public truth" concerning the nature of problems besetting the black poor resembles the dissent of neighborhood activist Robert L. Woodson. Like Crouch, Woodson exposits a social philosophy marked by pragmatism, one that identifies certain habits as instrumentally superior for preparing an individual to rise from poverty into economic freedom. Indeed, this holding of certain practices as essential vehicles for an individual's socioeconomic mobility is a central idea in the thinking of Woodson, and in the New Black Vanguard social vision as a whole. In this vein, rather than deny that many black students in inner cities do not take education as seriously as they should—or shoot the bearer of this bad news, as Donahue, Pozner, and Baraka were inclined to do—Woodson would have us take a serious look at this failure. "Last year in Washington, D.C.," he remembers, echoing the findings of the Ogbu and Fordham study, "six black kids who graduated from high school were presented with academic excellence awards, but were fearful of coming up and receiving them at graduation because they didn't want to be accused of being 'white.' I think that is sick!"[4]

Woodson is a unique figure in black advocacy. He is a Republican, though not blindly partisan. He is critical of the civil rights agenda followed since the late 1960s, though passionately committed to working for the well-being of blacks. He is academically trained, yet primarily active in the nonacademic environment of inner-city neighborhoods. Responsible for some of the most innovative and heartening transfor-

mations of neighborhoods from ghettos into safe and stable communities, Woodson remains an outsider in black politics.

Active in the civil rights movement and the NAACP in the 1960s,
Woodson began his dissent from conventional black advocacy during
the latter part of that tumultuous decade. Perhaps it was his experience
as a young military man that taught him this lesson of self-reliance, a
lesson he found antithetical to a "dependency strategy":

> After two years of running to bars and running around while in the army,
> I stopped and said, "I'm not going to be like a lot of Black people who
> say White people got their foot on my neck. The way not to become a part
> of that is to prepare yourself." I turned some of that energy and anger
> into achievement. I had more training than all the Whites in my squadron
> in missile science and technology. So they had to rely on me even though
> they outranked me, because I was the only one who knew how to run
> the dials. I learned from this experience that the way you get control and
> influence is through achieving.[5]

Sounding a theme of overarching concern for the least prosperous of
blacks, a theme that would be present in his social work for years to
come, Woodson further explained his dissatisfaction with civil rights
leadership:

> I didn't fight for integration, I fought against segregation. Their embrace
> of integration and busing really turned me off. Also I didn't like their
> embrace of the poverty program . . . when I knew it was ripping people
> off—that I didn't like. They seemed to be impressed with issues that were
> important to middle or upper-income blacks, but did little for lower income
> blacks.[6]

Woodson, then, sees the civil rights movement of today as genuinely
misguided in a number of ways. One is its understanding of racism. To
Woodson, the leadership of these organizations is addicted to using race
as an excuse for not forthrightly addressing the needs of poor blacks.
He repudiates "the old rhetoric that blame[s] racism for all social ills."[7]
Still, Woodson is brutally frank about the disgusting reality of America's
racist past and has no illusions about racial harmony today. "Racism,"
he acknowledges, "is a given."[8] But unlike the civil rights establishment,
Woodson is unwilling to allow racism to be a controlling factor in the
lives of black Americans. In fact, he would agree with Steele that some
"evidence" of white racism is actually a misinterpretation of the signs
of the times. For instance, he says, "In no way is everyone who voted

for [ex–Ku Klux Klansman] David Duke a racist. Their support was an expression of their alienation and resentment. There is frustration on the part of working America and people at the grass-roots level."[9] This capacity to step outside the frames of "acceptable" black advocacy and impute something other than the most nefarious of motives to white America, even to those who voted for Duke, is characteristic of the New Black Vanguard.

His qualms about black moral leadership are supplemented by his impatience with civil rights groups for their persistent failure to recognize that their present agenda, while helping middle-class blacks, inadequately serves the needs of the black underclass. He sees an inflexibility and dogmatism in these groups that he finds both troubling and humorous. "They continue to repeat the mistakes of the past," he suggests. "They remind me very much of old retired circus horses out there in the pasture. Every time the circus comes by, they just start prancing and dancing to the same old music!"[10]

THE POVERTY PENTAGON: WOODSON'S CRITICISMS OF WELFARE

If Woodson finds the civil rights leadership mechanical and stubborn, he finds the same sorry immutability in the mega-governmental structures charged with helping the poor. Woodson's conviction on this point was evident in his reply to our question, "What has most surprised you in your years of working for neighborhood empowerment?"

"What has surprised me is the tremendous resistance," he said. "When I began, I didn't realize that the industry benefited from keeping people poor."[11]

Commenting on the welfare industry, Woodson has written:

What we have built in the name of the poor is a *Poverty Pentagon*. And in this huge conglomerate of programs for the poor, the principal beneficiaries are not the poor but those who make their living from the poor. We have, in many cases, programs that do not improve the conditions of the poor but actually exacerbate the very problems they were designed to solve.[12]

Here we have Woodson's paradigmatic rebuke of the government-centered approach to aiding the poor that has held sway the last thirty years. Rather than achieving their averred goal of relieving the misery of the economically impoverished, the standard welfare programs have the tragic paradox of further impoverishing the poor. For while they are a source of nominal cash, they impede the development of the self-reliance and personal resourcefulness that alone can sustain the type of effort and outlook that escaping the provinces of inner-city poverty requires. With Sowell, Woodson is convinced that raw, bureaucratic self-interest at the "Poverty Pentagon" has displaced the aim of helping people achieve self-sufficiency. "Prior to 1960," he told an unusual meeting of left and right think tanks at the Heritage Foundation in Washington, D.C.,

> government expressed its concern for poor people by transferring cash directly to them. Seventy cents of every dollar went directly to poor people. Since then, we have seen a 25-fold increase in the amount of money that is spent in the name of poor people, but seventy cents of every dollar spent goes to the service industry.[13]

Central to Woodson's approach is the primary recognition, so elusive to those accustomed to looking for centralized answers to localized problems, that empowerment and riches extend beyond the merely financial. A vital family, a personal character grounded in the values of human dignity and community obligation, and voluntary associations embodying shared concerns and goals, all contribute to the interior wealth that is human flourishing in its fullest sense. Woodson thinks that only self-help strategies can bring the inner-city poor to this more complete and self-sufficient life.

In the wake of the Los Angeles riots—and politicians' calls for sluicing more federal dollars into the ghetto—Woodson voiced fear that the self-help strategies he had personally seen work so well (in black Philadelphia neighborhoods, in low-income Hispanic communities, and in native American reservations)[14] would be discounted in favor of government-based solutions. "My fears are that we will deal with this incident the way we did in the '60's, applying the same remedies that failed *then* to the conditions today."[15] Echoing this sentiment is self-government advocate Ezola Foster. A former Watts school teacher and long-term resident of South Central Los Angeles, Foster said after the 1992 riots, "Following the 1965 riots, inner-cities received upwards of 5 billion dollars in aid for education and job training programs. The Small Business Administration was created to assist black entrepreneurs. None of it appears to have solved the deeper problems that really plagued the black community."[16]

Underlying this comment and Woodson's whole self-help philosophy is the conviction, born of experience, that self-control and *self-determination* should reign in every person living under a democratic regime. Woodson further elaborated this idea in an exchange with rapper-politico Sister Souljah, during a panel discussion following the Los Angeles riots.

Powerfully influential among inner-city black youth, Souljah has gained fame for her hate-filled diatribes, as well as for her "fight the Power" raps as part of Public Enemy, perhaps the most lionized of the "raptivists." Souljah finds the System thoroughly and indefatigably racist, and believes this message must be instilled in the consciousness of black youngsters. Billed as Sister of Instruction/Director of Attitude in the liner notes of Public Enemy's album *Apocalypse . . . The Enemy Strikes Black*, Souljah carefully reflected on race relations in an earlier interview:

> Despite what we've been lulled into believing, it is a race war. . . . Call it prejudice. I don't care. When I see whites, I see people who for generations were oppressing my people. Knowing their history, how can I feel favorable toward any whites?[17]

The following exchange between this Director of Attitude and Woodson was, in many ways, paradigmatic:

> *Woodson*: Power was defined in the black community by how we controlled *ourselves*. Up until 1959, 78 percent of all black families were whole; less than 2 percent of black children were raised in households where the mother never married. This was at a time when we were being lynched every day, driven out of towns—[but] we never allowed, historically, whites to determine our destiny. When we weren't treated at hospitals, we had our own 230 hospitals. When we couldn't borrow money from banks, we had our own banks.
>
> *Souljah*: But that was before integration and migration.
>
> *Woodson*: No, no, no. All I'm saying to you is that power does not come from what someone concedes; it is in controlling your own behavior. . . . At the street level, people are less concerned about racism, than they are getting to the store, past the drug dealers.
>
> *Souljah*: Right—but the drug dealers are there because of racism. Because young brothers and sisters do not have money and they sell drugs for survival, and we shouldn't be dishonest about that fact.
>
> *Woodson*: We can keep talking about how somehow the destiny of these young people is determined by something external . . .
>
> *Souljah* [interrupting]: Finance in America is the number one reality for black people!

Woodson: The young Muslim brothers, the young Christian brothers, who are associated with Teen Fathers in Columbus, Ohio—two hundred of them have married the mothers of their children, and are reaching out to two thousand others. . . .

Souljah: I think that should happen—but once they marry, how are they going to put food on the table?

Woodson: At Kennilworth Parkside in Washington, D.C. [a self-supporting public housing project], 680 kids in seven years have gone on to college, teen pregnancy is almost eliminated. In other words, there are efforts like this where people who work with teens and others say, "Power, first of all, comes from controlling *yourself*. If you cannot control yourself, you cannot control your society."[18]

For the record, Souljah's belief that black youth must "sell drugs for survival" is, beyond its inanity, counterempirical. The work-availability statistics cited earlier and current studies all show that inner-city crime pays less, on the average, than even low-wage employment.[19] Also, Souljah's grave pessimism regarding the economic welfare of black husband-wife couples is inconsistent with Urban League findings, which show that the number of intact black families living below the poverty line actually dropped 34 percent between 1969 and 1978.[20]

As is clear from the above exchange, Woodson's primary emphasis is on self-determination. Since 1964, says Woodson, the primary beneficiary of government largesse—in the forms of employment programs, federal housing, public welfare, and so on—has been the social service "industry." While this bureaucracy has grown, its putative beneficiaries have remained largely unaffected, except for the demotivational and dependent ethos big government has inculcated in them.

Conservative black social critic Elizabeth Wright notes the most damaging consequence of this habituated institutional reliance: "[W]orse than anything else, we [have] failed to stop sending self-defeating signals to our youth, who grow up learning from the behavior of their elders, the role of 'dependent' that blacks are expected to play in our society."[21] Woodson summarizes: "A permanent underclass of more than one third of all black Americans, unskilled and undereducated remains [unhelped] by civil rights gains, the war on poverty, increased black political power, and a mammoth social welfare industry."[22]

Toward remedying the economic damage he sees resulting from this misguided government paternalism, Woodson turns not to the policy experts nor to the government, but rather, in glorious irony, to the poor themselves. Wishing to keep government intervention to a minimum,

Woodson would rather rely on the abilities and ingenuity of the individuals targeted to be "helped."

Underlying this approach is the bedrock belief that economic stability for the black poor can never be given to them or bestowed upon them from outside their own communities, whether from corporate benefactors or from government gifts. It must be developed from within, generated and cultivated by those who are suffering.

> Rather than accept solutions [provided] by middle-class professional service providers, black America must recognize and expand on indigenous, self-help neighborhood efforts. The originators of these self-help programs have unique, firsthand knowledge concerning the problems and resources to be found within their communities.[23]

THE NATIONAL CENTER FOR NEIGHBORHOOD ENTERPRISE

In 1981, after leaving his position at the American Enterprise Institute, Woodson founded the National Center for Neighborhood Enterprise (NCNE), described by Clint Bolick as "by far the most successful pro–free enterprise grass-roots organization dedicated to solving black and urban problems."[24] Woodson intended it to provide to low-income communities an empowering alternative to the welfare state's "Big Daddy government." The structure of such a system had proven tragically ineffective—indeed, inimical—to the economic improvement of poor black Americans and should never have been regarded as an omnicompetent source of service delivery in the first place. "The poor and the disadvantaged," says Woodson, "if pulled into the government's social welfare industry machine, were turned into passive "clients" . . . and were led by the hand into poverty limbo."[25] Detailing the effects of these policies, Woodson finds that they exacted an enormous price from the black community.

> This government-knows-best policy herded low-income families into high-rise buildings that bred crime and frustration, discouraged the work ethic, fostered dependency on public assistance and stifled the initiative of small entrepreneurs with programmed-to-fail bureaucratic restrictions.[26]

One of NCNE's more innovative programs was a demonstration program in housing projects in several cities to show the benefits of resident management, economic development, and conversion of public housing to home ownership.[27] The infusion of private enterprise and private property incentives in these housing projects has helped reduce government costs, decrease welfare dependency, increase on-site jobs, and reduce crime.

Woodson's appreciation of free enterprise, like that of Peter L. Berger, his former colleague at the American Enterprise Institute, has a strong empirical base.[28] "We want to be judged by our work," Woodson insists, "and not by our theories."[29] In fact, Woodson credits Berger with a critical role in shaping his own social viewpoint. "The whole self-help movement," Woodson affirms, "owes a debt of gratitude to Peter Berger and his work."[30]

With Berger, Woodson has both a commitment to empiricism in social measurements and a recognition of social cohesion as a virtue in society. Berger puts his imprimatur on the value-laden activism of Robert Woodson. "What . . . appeals to me (both as a sociologist and a citizen) is Woodson's emphasis on values." Berger, like Woodson, sees neighborhood empowerment as largely a "moral enterprise."[31]

Woodson's emphasis on moral enterprise has prompted others to describe him as a conservative, though he resists the label as exclusively defining his position. "I think of myself more as a pragmatist, because I'm more concerned about concrete prescriptions than labels. My views contain elements of liberalism, conservatism, black nationalism, and American patriotism."[32]

BLACK UNITY AND RACIAL PRIDE

An important component of Woodson's self-help strategy is an understanding of the value of neighborhood unity and of the positive contribution ethnic fraternity can make to economic mobility. Woodson recounts, with unabashed pride, his experience of growing up in a segregated neighborhood:

> I guess my mother never had to adapt [his father died when he was nine.] They just worked for white folks and they went their way and did their work and came back to the black community. White people were never discussed in the family, in the neighborhood, or in the black community. Race was never talked about. They listened to Joe Louis on the radio, and celebrated the victories of Roy Campenella.[33]

Woodson's experience taught him something that the service providers and policy architects of today seem to have forgotten: Black people can think for themselves and manage their own affairs. Though Woodson fought in the 1960s against de jure segregation, he is convinced that forced integration, especially in the form of school busing, has been a mistake, as it has broken up natural, organic ties in black neighborhoods that were serving blacks well; what Bob Teague termed in Chapter 2 "a sprawling black conspiracy that really worked."

Woodson's skepticism about the need for forced integration of white students and teachers into black neighborhoods is given credence by the civil-rights-era experience of a black teacher in the South. She had taught for many years at a successful and award-winning black grade school, which like many other black schools would be changed (not for the better) by the onset of the integration eschaton. Entering a first-grade classroom one day, she was surprised to find a young white teacher sprawled supine on the floor of a once-orderly, but now chaotic, classroom. He had a red rose in his teeth and a serene look on his face, as the children gaily pranced around him. Less than enchanted with the young man's *nouveau* pedagogy, this veteran teacher resigned the next day. The "educrats," in Polly Williams's phrase, had won the day, and school achievement slid rapidly.

Some of his critics may chide Woodson's ethical and pragmatic objection to forced integration as nothing but a strange romanticization of the "good old days" of forced segregation. But to do so is to falsely dichotomize the issue and absurdly caricature his thinking. Woodson's main point is that social policy that insists that black people need to be "rescued by outsiders" borders on bigotry and is historically naive.[34] He believes that black neighborhood residents are best qualified to recognize and overcome their own problems, rather than those who do not live in the presence, and under the effects of, those problems. Political scientist William Allen also stresses this point. Writing the weekend after the havoc in Los Angeles, Allen found it strange that the disorder had been policed largely by authorities and officers who did not live in the neighborhood. "Is it not clear," he asked, "that communities that are not self-governing are incapable of avoiding such crimes as this?"[35]

Interestingly, some in the black community have argued that a school voucher program could serve as a gateway to widespread "self-governance," in the sense advocated by Woodson and Allen, by fostering student interest in, say, careers in local law enforcement and firefighting.[36] Many residents believe that the flexibility and decision making that a voucher program accords to students and their families offers a unique opportunity for early career training and, as a result, practical community building. This community building could remedy such destabilizing social disparities as the current gap between the proportion of Los Angeles residents who are black (17 percent) and the proportion of police officers who are black (7.3 percent). Still, traditional civil rights leaders, as noted, have dug in their heels in opposition to school choice plans. Jesse Jackson, for example, has mischaracterized school vouchers as little more than a divisive racist scheme.

Woodson, perhaps more than some other dissident figures, emphasizes racial fraternity as a helpful force for community building.[37] While Woodson does recognize that emphasis on racial identity and racism can be a distracting and demotivating force for the black community, often hindering needed efforts to redress critical problems, he consistently affirms its positive potential.

> The degree to which people feel self-sufficient is often determined by how the neighborhood defines itself and how others define it. Neighborhoods with strong ethnic, racial, or class identities often have great ability to deal with their problems. Such neighborhoods have a unique sense of pride, which affects the way they resolve difficulties. Yet public officials and scholars often refer to these communities in condescending, even pejorative terms, and policymakers neither build on the strengths of the neighborhood nor understood neighborhood social and cultural dynamics.[38]

Although Woodson sees a positive role for ethnic fraternity, he is qualified in his endorsement of the usual calls for Afrocentric unity and consciousness.

> My attitude toward "Afrocentrism" depends on how you define it. Certainly not as some alternative to traditional values that are gospel based, based upon Judeo-Christian values. . . . If Afrocentrism is defined as a desire to have the accomplishment of black Americans *included* in American history and in American life, I embrace it. But it is not a substitute for anything—it could be a supplement. For instance, that's why I think there should be nothing called Black History Month. If we teach accurate American history, wherein the accomplishments of black Americans are acknowledged along with the accomplishments of others, then I think that's the goal we should seek. Then it's a tool of inclusion, not a tool of exclusion.[39]

MEDIATING STRUCTURES AND "CIRCLES OF CARE"

The theoretical force behind Woodson's NCNE project hails back to seed work done in mediating structures at the American Enterprise

Institute (AEI). Though the designation "mediating structures," is not a common one, the idea itself is intimate and experiential in American life. Mediating structures are the familiar organic and voluntary associations of our daily living, including family, church, neighborhood, clubs, and schools. If the New Black Vanguard's plan for black progress is to be realized in the twenty-first century, it will be through the work of mediating structures, which by their very associative nature confer meaning and a sense of *communitas* on the individual and society.

The practicality of Woodson's "neighborhood enterprise" belies something of its rich philosophical base. The work on this base at the American Enterprise Institute reflects a wide confluence of ideas, both modern and ancient. The principle of *subsidiarity*, with its philosophical roots in Thomistic theology, is one of these ideas. Associated with Catholic social teaching, subsidiarity is essentially the concept Woodson is employing in calling for a return of authority to the neighborhood.

Holding that the decisions of government should take place on the level closest to the people affected by them, subsidiarity is the antithesis of totalitarian rule. It respects the dignity and capacity for autonomy resident in all people, and it recognizes the connection of that dignity and autonomy to family and community. Every individual life is lived in the context of "rings of care"—concentric circles of care and responsibility—made up of family, friends, and associations, with the individual at the center. The family, as the inmost ring of care, bears a special significance to the person. An example of this unique significance of the family was provided in a talk by Allen:

> My mother would tell me as a young man, "Hold your head up." Now, I know that you've all heard that before—Jesse Jackson has his "I want to be somebody" drill that he leads young people through in large auditoriums. But it's different when your mother tells you, "Hold your head up," than when you hear this as a group exercise in a large auditorium.[40]

Allen's point is that the inmost "ring of care and responsibility" in a child's life is naturally the family, and that professionals beyond that ring, even well-meaning and credentialed ones, are typically only paper maché substitutes for the kind, intimate concern that is proper to family life. (Recall Loury's idea of the family as "the locus of formation of personal character.")

Woodson would make this principle of subsidiarity the new starting point of American social policy. That is, he would see government harness this natural disposition to seek guidance and material assistance first from family, friends, and neighbors, and have government trust the judgment of the common man and woman. Woodson believes that when this is done, the responsibility accorded to parents, including single parents, works to strengthen them, to improve their ability to supervise their children. He reports that inner-city residents would prefer to look to the government as little as possible.

> What we discovered in our own "needs assessments" was that poor or low-income people faced with a problem want to turn, in order of importance, to friends, relatives, the local church or the ethnic community in their immediate environment. Last on the list, in most cases, is the professional service provider. In light of the fact that we tend to deliver services through government programs, it is no wonder that we fail to reach the poor.[41]

Though the civil rights establishment has paid lip service to these and related principles, says Woodson, it has habitually opposed their *practical application*. He offers an example, recalling the heyday of civil rights victories, and the lost opportunities: "We had black parents for the first time wanting to improve the quality of education in their neighborhood, while civil rights leaders said, 'No, that's not what is needed. They need busing and integration.' "[42] Black parents—the innermost ring—knew that forced busing was not necessary for a good education; but the civil rights establishment went over their heads. The establishment continues this mistake; a month after the riots in Los Angeles, the city's board of education approved a $405.7 million "integration budget."[43] It is no wonder, then, that according to United Teachers Los Angeles, only 36 percent of school funding finds its way past such a bureaucracy and into Los Angeles classrooms.[44]

Again, in Woodson's support of school vouchers and the civil rights establishment's resistance to them, we see the battle line drawn over the practical application of the principle of subsidiarity. Woodson would put the ultimate decision about where youngsters attend school in the hands of their parents. Parents are free from the encumbrances of the educational bureaucracy, while public school principals are under the thumbs of dozens of masters, accountable to special rights groups such as the ACLU, to special interest groups such as the teachers unions, and to political pressure groups such as the NAACP. Such many-mastered schools do not effectively serve children, nor can they effectively help parents realize their best intentions for their children. The effects of this accountability to the wrong parties can be seen, for instance, in the New York City public schools, where during the 1988–89 school year, out of roughly 62,000 teachers, fewer than 1 percent were rated unsatisfactory by their principals.[45] Principals were even more secure in their positions; during the same year, only 1 in 1,000 New York City principals was rated unsatisfactory.[46] Is the New York City public school system really that efficient? It is more likely that there is a lack of vigorous peer review because these teachers and principals are not finally accountable to the parents, but to union-pressured administrators and school boards. Woodson's experience with grass-roots activism has taught him this: Accountability to the wrong parties redraws the "circles of care" into unnatural and artificial designs.

In a more academic vein, in *To Empower People* (1977) Peter L. Berger and Richard John Neuhaus outline a broad, but cogent, theoretical foundation for the viability of mediating structures as instruments of social change and cultural cohesion. Beyond these two goals, Berger and Neuhaus see mediating structures as a hedge against the totalitarian tendencies of government. Without the middle term of "society," government tends to swallow the individual, usurping the autonomously selected values of its members with its own vision of the good life.

Reconciled to the existence of the welfare state, and approving of many of its services, Berger and Neuhaus see mediating structures as superior mechanisms for delivering benefits. Believing that not everything *public* must be superintended by government, they point to mediating institutions as better able to administer distributive programs.

The AEI Project on Mediating Structures formulated two normative propositions concerning the relationship of government to mediating structures. Minimally,

> public policy should cease and desist from damaging mediating structures. Much of the damage has been unintentional in the past. We should be more cautious than we have been. As we have learned to ask about the effects of government action upon racial minorities or upon the environment, so we should learn to ask about the effects of public policies on mediating structures.[47]

Berger and Neuhaus, discussing intermediate structures in a completely pluralistic context, nonetheless recognize the power inherent in particularized associations, including ethnic and racial ones.

> Strong neighborhoods can be a potent instrument in achieving greater justice for all Americans. It is not true, for example, that all-black neigh-

borhoods are by definition weak neighborhoods. As we shall see, to argue
the contrary is to relegate black America to perpetual frustration or to
propose a most improbable program of social revolution. . . . If our hopes
for development assume an idealized society cleansed of ethnic pride and
its accompanying bigotries, they are doomed to failure.[48]

Maximally, "Wherever possible, public policy should utilize mediating
structures for the realization of social purposes."[49] Woodson's NCNE
represents a concrete attempt at implementing this "maximalist proposition." Woodson's embrace of this maximalist proposition is comprised
of community action on a number of fronts, including family support
programs, community job training, resident management of housing
projects, and privately run neighborhood schools. All of these programs
engender what he calls a "culture of self-sufficiency" among the inner-
city poor.[50]

One example of the efficiency that tends to inhere in the kind of self-
sufficient voluntary associations Woodson is advocating is the Catholic
schools system. Michael Barone, in the Almanac of American Politics,
indicates that New York City's Catholic schools, with a central bureaucracy of just 35 people, typically outperform the public schools, which
employ 20,000 central bureaucrats.[51] Woodson is convinced that when
people are allowed deep involvement and a personal stake in the institutions that impact their lives and neighborhoods, they can rise to the
challenge of self-governance.

"COMMUNITY ACTION" IN THE 1960s

On the surface, Woodson's neighborhood vitality project sounds
much like the Community Action Program (CAP) created as a component of President Johnson's war on poverty. One project in particular,
the first director of which was the distinguished black psychologist Kenneth Clark, was the Harlem Youth Opportunities Unlimited project
(HARYOU). Growing out of Clark's 1964 delinquency plan, Youth in
the Ghetto, which—foreshadowing Woodson—said that black ghettos
were essentially colonies "whose inhabitants were subject peoples, and
whose pathology derived from their powerlessness,"[52] Clark purposed
to establish neighborhood boards "that would empower the poor to deal
with their own problems and press for institutional change."[53] But HAR-
YOU became mired in political squabbles, power grabs, and corruption
and ended up being a dismal and complete failure. Kenneth Marshall,
who worked with Clark on the original HARYOU plan, eulogized,

"None of it worked, . . . and the 20 million dollars that went into it has disappeared without a trace."[54]

But Woodson's philosophy of neighborhood empowerment is markedly different from these predecessors. Most obviously, his approach *works*—and he has evidence to prove it. But beyond that, Woodson is stressing change for the sake of neighborhood improvement, not for the sake of larger "institutional" restructuring, although he would also like to see reformation of the national welfare policy. Woodson's intensive concentration on neighborhoods for their own sake translates into residents' felt pride and assumed responsibility, two emotions that directly confer meaning and importance on the task of remaking their neighborhoods.

Another fundamental difference between Woodson's work and that of the CAP programs of the 1960s is that

> the poverty programs imposed plans and requirements from above. For instance, community outreach workers had to have a bachelor's degree. They prescribed who the board would be. It was never controlled by the community. That's a dramatic difference from the [way National Center for Neighborhood Enterprise operates]. The way we operate the "empowerment" agenda is set by the people experiencing the problems. They control the resources, they control the direction of the program.[55]

In CAP's HARYOU it was understood that there was an adversarial relationship between the victims of the Establishment and democratic capitalism. The Marxist undercurrent of revolution and "liberation" that imbued so many movements and projects of that decade, fomented hostility and encouraged movement toward withdrawal from the social mainstream. Woodson's appreciation of democratic capitalism as a vehicle of upward mobility for the inner-city poor is in bracing contrast to the contempt with which democratic capitalism was held thirty years ago. Woodson's self-help approach encourages confidence in the possibility of economic success. As Raspberry wrote, describing Woodson's philosophy, his "is no zero-sum redistribution game, in which blacks can gain only at the expense of whites, but a wealth-creation agenda."[56] It was just this kind of agenda that Christina Montague, a 38-year-old county commissioner from Ann Arbor, Michigan, said was absent at the NAACP convention she attended. "I want to know about economic development," she said. "I will live in the ghetto as long as I can control the jobs, the stores, the economic vitality. . . . There's nothing here [at the convention] for us to learn."[57]

A further feature of the difference between Woodson's approach and the CAP programs lies in their respective attitudes towards bourgeois values. Although the antibourgeois outlook of the 1960s did not permeate every aspect of programs like HARYOU, it certainly colored the thinking of some of their leaders, sometimes in extreme ways. For example, the ever-provocative Amiri Baraka (formerly Leroi Jones) is described in Alan Matusow's *The Unravelling of America* (1984) as having obtained $100,000 of CAP funds by "simply barging into [the director's] office one day and emphatically demanding it."[58] Jones is one whose call for America to be invaded "by twenty million spooks . . . with furious cries and unstoppable weapons,"[59] would seem to qualify him as somebody uniquely inimical to middle-class values. Matusow goes on to tell how Jones handled his CAP money:

> That summer Jones . . . employed 242 people to stage plays nightly on the streets of Harlem. Blending racism with Marxism, the plays included one by Jones himself—*Jello*—in which Jack Benny's valet, Rochester, rises up and kills his white oppressors.[60]

Woodson obviously embraces middle-class virtues in a way that the neighborhood programs of thirty years ago, and leaders like Jones, did not. Woodson is not engaged in a Kulturkampf, except insofar as he opposes government manipulation of the affairs of the inner-city poor.

Woodson's *On the Road to Economic Freedom* (1987) is rife with examples of American blacks who with great diligence struggled against severe economic handicaps. Despite these hardships, they advanced and were proudly self-sufficient. Woodson's respect for the power of bourgeois values is further seen in his estimation of the importance of personal responsibilities, and their fulfillment, in aiding the urban poor in their climb out of poverty. Woodson believes that the language of entitlement can ill serve the very poor, and so approves of states that are "passing some laws that are not only talking about the rights of people on welfare, but their responsibilities for themselves."[61]

Woodson's vision of self-responsibility (responsibility for oneself and one's community) as a humanizing concept for the inner-city poor, bears a clear resemblance to the attitudes of Steele, Sowell, and Loury. Together they understand that human beings, whatever their racial or economic standing, to be fully human must accept duties of performance as well as rights of entitlement. The responsibility to care for one's family, one's society, and one's own self lies with all who consent to dwell

among others and expect their own natural and legal rights to be ob-
served.

POPULAR CULTURE AND VALUES

"The American Dream is not for Blacks," insisted millionaire rapper-
politico Ice Cube at a 1991 news conference. "Blacks who [still believe
in that dream] are kidding themselves. There's only room in that dream
for a few Blacks."[62] Ice Cube's dismissal of the American capitalist system
recalls Baraka's similar pessimism a quarter-century ago. Such routinized
denunciations of democratic capitalism in popular black political culture
impede economic mobility. Of course, Woodson rejects the idea—the
base line of political rap—that the odds against black economic success
are insuperable in America. Statistics just do not support this view, he
says: the fastest-growing income group in America is black families with
incomes of more than $50,000.[63] "My basic message to any who complain
of the power of discrimination to limit their prospects is to keep in mind
that the best antidote to disrespect is performance."[64] Woodson is a
pragmatist, and he is convinced that reciting to oneself the history of
racism in America and repeating the rhetoric of the black youth culture
or civil rights professionals will not move the black poor one whit closer
to self-sufficiency and economic freedom. It is unrealistic to imagine, as
most civil rights leaders seem to, that eradication of racism is the prerequisite to black social mobility. In fact, such an insistence, in Woodson's eyes, is a "confession of impotence" and a flight from
responsibility.[65] Instead of such confessions, Woodson would have African-Americans embrace the middle-class values that have historically
informed black experience.

But today there is hostility to these values, in some camps. Simple
bourgeois or instrumental values and their corollates (e.g., monogamy,
thrift, respect for traditional religious ideas) are sometimes reviled by
the hip-hop culture as "white," by the civil rights establishment as "ineffective," and by the "adversarial culture" of today's academy as unen-
lightened.[66] These mentalities are completely counter to that of
Woodson, who unabashedly recommends "traditional values that are
gospel-based." He does not glibly reject such values as concoctions of
the "white establishment," as though George Gilder had invented them
to comfort white conservatives. Advocacy of these instrumental values
does not amount to some kind of religious triumphalism, but rather the
adoption of a moral-ethical system suited to democratic capitalism. For

Woodson, to think of these values as "white" (recall the tendency, noted in the Ogbu and Fordham study mentioned in Chapter 2, to identify studiousness as "acting white") is to misread the historic achievement of blacks in America, which was powered by these virtues. To regard these values as irrelevant to black advancement in American culture is to ignore ample empirical evidence of their sheer practicality. For instance, according to a 1986 study, young black women who graduate from high school (and avoid unwed parenthood) have a better than 90 percent chance of living above the poverty line.[67]

Such evidence also supports Sowell's prescription: "Those who want to share their good fortune can share the sources of that good fortune—the skills, values, and discipline that mean productivity."[68]

It would be difficult to overemphasize the importance to Woodson of the Judeo-Christian moral heritage. It has, he argues, sustained the black family and community through the harshest of times.

> [Judeo-Christian values] have been an essential ingredient in the survival of black America over the centuries. They have kept the fabric of the community together. It enabled us to maintain strong families up to 1959, when 78 percent of our families remained whole even in the face of virulent racism, low political participation even before we had voting rights. Then, less than 2 percent of black children were raised in households where the mother never married.[69]

But these impressive statistics are no more. The values that generated such family and community cohesion have been undermined.

> We never in the past used racism as an excuse for abandoning the moral and ethical principles that are based upon the gospel. We must not abandon them—they certainly have been undermined in the last 25 years. I think one of the reasons why problems plaguing the black community have escalated is that we have abandoned the moral highground.[70]

One arena in which the moral high ground has obviously been lost is in hypersexual rap. Woodson calls it "a kind of verbal pornography" and stresses that many in the black community, especially those who have retained the Judeo-Christian value system, do not approve of it. "Neighborhood people rail against it all the time. It, too, will be crushed under the rush of the self-sufficiency movement," says Woodson.[71]

The decline of values that Woodson here describes may be largely the result of a larger trend described in books such as *The Naked Public Square* (1984).[72] In it, Richard John Neuhaus discusses the banishment from public discourse—under the auspices of tolerance and pluralism—of substantive discussion of values having a religious basis. This elitist tilt away from religious values is radically undemocratic, inasmuch as Princeton University researchers recently released a study which found that 59 percent of Americans are convinced that religious values are the answer to the nation's many-faced social and political problems.

Predictably, this tilt hit the poor hardest, since as "clients" of government, they were the object of the government's secularized form of compassion. This state-supported mission, with its seminaries in the public administration and social work departments of academe, deliberately tried to speak in a nonnormative voice, not wanting to impose sectarian dogma on the citizens. But in so doing, they unavoidably employed the antinomian normativity of normlessness; that is to say, in their quest for value neutrality, public policy makers merely replaced one particularity with another. This placed the poor in the precarious condition of freedom from responsibility, driving them into an anomic dependency on government, in which they must find their own meaning and moral structure. Berger and Neuhaus wrote in *To Empower People*, "One of the most debilitating results of modernization is a feeling of powerlessness in the face of institutions controlled by those whom we do not know and whose values we often do not share."[73]

Berger and Neuhaus go on to say:

> Upper-income people already have ways to resist the encroachment of megastructures. It is not their children who are at the mercy of alleged child experts . . . not their neighborhoods which are made the playthings of utopian planners.[74]

IDEAS ON EDUCATION

Woodson sees this fiddling with children as an unnecessary infringement on the role of the family. He notes that when middle-class parents sense that the moral temper of the public school their child attends does not reflect their own values, they can "resist" this trend by enrolling their child elsewhere. But poor parents do not have this option. Their children are often funnelled into schools that not only poorly educate, but do not contribute to their attitudinal development—in Woodson's phrase, to the "wholeness of character that lends itself to fuller student participation and receptivity."[75]

Acknowledging persistent educational underachievement (SAT scores for black students typically trail those of white students, in both the verbal and mathematical components, by more than 100 points[76]), the civil rights leadership habitually attributes this failure to poorly funded schools. Though many leaders would agree with Woodson that character education, classroom decorum, and parental involvement have intrinsic value, their primary call is for increased educational funding. But in the 1980s the District of Columbia was ranked third in the nation in per-pupil school expenditure, had some of the highest teacher salaries in the nation, and *still* ranked fourth from the bottom among regional districts using SAT scores.[77] Decidedly more ominous are statistics that indicate that 42 percent of young black men in Washington, D.C., were embroiled in the criminal justice system on any given day in 1991.[78] Though well funded, the Washington, D.C., public schools are not help-ing students develop the "wholeness of character" that would help them see the importance of education, on one hand, and help them resist the pressures and lures of the street, on the other.

Better-funded public schools will not do the trick, assures Woodson. Polly Williams captures the mood of a growing number of black parents in Washington, D.C.: "If you keep giving money to the same doctor and the patient continues to get worse, you'd better seek a second opinion."[79] That "second opinion," for Williams and Woodson, is a mediating-structures approach that puts the time-tested practicality and efficiency of private schools to work for black students and their parents.

Woodson sees parental control of schools as especially valuable, given the flexibility such schools have in the teaching of values. He is saddened by the current *Nein!* of public schools to parental pleas for the incor-poration of basic, unambiguous moral teaching in school curricula. This divorce of education from what are widely accepted, though essentially religiously informed values in the name of an exaggerated separation of "church" and state is emphatically seen in the censoring of prayers at commencement ceremonies in California and elsewhere. Not only has the most ecumenical of religious ceremonies been exorcised from the secular campus, but the exclusion of religious ideas has substantially impacted the curriculum as well, leading to some perverse ironies. Mar-tin Luther King, for example, as a Christian clergyman, regularly ex-horted his followers to observe a Christian ethic of suffering with humility and forgiveness.

> Frequent meetings were held to inform the participants of Christ's teach-
> ings on loving one's enemies. Training sessions were held to develop

proper responses among the people. They were advised that they must be willing to suffer physically and mentally. King emphasized that as Christians they were to expect it and were to face it as Christ would have.[80]

But in today's public school environment, King's religious faith, the ethical wellspring of his thought and political action, is likely to receive only passing reference and inadequate emphasis when King is studied. Indeed, this is reflective of a larger social trend: the removal of religious values from the public square. Neuhaus ironically notes that at Martin Luther King's funeral, an announcer remarked on the appropriateness of religious themes in the ceremony by calling Dr. King, "the son of a minister," completely oblivious to King's own standing as an ordained clergyman.[81]

Even though schoolchildren study the civil rights movement, observe the King holiday, and celebrate Black History Month, the true moral provenance of the King legacy is still eclipsed, if not altogether hidden.

To make these observations is hardly to suggest establishing a sectarian religious curriculum in public schools, but simply to point out a sociological fact widely experienced. This fact means a great deal to Woodson, who argues that the presence or absence of a given ethical-cultural frame in a school can have an enormous impact on the mind of a child.[82] As a point of sociological fact, public schools have shown themselves disinclined—or simply incapable, under prevailing First Amendment interpretations—of providing such frames. Woodson thinks it is unreasonable that low-income parents who see such ethical-cultural frames as enriching their children's lives are denied the right to send their children to schools patterned on them, while well-off parents can select such schools. After all, school attendance is compulsory, as well as parental funding of school operations. While our public schools have shown themselves disinclined or unable to provide such frames, America's private schools—Black Muslim, evangelical, Lutheran, Catholic and so on—have a proven track record here. For decades they have been providing consistent ethical-cultural frames for children, and children from all backgrounds have flourished in these atmospheres. One study suggests that the several hundred private schools that currently are "owned, operated, and designed to teach black children" send at least 52 percent of the children to college.[83] Woodson points out that this is far above the national average for largely black public schools in the inner cities.

One private school serving black students is the Ivy Leaf School of Philadelphia, Pennsylvania. The school's emphasis on reading and math has resulted in 85 percent of its students scoring above the national average on the California Achievement Test.[84] Says Liller Green, who cofounded the school with her husband in 1965, "We stress both a strong academic program *and* a strong social program."[85] The results are impressive:

> Student attendance is high, and absent are the problems common to public schools. The incidence of student drug use, the high level of academic failure and the rowdiness of most schools is virtually unknown at the Ivy Leaf school. A dress code, which would be impossible to enforce at a public school, is well received by Ivy Leaf students who display a love for the dignity that graces the school.[86]

Woodson has also studied such schools. Ivy Leaf and other mediating institutions, he says, "give youngsters a sense of identity, a sense of direction, and a purpose in life."[87] Garnering secrets of educational success from these schools, Woodson shares these with black educators across America though NCNE programs. His focus is on disseminating information on *practical* success in education, and not mere theoretical novelty.

Commenting on the fundamental reason for the success of private, parent-run schools, he says:

> The difference is who controls the curriculum, and the control of the program by the people experiencing the problems. The bureaucracies and teachers of public schools are not answerable to their customers, but rather they are answerable to the school boards. And so they are detached from the people they serve. That is what state communism was all about in Russia and the Eastern Bloc countries, and why these regimes have fallen. We think life should be prescribed and determined by the people, so we're trying to bring about a kind of *perestroika* here, in the United States.[88]

Woodson is not calling for wholesale dismantling of the public schools system, but for the option of parent-selected education. "Every city can boast," he says, "of one or several model schools."[89] But in this arena, which is so critical to black progress and to the welfare of the nation as a whole, occasional successes in the inner city, dwarfed by well-publicized failure, are not good enough for Woodson. Most blacks agree with him, and have expressed a definite discontent with the proliferation of substandard public schools. In fact, recent data has shown that blacks, even more than whites, wholeheartedly favor school choice and voucher plans.[90] Increasingly, blacks are losing faith in the "higher funding" school solutions of the "educrats." Justice Thomas reflected this mood when, remembering his days at St. Pius X High School in Savannah, Georgia, he said, "We did have a bad physical plant; we did have constant problems with paying the bills, and so forth, and we did have poor books. [But] we also had an excellent education."[91]

GRASSROOTS LEADERSHIP

Not only would low-income children benefit from such a plan, but so would low-income parents, according to Woodson. Severely limited parental choice in education has had a cruel, disempowering effect on these parents, he contends. He has evidence that a voucher plan would have an opposite, healing effect. The presence of choice in education confers feelings of dignity and self-worth, as well as a sense of involvement, which, Woodson says, leads many families to "pool their resources for the common good of the community."[92]

Woodson's reasoning here is typical of his "turning problems into opportunities" motto. The "problem" of how to help inner-city children can assume the face of an opportunity if responsibility for change is placed with the neighborhood itself. This is the theme of his grass-roots style of community leadership.

Woodson's faith in indigenous leadership and its effectiveness animates his confidence in self-help strategies. In neighborhood empowerment philosophy, the unsung heroes of black leadership are those grass-roots pioneers whom we have elsewhere labeled "interior activists." But too often, according to Woodson, these community builders take a backseat in the media to political figures whose adversarial politics make interesting and exciting stories. Something of Woodson's discontent with media coverage of interior activists was evident at a 1991 press conference he called to announce the formation of a coalition of black grassroots leaders who supported the confirmation of Clarence Thomas. Woodson sardonically told the reporters present that they "probably won't recognize these guys" as important black leaders. The clear insinuation was that the media, for some time, had had their microphones directed at hollow political voices, rather than authentic, neighborhood-backed leaders.

WOODSON'S CRITIQUE OF BLACK LEADERSHIP

The term "hollow voices" nicely captures the essence of Woodson's dissatisfaction with liberal black politicians and the civil rights movement of today. Woodson does not think they speak for most blacks, especially the poorest.

> The civil rights leadership has very successfully imposed a gag rule on the black community: unless you espouse the liberal Democratic ideology, you're out of step, and we'll accuse you of being anything but a child of God. People have been intimidated by that.[93]

While the "old-guard" civil rights leaders are vociferous in their calls for assistance and equity, their voice is not filled with the plans for action that will empower the needy. Woodson also sees them as double minded. On the one hand they echo the historic call to be judged based on the content of their characters, but on the other hand they fail to evidence the moral leadership this kind of commitment requires. Woodson is unflattering in his descriptions of black politicians who "use affirmative action to pad their pockets then pull out their civil rights credit card and plead race when they get caught.[94]

Much of Woodson's dissatisfaction with civil rights groups and black politicians stems from what he sees as poor management of resources. Woodson says that of every dollar of government money that goes into what he calls "black-run cities" (major urban centers like Washington, New York, and Los Angeles) only twelve cents goes directly into black areas, with the rest going to downtown development, frequently improving real estate or buildings that are foreign owned. He sees this as a travesty, and maintains that black leaders "hustle" poor blacks to obtain these funds, only to spend them elsewhere. With the intensity of a hellfire evangelist, Woodson declares that "poor blacks will rebel when they find out that they are being hustled."[95]

Woodson is dissatisfied not only with these leaders' stewardship of government monies, but also with the interior management of funds within their organizations. He is fond of rebuking black organizations' cries for increased funding by arguing that

> if the 150 black organizations that meet annually and spend $5 billion on liquor, food, clothes, and hotels around the country complaining about white folks, instead met in groups of ten once every five years, they would save huge amounts of money that they could then direct into developing the human capital of the black urban poor.[96]

These criticisms highlight Woodson's constant but unique call for leadership by example from black civil rights groups and politicians. When such calls for personal moral credibility on the part of political leaders are issued, it is usually from conservative religious quarters. But to Woodson leadership by example is essential to genuine community advocacy. Woodson thinks it is a red herring to posit, as he says many black leaders do, an elaborate conspiracy theory

> which charges that a racially motivated campaign is being waged to attack black leaders. I [have] stressed the importance of recognizing cases in which blacks in leadership were truly failing and misusing their people and the necessity for holding such leaders responsible for the corruption and incompetence that has been more damaging to the black community than years of racist policies. . . . It is unconscionable to let blatantly self-serving officials hide behind the cloak of "racism" defense.[97]

Woodson's normative criticisms concerning lassitude and corruption in black leadership speak to the larger anthropological question of man's common capacity for evil. Like other dissenters, Woodson is willing to criticize, sometimes harshly, the personal foibles of the black leadership. Rather than being understood as a kind of betrayal or insensitivity, such forthrightness should be seen as realistically affirming the common humanity of everyone. This is hardly a moral innovation, but in the politicized world of American race relations, it is a refreshing notion.

For Woodson, moral behavior is not a luxury. It is the very backbone of personal well-being and public responsibility in the context of a democratic polity. This comports with Michael Novak's understanding of the role of character in human government.

> If one cannot govern oneself, how can all of us collectively govern either ourselves or the republic? Character is necessary to release the spiritual energy for self-government. If we could not be responsible, we could not govern ourselves.[98]

Woodson has demonstrated, at considerable personal cost in terms of celebrity and quite possibly money, that his commitment to neighborhood activism is tenacious. Offered an influential job under housing director Jack Kemp, Woodson turned it down, explaining, "I couldn't serve my folks. I figured I could serve better as president of the National Center for Neighborhood Enterprise."[99]

Service to the black poor is important to Woodson. This is part of the cause of his disaffection from the "old guard" civil rights leadership. These leaders are not, in his mind, truly representing the interests and thinking of the black poor. For Woodson, the Clarence Thomas nomination was a test case for the leadership qualifications of the "old guard."

> They [civil rights leaders] are in descendance. Seventy-eight percent of the black public came out forthrightly for Clarence Thomas, while black leadership opposed him. . . . The Thomas nomination became a surrogate for the pent-up frustrations of millions of black Americans, who have not had an opportunity to voice their views and opinions on this issue. Clarence is a strong believer in traditional values and puts principle above position—black Americans supported him up to 70 and 80 percent in the polls, even in the face of opposition from civil rights officials and black elected officials. That tells me the civil rights leaders are declining. The only ones who don't realize that are the press.[100]

According to Woodson, the national media tend to downplay or even ignore the gathering momentum that self-help strategies are enjoying. This view stems from his feeling that they are ideologically disinclined to recognize the potential self-sufficiency of the poor. "There is a disbelief, a bias, against anything that appears to be empowering poor people. It just violates a lot of reporters' understanding of how the world works."[101]

This assumption against the ability of the urban poor to transform their own conditions is so powerful that even Nicholas Lemann, in his majestic work *The Promised Land* (1991), seems to be resigned to it. "There are quite a few successful community development organizations in black neighborhoods," he writes, "but they are subsidized by philanthropists, and located in areas that people with jobs haven't left yet. The high-rise projects are operating at such a heavy loss, that simply turning them over to their tenants is impracticable."[102]

Woodson, who has been on the front lines of public housing "reclamation" for many years, offers an opposite picture. Self-help efforts have hardly proved "impracticable," even in the poorest of neighborhoods. Indeed, a key index to the popularity and efficacy of today's black self-help movement can be found, says Woodson, in the growth, and the success, of resident-managed inner-city public housing.

One of the more famous recent instances of such success is the Cochran Gardens project in St. Louis, Missouri, once called by the *New York Times* "a squalid den for narcotic dealers where garbage was flung from windows and residents urinated in the hallways." The tenants took control, evicting the criminals and renovating the project. Since the project's inception, more than 250 residents have been employed by the

tenant management corporation. The story of tenant-management public housing successes continues in other large cities, like Cleveland,
Chicago, and Washington.[103]

Woodson points out that six years ago there were only six developments under resident-management in the United States. Today there
are about two hundred in various stages of becoming self-managed, and
Woodson predicts some two hundred and fifty at the end of 1992. "We
had a handful of people at our first conference six years ago," remembers
Woodson. "This year, we had seventeen hundred."[104]

THE ACCOMPLISHMENT OF THE RESIDENTS OF KENILWORTH

Viewing Watts after the riots of the late 1960s, Milton Friedman recalls,
in *Free to Choose* (1980), commenting to a resident on the attractiveness
of a newly built development. He was surprised at the man's heated
reply:

> That's the worst thing that ever happened to Watts. That's public housing.
> How do you expect youngsters to develop good character and values when
> they live in a development consisting entirely of broken families, almost
> all on welfare?[105]

The anger of Friedman's companion was not without justification.
"The projects," as they are called, were perhaps the most misbegotten
fruit of urban renewal. An enduring problem in American cities, their
transformation is a primary focus of the NCNE.

A nationally recognized success of Woodson's neighborhood approach is the transformation of one "project" in Washington, D.C., the
464-unit Kenilworth-Parkside public housing complex. Plagued by soar-
ing teenage pregnancy, crime, vandalism, and a 76 percent welfare dependency rate, the development had been overcome by such profound
dysfunction that for a two-year period the residents did not receive hot
water or heat.[106] Woodson's organization served as a support system
for the efforts by the residents of Kenilworth to gain control of their
neighborhood and administer the operations of the housing project
themselves, remaking their community in the image of their own needs
and values. NCNE's specific support efforts included legal counsel,
fund-raising assistance, public relations work, and an economic analysis
measuring the project's progress.

The director of the Kenilworth-Parkside Resident Management Corporation (KPRMC), Kimi Gray, said of Woodson's contribution to the resuscitation of her neighborhood, "Some people, they come in and it's, 'I'm here to help you, let me show you how it's supposed to be done.' The reason we respect Bob Woodson is he lets us dream our own dreams."[107]

The KPRMC, under contract to the Washington, D.C., Department of Housing and Community Development, was responsible for collecting rents, maintaining the buildings and grounds, enforcing housing regulations, screening residents, keeping up the housing records, and developing policy.[108] The results, which Woodson attributes in part to the community spirit and enthusiasm created by resident control of the housing project, were astounding. Woodson estimates that the KPRMC will have saved the District of Columbia $4.5 million over its first ten-year period. After two years of resident management, teenage pregnancy in the development was reduced by 50 percent, welfare dependency declined from 85 percent to 35 percent, the crime rate fell 75 percent, and rent collections increased 130 percent.[109] The Kenilworth development is self-supporting, generating enough revenue to cover its own expenses.

Formerly, only a few children at Kenilworth went on to college. Many dropped out of high school. This changed after Kimi Gray began a self-study program, College Here We Come, at Kenilworth. Gray recruited students with different proficiencies—one in math, another English, and so on—to tutor one another and gain help in their weaker areas. Seven years later, more than 580 students from Kenilworth had gone on to college.[110]

In addition, under this self-management, many tenant-owned and -operated businesses have sprung up at the complex, including a barber shop, a day care center, a snack bar, a thrift store, and a screen door repair shop. These businesses have also served as a source of employment to many of the residents. Allowing residents to manage their neighborhood at Kenilworth-Parkside has not only taken people off welfare dependency by creating new jobs, but also preserved families.

The profitability of such ventures only contributes to further profitability. In 1983, after an impressive performance in the preceding two years, the KPRMC received $13.4 million in grants from the U.S. Department of Housing and Urban Development. The KPRMC plowed this money back into the project. For example, the 1983 money was spent on contracts with residents to replace doors, install windows, and fix bathrooms and kitchens. Money was also spent on the training of new and current resident managers. Woodson puts his finger on a crucial point when he says, "The key to this success is their firsthand knowledge of the problems, needs, and preferences of residents."[111]

Unfortunately the KPRMC has encountered obstacles from government management professionals. Stuart M. Butler and Anna Kondratas, who have carefully studied community-based solutions to poverty, comment on this in *Out of the Poverty Trap*:

> The Kenilworth-Parkside managers, for instance, have had to overcome years of foot dragging and outright hostility from District of Columbia officials. The management board has been forced to obtain extra insurance, has suffered crippling delays in recovering rent money from the housing authority to cover essential bills, and has faced enormous union opposition to hiring its own residents.[112]

To Woodson, programs like the one at Kenilworth-Parkside represent the only proven way of transforming whole communities and peoples from frustrated wards of the government to vital and safe communities and families, thriving on the *applied* human potential of their members.

Analyzing the success of Kenilworth, Butler and Kondratas isolate three characteristics of successful community ventures. The first is "that they demand obligations on the part of those being assisted" and "encourage individuals to look to their own strengths to fulfill those obligations."[113] The second is that the successful community organizations are "primarily social and economic in nature, not political."[114] The third feature of successful neighborhood ventures is their "frontier approach," in the phrase used by Butler and Kondratas, to problem-solving. They write, "Just as on the frontier in the great movement west, the [present-day] leaders of successful community organizations use unusual methods to deal with unusual situations," and they adduce two examples from Kenilworth-Parkside.

First, Kimi Gray has seen to it that drug dealers are discouraged from doing business in the complex through an aggressive neighborhood watch. Because of this kind of neighborhood control effort, drug dealing and other crimes have been dramatically reduced. Woodson reports that before resident management, a death a month at Kenilworth was commonplace. Today, according to Woodson, "the most serious illegality in the development is parking violations."[115] The second illustration of Gray's "frontier" approach to problems is her handling of graffiti in the laundry room. She solved the persistent problem by assigning to the suspected vandal's mother the task of supervising the laundry room. The problem quickly disappeared. (We have had no word from the ACLU about whether this violated "tenants' rights" and jeopardized the Constitution.)

An axiom of Kimi Gray's successful approach to problems of neighborhood crime recalls James Q. Wilson's famous "broken window" thesis: If one broken window is left unrepaired, the likelihood of further vandalism is heightened. The larger point, for Wilson, which the residents of Parkside perceived, is that the covenant between individuals and the rule of law is a tenuous one, and that once that covenant is breached, the social fabric is weakened. Unquestionably, neighborhood self-government strengthens that covenant. Proof is to be seen in the fact that, despite nearly a billion dollars in damage wreaked by the Los Angeles riots, public housing developments that were under tenant management survived damage free. Former housing czar Jack Kemp comments, "That should come as no surprise. When people have a stake in their neighborhoods, they will not only defend their homes and property, but their neighborhoods as well."[116]

Kimi Gray's vigilance at Kenilworth helped create a culture of care and an ethos of respect. Commenting on the marvelous transformation of Kenilworth-Parkside, Woodson said, "It happens when people get inspired. It happens when a whole ethic and culture of self-sufficiency becomes pervasive."[117]

The common perception of the inner-city black poor is that they cannot succeed. Whether due to racism or government underfunding, cues are sent throughout the culture that posit an insurmountability to the condition the black poor find themselves in.

These cues are reinforced by such tragedies as the Los Angeles riots of 1992. But the causes of such a profound social breakdown are so deeply rooted in the history and fabric of a community that their blame must be shared across the political and social spectrum. The riots represented, for Woodson, "a failure on the part of Democrats who failed to link assistance with responsibility, and the cynicism of Republicans who refused to address the problems of poor people."[118]

Woodson rebukes the assumption that the black poor are doomed but for the brilliant intervention of civil rights politicians, cajoling an ever-recalcitrant racist government to "do the right thing." He has evidence that the poor possess the capacity to help themselves. They lack neither the ability nor the will to overcome the problems associated with inner-city poverty. What they need is a government and professional bureaucracy willing to let them take the reins.

NOTES

1. Dinesh D'Souza, *Illiberal Education* (New York: Macmillan, 1991).

2. Timur Kuran, "Private and Public Preferences," *Economics and Philosophy* 6 (1990): 1–26.

3. Stanley Crouch, television appearance on "Donahue and Posner," first aired 23 February 1992.

4. Quoted in television documentary, "Black American Conservatism: An Exploration of Ideas," Clarence Page, host and scriptwriter, a presentation of South Carolina ETV, New York City broadcast, 13 February 1992.

5. Lois Benjamin, *The Black Elite* (Chicago: Nelson Hall, 1981), p. 206.

6. Brad Stetson, interview with Robert L. Woodson, 12 February 1992.

7. Robert L. Woodson, "Civil Rights and Economic Power," *Think*, no. 2 (1987).

8. Quoted in Benjamin, *Black Elite*, p. 206.

9. Robert L. Woodson, "The New Politics in Action: Beyond the Welfare State," in Left and Right: The Emergence of a New Politics in the 1990s? a conference sponsored by the Heritage Foundation and the Progressive Foundation, Washington, D.C., 30 October 1991, p. 47.

10. Stetson, interview with Woodson, 12 February 1992.

11. Stetson, interview with Woodson, 12 February 1992.

12. Robert L. Woodson, "Saving the Poor from the Saviors," *Destiny*, June 1991, p. 35.

13. Robert L. Woodson, "New Politics in Action," p. 46.

14. Ibid., p. 48.

15. Robert L. Woodson, interviewed by Bernard Shaw, CNN, 1 May 1992.

16. Ezola Foster, quoted in Matt Rees, "The Politics of Rebellion," *Destiny*, June 1992, p. 16.

17. "She Gives Voice to Black Anger," *Los Angeles Times*, 7 March 1992.

18. "Bill Moyers: Listening to America," PBS broadcast, 10 May 1992.

19. Lawrence Mead, *The New Politics of Poverty: The Nonworking Poor in America* (New York: Basic Books, 1992), p. 135.

20. Lawrence Mead, *Beyond Entitlement: The Social Obligations of Citizenship* (New York: Macmillan, 1986), p. 36.

21. Elizabeth Wright quoted in Robert C. Newberry, "Blacks Should Put Energies into Self-Help Enterprises," *The Houston Post* 27 August 1990, p. A7.

22. Robert L. Woodson, *On the Road to Economic Freedom* (Washington D.C.: Regnery-Gateway, 1987), p. x.

23. Ibid., p. 23.

24. Clint Bolick, *In Whose Name? The Civil Rights Establishment Today* (Washington, D.C.: Capital Research Center, 1988), p. 43.

25. Robert Woodson, *Orlando Sentinel*, 18 January 1989.

26. Ibid.

27. Bolick, *In Whose Name?* p. 44.

28. See Peter L. Berger, *Capitalist Revolution: 50 Propositions about Prosperity, Equality, and Liberty* (New York: Basic Books, 1986).

29. Stetson interview with Woodson.

30. Ibid.

31. Robert L. Woodson, *A Summons to Life* (Cambridge, Mass.: Ballinger, 1981), p. xi.

32. Robert L. Woodson, quoted in Lee A. Daniels, "The New Black Conservatives," *New York Times Magazine*, 4 October 1991, p. 23.

33. Benjamin, *Black Elite*, p. 157.

34. Woodson, "New Politics in Action," p. 47.

35. William B. Allen, "We've Slaked Our Thirst with Poison," *Los Angeles Times*, 3 May 1992.

36. Joseph Conti, interviews at a meeting, Brotherhood Organization of a New Destiny (BOND), Los Angeles, Calif. 17 May 1992.

37. *Los Angeles Times*, 11 May 1992, p. T8.

38. Woodson, *Summons to Life*, p. 123.

39. Brad Stetson, interview with Robert L. Woodson, 27 February 1992.

40. William B. Allen, talk at BOND meeting, Los Angeles, Calif., 10 July 1990.

41. Robert L. Woodson, "Poverty: Why Politics Can't Cure It," *Imprimis* 17, no. 7 (July 1988): 3.

42. "He's Black, Conservative, Hates 'Elitism'," *Washington Times*, 14 August 1991, p. E1.

43. *Los Angeles Times*, 16 June 1992, p. B1.

44. Russ Howard, "20 Questions: Parental Choice in Education Initiative," draft V4.2, Los Angeles, Calif., ExCEL, p. 1.

45. Emily Sachar, *Shut Up and Let the Lady Teach!* (New York: Poseidon, 1991), p. 248.

46. Ibid., p. 249.

47. Peter L. Berger and Richard John Neuhaus, *To Empower People* (Washington D.C.: American Enterprise Institute, 1977), pp. 6–7.

48. Ibid., pp. 8–9.

49. Ibid., pp. 6–7.

50. Stetson, interview with Woodson, 27 February 1992.

51. George F. Will, "Smart Money Is Buying Up Assets," *Los Angeles Times*, 15 June 1992.

52. Alan Matusow, *The Unravelling of America* (New York: Harper and Row, 1984), p. 257.

53. Ibid., p. 257.

54. Ibid., p. 260.

55. Stetson, interview with Woodson, 12 February 1992.

56. Quoted in Woodson, *On the Road to Economic Freedom*, p. xiv.

57. "Blacks on the Right: Voices Rise," *Los Angeles Times*, 15 July 1992, p. A1.

58. Matusow, *Unravelling of America*, p. 259.

59. *U.S. News and World Report* 59 (13 December 1965): 16–17.

60. Ibid.

61. Specifically, Woodson is alluding to Maryland and New Jersey, which have enacted self-help welfare reform in the early 1990s.

62. A. S. Doc Young, "Negatives and Positives," *Los Angeles Sentinel*, 14 November 1991.

63. Woodson, "New Politics in Action," p. 47.

64. Robert L. Woodson, "In a Word," *From the Center* 2, no. 2, p. 2.

65. Woodson, *On the Road to Economic Freedom*, p. x.

66. For a discussion of the "adversarial culture," see Irving Kristol, *Reflections of a Neoconservative* (New York: Basic Books, 1983), and Peter Berger, ed., *The Capitalist Spirit*, (San Francisco: Institute for Contemporary Studies Press, 1990).

67. William Bennett, *The De-Valuing of America* (New York: Summit, 1992), p. 197.

68. Thomas Sowell, *Compassion versus Guilt* (New York: Morrow, 1987), p. 17.

69. Stetson, interview with Woodson, 12 February 1992. Woodson's point is borne out by the fact that black youths who go to church have been shown to be more likely to remain in school and avoid crime. See Mead, *New Politics of Poverty*, p. 312, note 69.

70. Ibid.

71. Stetson, interview with Woodson, 27 February 1992.

72. Richard John Neuhaus, *The Naked Public Square* (Grand Rapids, Mich.: Eerdmans, 1984).

73. Berger and Neuhaus, *To Empower People*, p. 7.

74. Ibid., pp. 8–9.

75. Woodson, *On the Road to Economic Freedom*, p. 100.

76. Clint Bolick, *Changing Course* (New Brunswick, N.J.: Transaction, 1988), p. 108.

77. Ibid., p. 106.

78. *San Francisco Chronicle*, 20 April 1992, p. A2.

79. Spencer Holland, "Education: The Battle Is On for the Minds of Black Children," *Destiny*, March/April 1991, p. 33.

80. Lynn Buzzard and Paula Campbell, *Holy Disobedience* (Ann Arbor, Mich.: Servant Books, 1984), pp. 115–16.

81. Neuhaus, *Naked Public Square*, p. 98.

82. Woodson, *On the Road to Economic Freedom*, p. 100.

83. Holland, "Education," p. 33.

84. Woodson, *On the Road to Economic Freedom*, p. 105.

85. Quoted in ibid., p. 104.

86. Ted Mann and Emmanuel McLittle, "Education," *Destiny*, March/April 1991, p. 33.

87. Woodson, *Summons to Life*, p. 109.

88. Stetson, interview with Woodson, 27 February 1992.

89. Woodson, *On the Road to Economic Freedom*, p. 99.

90. Thomas Sowell, "Black Leaders: Slaves on a Liberal Plantation," *Orange County Register*, 26 February 1992.

91. Clarence Thomas, response to Thomas Sowell's "False Assumptions about Black Education," in Institute for Contemporary Studies, *The Fairmont*

Papers: *Black Alternatives Conference, December 1980* (San Francisco: the Institute, 1981), p. 81.

92. Woodson, *On the Road to Economic Freedom*, pp. 99–100. For an example of a highly successful community-based school that is self-supporting, see case study no. 3, "Ivy Leaf School" in Woodson, *On the Road to Economic Freedom*, pp. 104–7.

93. *Washington Times*, 14 August 1991.

94. Robert L. Woodson, television appearance on "Tony Brown's Journal," first aired 13 July 1990.

95. Ibid.

96. Ibid.

97. Woodson, "In a Word," p. 2.

98. Michael Novak, "The Neglected Cultural Frontier of Public Policy," in *Welfare Reform: Consensus or Conflict?* edited by James Denton (Lanham, Md.: University Press of America, 1988), p. 2.

99. Stetson, interview with Woodson, 12 February 1992.

100. Ibid.

101. Ibid.

102. Nicholas Lemann, *The Promised Land* (New York: Knopf, 1991), p. 291.

103. *Orange County Register*, 8 May 1992, p. B15.

104. Ibid.

105. Milton Friedman, *Free to Choose* (New York: Harcourt Brace Jovanovich, 1980), p. 110.

106. Woodson, *On the Road to Economic Freedom*, p. 24.

107. National Center for Neighborhood Enterprise, pamphlet "Turning Problems into Opportunities," Washington D.C. (undated).

108. Woodson, *On the Road to Economic Freedom*, p. 24.

109. "Civil Rights and Economic Power," *Think*, vol. 2 no. 2 (1987).

110. Woodson, "Poverty: Why Politics Can't Cure It," p. 4.

111. Woodson, *On the Road to Economic Freedom*, p. 26.

112. Stuart M. Butler and Anna Kondratas, *Out of the Poverty Trap: A Conservative Strategy for Welfare Reform* (New York, Free Press, 1987), p. 126.

113. Ibid., p. 125.

114. Ibid.

115. Stetson, interview with Woodson, 12 February 1992.

116. Jack Kemp, "Federal Policy Must Facilitate Property, Business-Ownership," *Orange County Register*, 10 May 1992.

117. Stetson, interview with Robert Woodson, 27 February 1992.

118. Bernard Shaw, interview with Robert Woodson, CNN, May 1, 1991.

───── 6 ─────

GLENN C. LOURY: BLACK DIGNITY AND SELF-HELP

Time, patience, and constant achievement are great factors in the rise of a race.

Booker T. Washington, *Black Belt Diamonds*

Our leaders will boycott for jobs and money, but not for decency.

Maxine Hankins Caine, *Destiny* magazine

As a member of the third generation [after slavery], Patience Gromes worked to civilize a city neighborhood. And, as one who lived within a stone's throw of bootleggers and gamblers for sixty years, she knew that the prizes of civilized life are always in jeopardy and must be achieved again and again by each generation or they will wane and be lost.

Scott C. Davis, *The World of Patience Gromes*

On the eve of the Clarence Thomas confirmation, a phone-in segment of a CNN broadcast featured a call from a black woman who opposed Thomas's confirmation with this reasoning: "There is something wrong when white men rally around a black man. Why would all these white senators rally around this black man? After all, this is America." Her doubt is not unusual. Not a few black Americans are convinced that the overwhelming majority of white Americans are hostile to black progress, and that therefore their political support must be disingenuous and a prelude to some nefarious end.

Something of the same viewpoint is part of the interpretive frame of books such as *The Day America Told the Truth*, which we mentioned in Chapter 4. "Are you a racist?" asks the title of a quiz survey in James

Patterson and Peter Kim's book, under which appears a series of yes or no questions, including:

—Do you believe that the United States has an obligation to compensate blacks for discrimination suffered in the past through affirmative action, even if such programs sometimes put white Americans at a disadvantage?

—Do you think that black people feel uncomfortable around you?[1]

But these questions are not really authentic indices to personal racism. It seems to us, rather, that they are prime examples of the seriously flawed sociology of *The Day America Told the Truth*. For instance, is it true that persons who oppose affirmative action are necessarily racist? Must we assume that a reasoned opposition to it, say, on libertarian grounds as a "reverse-discrimination" violation, is simply rationalized bigotry? Does such a view red-flag the closet racist? Common sense and the testimony of experience would say no, that racism is not an inherent component of libertarianism. More empirical analysis, such as that found in Paul Sniderman and Michael Gray Hagen, *Race and Inequality* (1985), disconfirms the necessary identity of racism and libertarian individualism.[2] In light of this datum, the easy identification by Patterson and Kim of an anti–affirmative action stance with racial intolerance appears not only unwarranted, but slanderous.

Another of the questions Patterson and Kim have designed to sniff out racism—"Do blacks feel uncomfortable around you?"—rests on similarly disturbing premises. It ascribes to African-Americans a sort of racial ESP. It also implies an arbitrary privileging of one race's perception over another's. Even more fundamentally, the question is disturbing as an example of the suspect logic of "perceptual rhetoric."[3] That is, it resists any commonsensical cross-checking of the perceiver's conclusion against available evidence for its truth or falsity—including the remarks of the alleged "racist" in his or her own defense!

In sum, to use the question, "Do black people feel uncomfortable around you?" as an index to personal racism is to promote racial subjectivism. Essentially it declares, "If X is perceived by Y to be racist against Y's group, X is a racist."

The danger of such racial solipsism hardly needs elaboration. It is clearly at odds with a first principle of the civil rights struggle, that a nonblack's belief that black persons are inferior does not make black persons inferior, because a belief is not a fact. A strongly held and powerful proposition, which some (Thomas Jefferson) have thought self-evidently true, is that "all men" are of identical intrinsic worth, that people are quite literally equal. The logic of the civil rights struggle was: A black person is not inferior to a white person merely because a white person thinks or feels the black person is inferior."[4] But Patterson and Kim's racism quiz reverses this logic. 'You are what others feel you are.'

If the Patterson and Kim theory of race relations were not so dangerous, it would be comical. A nonblack who is suspected by black co-workers to oppose affirmative action is doubly damned, by this paradigm. Not only does opposition to preferential policies expose this worker as a racist *ab initio*, but if the black co-workers learn of his or her opposition to such policies, and so feel uncomfortable, their very feeling is the second and definitive "proof" of racism!

"Surely we do not seriously advance the notion," insists Loury, "that white middle-class anger and concern about street crime in the central city—crime often associated with urban minority youth—is racist in motivation."[5] This statement from Loury, with its implicit rebuke of the dichotomizing of political opinions into starkly defined clashes between racists and non-racists, is clearly at odds with the Patterson and Kim vision of race relations and politics. Loury is not naive; racism persists as an ugly and palpable social fact. But he refuses to loosely apply the racist tag to persons, political stances, and economic structures that are not evidentially and clearly motivated by racial animosity—a refusal that distinguishes the thought of Loury for its sanity in the midst of today's irrational racial rhetoric.

LOURY'S VISION OF AMERICA

In his well-publicized "Open Letter to Justice Clarence Thomas from a Federal Judicial Colleague," A. Leon Higginbotham, Jr., Chief Judge Emeritus, U.S. Court of Appeals, Third Circuit, remarks:

> During the last ten years, you have often described yourself as a black conservative. I must confess that, other than their own self-advancement, I am at a loss to understand what is it that the so-called black conservatives are anxious to conserve?[6]

Glenn C. Loury, who rose from the ghettos of South Chicago to a tenured post at Harvard and later Boston University, does not share Judge Higginbotham's view of the bankruptcy of a conservative philosophy of politics as a tool for securing the advancement of black Americans. For all their present flaws and past failures, Loury deeply appreciates the American traditions of free enterprise and limited government intervention, both hallmarks of a conservative orientation to politics. He, along with other conservatives who are black, is quite "anxious to conserve" these and other institutions that have shown the ability to deliver Americans of all ethnicities from economic bondage to economic freedom. Loury is also intent on preserving the American tradition of self-help, which he sees as uniquely tied both to a conservative political philosophy and to the history of African-American achievement. For Loury, this philosophy of self-help "stems not from a sense of what is politically pragmatic but from a distinct vision of America"[7]—a vision he sees resting on

> an appreciation of (1) the extent of opportunity afforded all persons in this free society; (2) the consequent responsibility of the individual to apply himself in the pursuit of opportunity; and (3) the primacy of family, church, and local private organizations [and the values they convey]. . . . It is from principles such as these, which are in fact nothing new to black Americans, that the advocacy of self-help in the black community ultimately springs.[8]

The balance of this chapter will examine these ideas in more depth.

THE NATURE OF AMERICAN OPPORTUNITY

Although Loury believes that the American free market and political polity does conduce to social mobility, there is nonetheless present in his exposition a pronounced realism that is often overlooked, for different reasons, by those who both approve and disapprove of his ideas. This realism consists of a blunt recognition of the perduring legacy of discrimination against black Americans. In unequivocal terms, Loury insists that black Americans have been constrained by a history of racism and limited opportunity. Blacks, for instance, have had a harder time than whites in amassing financial capital. The passing down of wealth, part of the American Dream of generational improvement, has been impeded. Still, Loury is deeply aware of the progress made by his people—"a great people striving under terrible odds to overcome the effects of profound historical wrongs."[9] And, with many other black dissidents, he readily acknowledges that this improvement in the quality of citizenship for blacks was largely effected by the "efforts of advocates working in the tradition of the NAACP," which had its genesis in the thought of W.E.B. Du Bois.[10]

As for Loury's critics on the left—those who fail to see anything of merit in the projects of black conservatives and accuse them of being merely flag-waving race-traitors—Loury's nuanced assessment of the historical shaping of opportunity in America for blacks totally escapes them, much as Judge Higginbotham dismissed out of hand the possibility of rational black conservatism.

On the other hand, some of Loury's supporters on the right fail to take notice of his frank assessment of the residual effects of racism. This failure deeply disappoints him. Their denial, in his mind, betokens a sorry narrowness of thinking and a retreat from the noble American project of public responsibility. Moreover, to Loury this evasion of social responsibility represents a dereliction of religious duty for those who stand in the Judeo-Christian tradition.

This retreat by conservatives is manifest in a tepid lack of urgency on their part for pursuing creative approaches to fully righting this historical injustice. When addressing them, Loury urges that they not take his criticisms of the "civil rights strategy" as some blanket exculpation of public responsibility for the condition of needy American blacks, that they not be lulled into complacency by what they find as the agreeable diagnoses of black dissenters while life-and-death ghetto exigencies continue unaddressed by them. Recalling the many congratulations he has received on his renegade "courage," during a speech at the Smithsonian Institute Loury offered, with no small pique, this recollection of one supporter's approbation:

> He [saw] personified before him courage and license. I'm going to make it O.K. Tom Sowell and I will come running in, battle-scarred, to say that all is well, and to tell the runny-nosed black kids who have been tyrannizing these well-meaning liberals to go to hell.[11]

Loury's remarks suggest something of the complexity of his existential position. As a careful scholar and a man of heartfelt concern for the needy, Loury must be chagrined when the *raison d'etre* of his life's work is described as "giving aid and comfort to people who want to be critical of black leaders and of government programs," as an official of the U.S. Civil Rights Commission once put it.

Loury's speech at the Smithsonian, and an address on a similar theme that he gave at the Heritage Foundation in 1990, indicate that he recognizes some truth in the "aid and comfort" criticism. However, this is not a truth that Loury has inculcated in his writing, but rather one that his supporters have established by failing to recognize the full range of his ideas. For while Loury's criticisms of the contemporary black leadership resonate favorably with conservative audiences, his criticisms of conservative lassitude and lack of urgency about remedying the problems of the black poor are overlooked by many of them. So, through no fault of his own, his work serves to further entrench some conservatives in their stolid attitude toward the problems of the black poor.

And yet it would be sour cynicism to wholly attribute conservatives' appreciation of Loury's thought mainly to their misconception that his project relieves them of further responsibility for the black poor—no honest reading of his work would allow that reductive understanding.

> My point to conservatives should be plain. Rather than simply incanting the "personal responsibility" mantra, we must also be engaged in helping those people who so desperately need our help. We are not relieved of our responsibility to do so by the fact that Ted Kennedy and Jesse Jackson are promoting legislation aimed at helping this same population.[12]

More reasonable is the idea that conservatives, in the main, respect Loury's dissident analysis for legitimate reasons: its solid empirical foundation, its prescriptive grounding in democratic capitalism and hoary constitutionalism, its courage, and its unembarrassed embrace of the spiritual dimension to the human person. Of course, self-respect also plays a role. Loury's powerful foil to the reckless demonizing of American conservative thought by the black leadership strikes conservatives as exactly on target. The direct and naive equation of conservatism and racism is perceived by conservatives as a cheap shot, but by sheer force of the repetition, the equation has become part of what we have been calling the deposit of public truth, as its implicit syllogistic presence in *The Day America Told the Truth* testifies:

a. All conservatives oppose preferential treatment policies.
b. All opposition to preferential treatment policies is necessarily and unerringly indicative of racism on the part of those who hold such opposition.
c. All conservatives are racists.

Conservatives resent such wild portrayals as unfair and slanderous. Naturally, they appreciate Loury's effective demonstration that conservative opposition to the agenda of the liberal black leadership may spring not only from a principled belief in limited government action, but from a distinctive, and no less zealous, concern for the welfare of black America.

The variety of reactions that Loury's and the other dissidents' work has met with makes two social facts clear. The first is that a wide cross-section of the American political spectrum (not just conservatives), weary with the doublespeak of the civil rights leadership, is emboldened by black dissident thought. The second is that reflexive charges of racism still await those who dare challenge the civil rights establishment. Even to criticize the present structure of welfare benefits in a public forum is to be accused of cynically provoking one's listeners to racism. (Recall the public truth, articulated by CNN's Bernard Shaw, that "welfare" is a codeword for demagogic race-baiting; similarly, in post-riot commentary John Chancellor upbraided those who "have fanned these flames with codewords about 'welfare queens,' 'equal opportunity,' and 'quotas.' Language designed to turn whites against blacks."[13])

It is hardly surprising, then, that voices are not raised more commonly in public criticism of welfare and the racial discourse conducted by civil rights "leaders." Loury wishes that people would thoughtfully speak up. Too often, he says, echoing an idea we heard from Wortham in Chapter 2, people "sit quietly and wait for me (a man of courage) to do their work." He adds wearily, "Well, I'm tired of doing y'all's work."[14]

DENIGRATION OF OPPORTUNITY

Loury sees the fate of America as tightly connected to the fate of its black citizens, especially those who constitute a frustrated underclass. Loury the communitarian is corroborated by Charles M. Sherover, who writes in *Time, Freedom, and the Common Good* (1989):

> Aside from a moral concern for these individual citizens themselves, the presence of any sizeable group that sees itself excluded from participation in the common good is a threat to the health of the common good itself; attendance to its presence is an act of prudential self-protection.[15]

Sherover sees the polis as precarious, ever in need of tending—its survival, not only its vitality, is never a given. Loury points to this tentativeness, especially as it involves race:

I think we oughtn't to lose the sense of the tragic. After all, race has been intimately involved in some very tragic events in American history, from the L.A. riots recently back to this awful Civil War we fought. Reason doesn't have to prevail.[16]

Because Loury is morally concerned about the ghetto poor and about the project of democratic capitalism in general, his hackles are raised by cavalier dismissals of black social mobility as an impossible and naive pipedream. Loury's reply to a *New Republic* piece by Hendrik Hertzberg titled "Wounds of Race" is instructive on this point. Hertzberg had insisted that he has "yet to meet a well-informed, unbigoted black American" who would not agree that to achieve the same success as a white person, a black must be "twice as good . . . twice as talented, twice as ambitious, twice as determined." Rejoined Loury:

How quickly he forgets! We've met more than once, and in the course of our encounters never did I confirm, and often did I contradict [that idea]. . . . I can only conclude that my earnest denunciations of affirmative action failed to register as the legitimate sentiments of a black intellectual. These ideas, coming from me, must not have sounded "black." Perhaps he simply dismissed my opinions as a sickeningly familiar neoconservatism in blackface. I guess until it fits the agenda of white liberals, a political sentiment can't be imbued by him with the awesome "moral authority" of having issued from "informed and unbigoted" victims of the ravages of slavery.

Here's some advice for Hertzberg: Quit trying to imagine what it's like for a black person "to experience contemporary American political culture." He can't—his [liberal] partisanship gets in the way. . . . I, having risen from a Chicago ghetto to a tenured post at Harvard, most emphatically *do not feel excluded* from the "land of opportunity" tenet of America's civil religion. Got it? . . . Must my participation in the national enterprise be made hostage to Hertzberg's anachronistic need for a victim class whose inevitable alienation proves the bankruptcy of American ideals?[17]

This letter highlights two important themes in Loury's thought. The first is Loury's affirmation of the reality of social mobility for black Americans. He flatly rejects the truthfulness of Hertzberg's "exclusionary" thesis, thus maintaining, by implication, that blacks from all economic stations can advance and prosper. The second theme underlying Loury's vigorous response to Hertzberg is a palpable anger based at his perception that Hertzberg, and those of his ilk, are deploying the historic victimization of blacks in the service of their own cultural critique of "bourgeois America." They are not concerned so much with the challenges facing American blacks—especially poor ones—as with establishing the necessity of their political agenda, one that ladens government with the responsibility and *ability* to manipulate social forces into some idyllic equality, however mythic and dubious such an idea has proven to be. This is much like Walter Williams's notion of liberals using black Americans as "stalking horses" for causes unrelated to black progress.

Beyond that, Loury is frankly puzzled by the insistence of the left that, in academia, opportunity is crowded out by still-pervasive racial discrimination.

> As anyone who has spent time in an elite university community knows, these institutions are not racist in character, nor do they deny opportunities to blacks with outstanding qualifications. The case can be made that just the opposite is true—that these institutions are so anxious to raise the numbers of blacks in their ranks that they overlook deficiencies when making admissions or appointment decisions involving blacks.[18]

Supporting Loury in his contention that higher education is *at least* adequately "sensitive" to diversity is data from a recent survey, conducted by *Change* magazine, of 196 colleges and universities. Of the four-year public institutions surveyed 54 percent had formally instituted a multicultural general education requirement.[19]

Despite this national progress in attitudes about race, the black leadership—with the left—continues to emphasize, for strategic reasons, the bitter seed of racial animosity. Loury argues that this redounds to the special detriment of the neediest blacks, who are ill served by the rhetorical magnification of the odds against them. Certainly, says Loury, they would be better equipped by the truth that American society, at nearly every level, has markedly matured in its understanding of the moral imperative of racial justice; further, that this abiding moral imperative has driven American social institutions toward de facto fairness. Loury decries

> tracts [that] have been written "proving" that things have been getting worse for blacks as a whole, denouncing the "myth of black progress," showing that talk of an emerging black middle class is premature, and insisting that the role of racism as a fundamental cause of the problems of blacks has not diminished one bit.[20]

In contrast to Pinkney's *The Myth of Black Progress*, to which Loury is here alluding, Loury neither recognizes a seamless garment of social experience nor a common standard of living in the black community. He sees black politicians and community leaders as purposely holding up "their" people as continually victimized.

> He who leads a group of historical victims as victims must never let "them" forget what "they" have done; he must renew the indictment and keep alive the supposed moral asymmetry implicit in the respective positions of victim and victimizer. He is the preeminent architect of what British philosopher G.K. Minogue has called "suffering situations." The circumstance of his group as "underdog" becomes his most valuable political asset. Such a posture, especially in the political realm, militates against an emphasis on personal responsibility within the group and induces those who have been successful to attribute their accomplishments to fortuitous circumstance and not to their own abilities and character.[21]

VALUES AND PUBLIC PHILOSOPHY

Against the "myth of black progress," Loury sees the growth of the black middle class as a triumph of the democratic process and a vindication that America today is "an essentially good nation worthy of allegiance and support."[22] After the long struggle for equality under law, there has been a sufficient abatement of racism, he says, to make an "internal strategy" practicable—indeed, necessary.[23] Interestingly, Loury sees the black community as at a critical crossroads, which parallels the historical tension in black public life seen in the nineteenth century, between the self-help thrust of Booker T. Washington and the political agitation thrust of W.E.B. Du Bois. Lately, Loury has been explicating a public philosophy that draws specifically at the wellspring of Washington's thought. Ironically, a proposition in Washington's philosophy that Loury sees as centrally important is an idea that is anathema to today's civil rights establishment: Blacks should be concerned about the sensibilities of whites. In a speech delivered to the American Enterprise Institute, Loury said:

> Washington was a conservative advocate of a philosophy of self-help. . . . He saw two factors preventing blacks from enjoying the status in American society which was our due: actual defects of character as manifest in patterns of behavior and ways of living to be observed among the black masses; and the racist attitudes of whites. He believed that blacks had both an opportunity and a duty to address the former difficulty; and that, in so doing, [blacks] would go a long way toward overcoming the latter.
> . . . Today's orthodoxy holds in contempt the need to express concern for and acknowledge the legitimacy of the sensibilities of whites, when they

run up against the presumed interests of blacks. What Washington under-stood, and what remains as true today as it is difficult to say out loud, is that cultivating the sensibilities of whites is directly in the interests of blacks. Because we live in a democracy we bear the burden of persuading our fellows of the worth of our claims upon them.[24]

Again we see that Loury, as with Steele and Woodson, ascribes to white America a pool of goodwill—hardly ever publicly recognized by the black leadership—a pool that blacks can cultivate to their benefit. This is not to posit some kind of social servitude for American blacks, but rather to acknowledge the validity of common behavioral norms and the rightness of their observance.[25]

There seems to be both a pragmatic and a moral element at work in Loury's thinking. He sees a practical value for African-Americans—es-pecially the poor—in being aware of the public sensibilities of the ma-jority of the American population. This is coupled with his appreciation for the intrinsic value of bourgeois norms—norms that are by no means inherently "white." The following remarks from an interview function as an adept summary of Loury's public vision. Note its richness:

There is wisdom in [Booker T.] Washington's self-help strategy for us today, particularly in light of past civil rights successes and the oppor-tunities they've opened up.

One of the things that was wise about Washington's strategy was its recognition of the fact that respect had to be earned. Respect can't be demanded or brokered as the *quid pro quo* for peace, where whites say, "I'll respect you if you don't riot." The sense of the worth of the other has to be conveyed as a consequence of what fair-minded people conclude regarding the way people are living and contributing. You see, Washington recognized—and I argue, too—that many whites do not see in aspects of black life something worthy of respect. One can call that racist if one wants, and one can bemoan the fact that whites feel or think this way. But two things are true:

One is that we need their respect and their assistance to get anything done. This is a democracy after all. The other is, whether we bemoan it or not, the objective conditions of too many black communities are con-sistent with decent and fair-minded people being dubious about who these people are. "Do they hold the same view of the world that we do?" "Are they committed to our common values and goals in this political enter-prise?" These are not unfair questions.

Loury then noted the special social effect of the morally virtuous ac-tions of Martin Luther King:

King, too, knew that to succeed he had to persuade white people of the legitimacy of his claims. That's why nonviolence was so important to him, and that's why nonviolence is an extremely dignified mode of protest.

I believe that nonviolence is the morally correct position, independently of whether or not whites are assuaged or impressed by its practice. Indeed, it is because of the objective moral correctness of non-violence, rather than its contingent and pragmatic value, that the practice of it could serve as evidence of the dignity and worth of the protestors. That is, King was adhering to high principle, not just playing ordinary politics, when practicing the discipline of nonviolence.

What you have is the racist who is hosing people down, spitting on them, and setting dogs on them—and what they are doing is holding their bloody heads unbowed. They are persisting in adherence to some ideals that are higher than those that are reflected in their antagonists. So what happens, at the end of the day, is that they have proved themselves to be dignified, worthy citizens who earned the respect of the onlooking masses of the American electorate—who, upon seeing these events, are persuaded of the virtue and righteousness of the claimants. They earned their respect by adhering to nonviolence.

That's what is so dangerous in this contemporary elevation of Malcolm X to sainthood. What King understood is that when you are 10 percent of the population of a democracy, you have to persuade, not cajole. White people don't need to be taught how to be afraid of young black men—they already know that when they get off the subway in New York City. What needs to be taught is the humanity of [African-Americans]. And that's the kind of thing that's exhibited by what King did, and in my vision of a new, invigorated movement of self-help in black communities across the country.[26]

The moral nobility Loury is remembering, honoring, and recommending to blacks, now at a crossroads, is an alternative style of group advocacy. Will blacks continue to major in the political, à la Du Bois? Or will they turn to the personal, à la Washington? While Loury would favor the latter, he would also remind African-Americans that, as with the civil rights demonstrations of the 1960s, such a commitment may demand unusual personal virtue. As King knew, such practice commands the respect of one's antagonists and encourages the general goodwill—which, as Loury points out, is imperative for the mobility of a minority in a democratic society. Loury sees great practicality for social mobility in the widespread practice of sound values. "Discipline, orderliness, and virtue in every aspect of life contribute to the goal of creating an aura of respectability and deservingness. Such an aura is a valuable political asset."[27]

Interestingly, he recognizes the confidence this involves—that whites (and people in general), by and large, are fair minded, and that they recognize and respect performance from individuals of every race. Such an estimation of whites as moral beings is, of course, rare in the rhetoric of the civil rights leadership today—obviously a fact most whites find insulting. Evidence for this is found in an extensive, yet unpublicized, study commissioned by the Leadership Conference on Civil Rights, comprised of civil rights, labor, women's, and disabled groups. The white Americans surveyed rejected the idea that they were racist. They saw today's black leadership as less concerned about fairness and equal opportunity than about group advantage. They are not buying the idea, wrote William Raspberry, who reflected on the study in an article, that their opposition to preferential treatment policies makes them racists. "How could we expect them to buy a product we have spent 400 years trying to have recalled: race-based advantage enshrined in law?"[28]

Of course, inevitably some regard Loury's emphasis on the intrinsic and pragmatic value of "bourgeois virtues" to be nothing more than the peddling of "white values" and "white consciousness." The Afrocentric manifesto of Leonard Jefferies would seem to represent this view, inasmuch as it demonstrates a hostility to certain qualities frequently associated with such values and their capitalist context.

> The Ice People [of Europe] are characterized by the three D's—domination, destruction, and death. The I in Ice stands for individualism, the C for competitiveness, and the E for exploitation. At the core of the system is the belief that domination makes you better. On the other hand, the Sun People [of Africa] are characterized by the three C's: communalism, cooperation, and collectivity.[29]

This charge of imposing alien values bespeaks an odd, but familiar, identification of race and ideology. Such a view loses force in light of the point, made by Loury and also by Woodson, that the Judeo-Christian moral heritage, wherein lie the roots of bourgeois values, has both imbued and nurtured African-American life for many generations.[30] In addition, the achievements of the black middle class contradict the notion that, today, these instrumental values only drive white achievement—that these "value-batteries" power only the white "machine" and won't work in the black model.

The deprecation of middle-class values by some intellectuals and Afrocentrists (and in turn by their acolytes in rap culture) is an example of a dangerous discounting of the "good" in favor of the "perfect"—in this case the time-tested and *functional* "good" of instrumental values, in favor of some idealistic and anthropologically naive social perfection, where everyone's rise to economic freedom is unfettered by hardship of any kind. Joseph Amato has argued most persuasively, in *Victims and Values: A History and a Theory of Suffering*, that the utopian undervaluing of the "good" in favor of the "perfect" is one of the most disturbing tendencies of contemporary American political thought.[31]

Resistance to the inculcation of bourgeois values comes from other quarters as well, notes Loury. One is from the philosophical posture of moral relativism, which would see a privileging of the values of one group over another as at best arbitrary and at worst, a form of cultural imperialism.[32] Something of the insistence that public policy strive for the value neutrality demanded by the assumption of relativism is seen in the Carter Administration's failed attempt to convene a conference on "the family." Recalling the account of the affair in *Family and Nation*, by Sen. Daniel Patrick Moynihan, Loury writes that haggling over definitions delayed the event until 1979, at which time a rather meaningless conference on "families" occurred. Loury describes the result of this politically correct eggshell treading:

> Indeed, just recently the divorced black mother who had been slated to chair that conference wrote proudly of her principled resignation when the White House urged upon her a married white male vice-chairman. How dare they suggest that a husband and wife raising children together were preferable to a mother doing the job alone! Today, the growing influence within the Democratic Party of feminist and homosexual rights constituencies would probably render such a conference altogether out of the question.[33]

The upshot of this, for Loury, is that the public sector, given the current political climate, is impaired in its ability to suggest normative solutions to underclass problems. "Addressing these failures requires they first be acknowledged to exist," says Loury, "a task for which [some] liberals . . . clearly do not have the stomach."[34]

Another source of resistance to the strategic diffusion of instrumental values is "knowledge-class" skepticism about the possibility of widespread upward mobility by means of these values, as well as avantgarde contempt for the ordinariness of middle-class values. Irving Kristol locates this hostility to bourgeois values in this context:

> Today the old-fashioned animus against the market economy is being sublimated into an aggressive animus against the bourgeois society that

is organically associated with our market economy. If you delegitimize this bourgeois society, the market economy—almost incidentally, as it were—is also delegitimized. It is for this reason that radical feminism today is a far more potent enemy of capitalism than radical trade unionism.[35]

For our purposes, the strength of Kristol's point lies in the fact that to deligitimate bourgeois culture is to delegitimate the most effective means of entry into the market economy. Social competence is undermined by the rejection of those values associated with the middle class, the social core.

RESPONSIBILITY AND DIGNITY

Amplifying a point made in the influential work of Orlando Patterson, Loury's thought consistently distinguishes between *fault* and *responsibility* with respect to the current situation of American blacks. While Loury forthrightly assigns fault to white racists for having caused manifold difficulties that endure today, he is unwilling to ascribe to them the sole responsibility of remedying these harms.

> It is absolutely vital that blacks distinguish the fault which may be attributed to racism, and the responsibility for relieving that condition. For no people can be genuinely free so long as they look to others for their deliverance. The pride and self-respect valued by aspiring peoples throughout the world cannot be the gift of outsiders—they must derive from the thoughts and deeds of the people themselves. Neither the guilt nor the pity of one's oppressor is a sufficient basis upon which to construct a sense of self-worth.[36]

In these paragraphs we see the central elements of Loury's understanding of dignity and its importance for the black community. Loury takes it as axiomatic that the human spirit naturally values dignity. For blacks, the change in the exercise of freedom, brought about through the victories of the civil rights movement, carried with it certain implications for the holding of dignity. In the field of freedom—that is, in the sphere of free human action—dignity has room to flourish. When individuals have freedom and accept responsibility for their freely chosen actions, dignity is affirmed. Conversely, when free individuals refuse to assume responsibility, their dignity is eclipsed. Such refusal represents an existential cowardice, a refusal to embrace the full range of contingencies that the exercise of freedom gives rise to. Loury further develops and reiterates this principle in the following remarks from his speech, "Black Dignity and the Common Good":

> It is to make a mockery of the idea of freedom to hold that, as free men and women, blacks ought to nonetheless wait passively for white Americans, of whatever political persuasion, to come to the rescue. If our people languish in dependency, while the means through which we might work for our own advancement exist, then we have surrendered our claim to dignity and to the respect of our fellow citizens. If we are to be a truly free people, we must accept responsibility for our fate even when it does not lie wholly in our hands.[37]

Loury is disturbed by an ironic discontinuity: rhetoric and action have been cavernously disjoined by the civil rights establishment. On the one hand there is the black leadership's intense rhetoric on the importance of freedom and unfettered liberty to the black community; on the other, he sees a markedly constrained exercise of freedom. Some blacks, it seems to him, would prefer to have their freedom supplemented by political maneuvering, rather than enjoy the undiluted freedom of complete personal responsibility. But such a stance thwarts a primary personal benefit of dignity, one that cannot be obtained through coercion, pity, or guilt: "the freely conveyed respect of one's peers."[38]

Loury's affirmation of dignity in this special sense brings us to a consideration of his bi-level communitarianism. As the reader will recall, in his reply to Hertzberg Loury emphasized his participation in the "national enterprise." Such communitarian language permeates Loury's writings. As a point of interest, and to again underscore the diversity of ideas expressed by black dissidents, Loury's *communitarian* neoconservatism is markedly different from Sowell's *libertarian* conservatism. To Loury, all citizens are engaged in the forging of national community, interconnected by their mutual goals and obligations. To someone like Sowell, the national fabric is less dense, more a confluence of individual interests than the purposive result of citizens engaged in the shared project of nation building.

Understood in this way, Loury's communitarianism is a transracial project, which sees all individuals as having a moral obligation to foster and preserve the national commonweal. This national communitarianism is supplemented by a distinctly African-American communitarianism. He sees blacks as having special fraternal obligations to one another. Those prospering ought to aid the economic advancement of those who are impoverished. This obligation, he asserts, springs from the political capital accrued by the black middle class as a result of the publicized hardship of the black ghetto, as when the "squalor and hopelessness of the Harlem ghetto comes to ensure the legitimacy of preferential treatment for black medical school applicants from Scarsdale."[39] Later in this chapter, when discussing Loury's perspective on mediating institutions, we will further explore his understanding of the obligations of the black middle class to the black lower class.

THE IMPORTANCE OF ACCOUNTABILITY

Weaving throughout Loury's communitarian public philosophy and his explication of the centrality of dignity to any program of black upliftment is an emphasis on the concept of accountability. An implication that flows naturally from the principles underlying the self-help movement is that all individuals must be held accountable for their actions. Anyone who believes in autonomy and personal responsibility will not credit the argument that holding young men and women accountable for their failures amounts to "blaming the victim," or siding with the "sick society" that somehow makes their failure inevitable. To the contrary, such a person must hold, for example, that young men who father children and then walk away from their responsibility to support them are not society's victims, but their own families' victimizers.[40]

Loury is annoyed with those who, in the name of compassion and historical vision, exempt black citizens from common moral standards. So, though Andrew Hacker was sniping when he described black conservatives as insisting that African-Americans "must be judged by the same standards as other Americans,"[41] his point was truly made, at least with reference to Loury. It is the poor, Loury argues, who are the least served by a denigration of middle-class sensibilities, and by the "proclivity to avoid [public] discussion of values, norms and behaviors in the low income black community which are inconsistent both with achievement in America, and with the ethos characteristic of much of the black middle class itself."[42] Thus, part of the fraternal obligation the black middle-class leadership owes the lower class is normative honesty—the leaders ought not overlook moral failures in the name of "pitying the poor" or, worse, for their own political purposes. Such moral silence on the part of middle-class black leaders is inexcusable, whether done in the name of political subterfuge or by the application of a moral double standard.

A particularly sharp illustration of this moral double standard is the

explanation offered by Kenneth Clark following the newsmaking shooting of four black youths by Bernard Goetz, the "subway vigilante."
Pronouncing the four young men who accosted Goetz victims of "pervasive community, economic, and educational muggings" committed
by a "hypocritical society," Clark nimbly swept away their moral responsibility by anointing them with the mantle of victimhood. Loury's
response, in his article "Black Political Culture after the Sixties," repudiates Clark's moral exculpation of these four young black men. Loury
writes:

> Even in the harshest of slums the vast majority of residents do not brutalize
> their neighbors. . . . Moreover, even the black poor who are violent must
> be held responsible for their conduct. Are they not made poorer still when
> they are not accorded the respect inherent in the equal application of the
> obligations and expectations of citizenship?[43]

The impoverishment to which Loury is here referring is not economic,
but personal. It is the insidiously debilitating reduction of human dignity
that occurs whenever moral exceptions are made in the name of "fostering guilt and pity among the population at large."[44] Because of his
fervent commitment to the concept of civic community, which transcends race, Loury is unable to excuse the four youths. For him, these
individuals have the same civic obligations and responsibilities as any
other people. Their socioeconomic condition and the very real hardship
they may be enduring as inner-city youth does not exonerate them from
the ethical duties common to Americans, such as observance of other
people's legal rights and respect for property. In this idea we see once
again Loury's vision of national community. This is a recurrent and
distinctive theme in his work. It is reflective of his desire for an inclusive
political culture, one not balkanized by the illusion of race-specific personality.

   In the case of Clark's defense of Goetz's would-be muggers, the double
standard was patent; in other cases it is more subtle. It is seen, in
subtextual form, in the first edition of the black-owned *Los Angeles Sentinel* that appeared after the Los Angeles riots. Page two of the *Sentinel*
featured an exposé on hate crimes against minorities, reporting a sharp
rise in their incidence. A few columns away on the same page, a riot-
related article reported on the beating of a white truck driver, Reginald
Denny, at an intersection in South Central Los Angeles. Pulled from his
vehicle, kicked onto the pavement, then bashed in the head with a lamp
and brick, the trucker was eventually taken to the hospital by four *black*

strangers, according to the article. But conspicuously absent from this typically color-conscious *Sentinel* article was mention that the four men who nearly killed Denny were black, or a condemnation of the attack as a "hate crime."[45]

Oppositely, Loury fiercely insists on accountability, for everyone, of whatever race or social context. Witness his comments on the Denny beating:

> One of the things that is most disturbing to me in the wake of the Los Angeles debacle is that responsible people in the black community have come forward [with] the idea of a defense fund for these guys who beat Reginald Denny—it's a grotesque absurdity. They think they are engaging in a kind of partisan advocacy—"It's us versus them, and it's the white world out there that we are standing over against. We're not abandoning our boys once they're under attack." What in fact they are doing is selling out their own community by failing to establish and underscore and reinforce the difference between right and wrong. You don't say it for white people, you say it for black people, that these individuals behaved in a barbaric way.[46]

To Loury's mind, true dignity requires accountability. He is not willing to excuse criminal behavior because of the retarding effect such excusing has on the personal development and character of those it excuses, and when the criminal is black, on the ethos of the national black community.

Loury's view of the importance of accountability extends into other issues, including welfare dependency. Loury is adamantly opposed to what he sees as mechanical responses from the black leadership on this issue—especially the tendency to *externalize* responsibility for the failures of ghetto youth. The young man who impregnates his girlfriend and assumes no responsibility for the care of the child—is he not shirking a basic human obligation? Loury thinks he is, and decries the inclination, on the part of many black leaders, to obscure accountability in such cases in favor of recourse to deterministic theories about social forces.

> If our intellectuals and political leaders insist upon externalizing this responsibility, if they continue to tell this young man that it is a racist American society which has wrought his current circumstance, then they risk removing the single most important tool for change in that young man's life—namely his belief in himself.[47]

So to Loury, a solution to the myriad problems surrounding unwed pregnancy and welfare dependency is intimately connected to an emphasis on personal accountability. Without accountability, it is extremely unlikely that one will achieve the personal maturity that yields confidence in oneself, and in one's capacity for economic self-sufficiency. It is in this way that the dearth of accountability leads to perpetuation of poverty. The very real opportunity to escape from poverty, for a young woman born into it, is greatly lessened if, told she cannot help it, she has a child out of wedlock. In this context, Charles Murray's idea is worth recalling: "A poor woman who wishes to get out of poverty ought not have a baby out of wedlock. This is not a moral statement but an empirical one."[48]

While Loury would agree with Murray's conclusion, he does emphatically speak to the ethical dimension of welfare dependence and unwed childbearing. The poor are badly served, says Loury, by the unwillingness of those traditionally invested with moral authority in the community to speak normatively in this area. Such leadership, apparently, fails to really grasp how "the human spirit, as it were, could be the basis for overcoming incentives [to nonwork], in one way or another."[49] When Loury says "in one way or another," he is specifically referring to two competing theories of nonwork, one advanced by Murray and the other proposed by William Julius Wilson. In an interview, Loury highlighted certain points of these two theories:

> Murray, for example, says that if you give people money when they have single-parent families, then basically that's rewarding them for behaving irresponsibly. They will respond to those rewards by increasing the amount of the subsidized behavior. Wilson, on the other hand, says . . . that as long as the economy doesn't produce enough good paying jobs, people will have to live in a certain degraded state.[50]

Loury is not convinced, however, that these two viewpoints take into account the sensitivity of the human spirit to moral imperatives—that is, the capacity of human will and conscience to respond to calls to virtue, and to recognize and act to manifest its own highest good, even in the face of economic hardship (Wilson) or economic incentive (Murray). The individual freedom Loury has in mind here recalls, in some respects, Shelby Steele's existentialism.

This idea returns us to what Loury sees as the importance of normative discussions in the public square. Because the human spirit has the capacity for self-transcendence ("We stand outside ourselves and assess the meaning and quality of our lives," in Robert Benne's words[51]), leadership worthy of the title will speak normatively and honestly in the public square about issues of *personal virtue and values*. To do less, says Loury, is to understand and treat the poor as less than human. It is to refuse to acknowledge in them essential elements of personhood: conscience and will. It is tantamount to moral infantilization. The kind of "public conversation" Loury has in mind here—conducted in good faith, and in the context of mediating structures—is at the heart of what Loury conceives as the potential across the country for a

> new, invigorated movement of self-help in black communities. . . . If people are imbued with a sense of who they are and what their worth is as human beings, then the effect on individuals can outweigh the material incentives. I am not so concerned that welfare has the effect of dulling people's incentives to live in a particular way, I think rather that it is a failure to instill in people an understanding of how they ought to live and to exhibit for them examples of people living in that fashion.[52]

Of course, Loury recognizes that it is not enough just to tell people "not to have babies." Rather, leadership must engage in the "laborious, unromantic work," to borrow a phrase from Dennis Prager, both institutionally (though not necessarily governmentally) and interpersonally, that affirms, supports, and develops responsibility in needy African-Americans.

CRISIS OF VALUES

For Loury, the kind of crisis in neighborhood values, as illustrated above, calls for an internal strategy of black advocacy—what he calls playing the "inner game." Disagreeing with that tenet of progressivism that essentially finds, according to Lawrence Mead's characterization of the position in *Beyond Entitlement*, that "all social problems are due to denials of freedom,"[53] Loury insists that many of the problems that hinder the underclass (but are not peculiar to it), to a large extent have their provenance in personal behavior and values. He writes:

> There is a large and growing body of data and evidence, both in the scholarly literature and the popular press, suggesting that the behavior and values of persons in this underclass, especially during their formative years of adolescence, play an important part in perpetuating their poverty. Problems such as early unwed pregnancy, alcohol and drug dependency, and chronic long-term joblessness are all, at least in part, a reflection of individuals' behavior and choices that make their impoverishment more likely.[54]

But the common embrace of values that have long been integral to the black experience, including self-sufficiency and family solidarity, has been supplanted, in the inner city, by a widespread and hostile discontent with the establishment, with a sense of entitlement instead of a yearning for opportunity and *legal* fairness. Ethelbert W. Haskins puts it this way in *The Crisis in Afro-American Leadership* (1988):

> It is one of the ironies of the times that the black youngster in the ghetto is encouraged by those who claim to have his best interests at heart to spurn the opportunities the "system" offers and to scratch at his roots and maintain his identity until the system retools to conform to his lifestyle. Having been advised that he is life's victim and to feel sorry for himself, he sits seething in rage about his poverty and unemployment.[55]

This clearly mitigates against youngsters' chances of achieving social competence. Loury, with Stanley Crouch, notes that rather than address this, the black leadership has failed to speak clearly and unequivocally on the culturally destructive attitudes issuing from this kind of inner-city "nihilism," in Loury's phrase.[56] Indeed, as Crouch points out in the following passage, the liberal leadership strangely romanticizes dangerous strains in the youth culture:

> We [cannot] ignore the way in which too many irresponsible intellectuals— black and white—have submitted to the youth culture and the adolescent rebellion of pop music, bootlegging liberal arts rhetoric to defend Afro-fascist rap groups like Public Enemy, on the one hand, while paternalistically defining the "gangster rap" of doggerel chanters such as Ice Cube as expressive of the "real" black community.[57]

In contrast to the irresponsible intellectualizing Crouch is describing, Loury offers a commonsense approach: "I think you have to take the message of [political rap] seriously," he commented during an interview. He continued:

> When some of these rappers say, "I hate white people," and intellectuals interpret their words using models of French deconstructionism to mean that they don't hate white people, I think the intellectuals are wrong. When these kids say they hate white people, they do.[58]

Rarely has the shimmer of this kind of intellectual varnish glowed so brightly as in Robert Hilburn's breathless *explicacion de texte* of political rap in his article "Beyond the Rage."[59] Noting with reverence that Ice

Cube recognizes rap as the "CNN of black America," Hilburn recounts the expletive-laced lyrics of the most popular rappers with the clinical analysis of the most erudite music historian. But Hilburn drops the ball when he writes, without any sense of irony: "KRS-One, one of rap's brightest and most positive forces, even posed with an Uzi on the cover of his 'By Any Means Necessary' album in 1988."[60] Brightest and most positive? One can only wonder what poses less "positive" role models would have struck for the contemplation of black youth. But critic Hilburn should be excused this oversight, as he was no doubt swept away by the brilliant antinomy of armed-to-the-teeth role model "KRS-One."

But sadly, it is not the wealthy rappers and elite cognoscenti of this latter-day radical chic who suffer the most under its regime of trans-valuation—its cavalier denigration of the habits and attitudes that have led immigrants of all ethnicities to social competence in our political economy. It is instead the young, economically disempowered African-Americans. In the eyes of ghetto youth, the bulwarks of the undercul-ture—virulent forms of rap music, welfare dependency, poor schooling, and the constant message that they are the victim and white society the victimizer—delegitimate those virtues best fitted to our social and eco-nomic polity, as noted earlier by Kristol. This unexamined and reckless critique of mainstream middle-class values does not contribute in any discernible way to the socioeconomic deliverance of those presently dis-advantaged.

GOVERNMENT AND VALUES

As noted earlier, Loury does see a meliorative role for government in addressing social problems. It was on this score that he chided certain conservatives on their complacency and lack of passion for creative pub-lic (though not necessarily governmental) policies that manifest "public responsibility." While Loury does not demonstrate, with those on the left, a faith in the omnicompetence of the state and in political solutions to social problems, he does recognize a measured role for the state in addressing societal failures, such as the depressed economy, serious criminality, drug abuse, inadequate educational preparation, and unfair discrimination. But the government's positive action must be tempered by respect for the power of political measures, on the one hand, and the primacy of personal autonomy, on the other. Loury expresses this concept in a formal principle of public policy formulation:

The main public policy consideration is to avoid rewarding "vice" (i.e., individual actions which retard . . . [individuals'] ability to become self-supporting—like having a child before being able to properly care for and support it), and to avoid punishing "virtue" (i.e., individual actions which promote independence).[61]

Loury most assuredly does not believe that it is the state's proper role to train and school its subjects in private virtue. Still, he believes that individuals are badly served by a government that provides them with an incentive to avoid self-reliance. Such a dynamic is not, for example, a call for the abolition of welfare; it is, rather, a practical recognition of the formidable power of government to sway the behavior of its citizens through incentives and disincentives.

ON WELFARE REFORM AND MEDIATING STRUCTURES

Loury's tempered view of governmental intervention in the lives of its citizenry is seen in his view of welfare reform. In conservative political circles the ideas of Lawrence Mead and Charles Murray dominate discussions of welfare reform. Loury tends to be more persuaded by Mead's plan than by Murray's. While Murray would abolish welfare altogether, Mead would bring public philosophy "beyond entitlement" by imposing mandatory work requirements on recipients. What Loury likes about Mead's workfare plan, as sketched in *Beyond Entitlement* and *The New Politics of Poverty*, is its accent on social "obligations," which Loury sees as affirming human dignity. That is, work requirements show "respect for the recipients, by according them the expectation that they are capable of meeting commonly held norms about how people should conduct their lives."[62] On the other hand, Loury is convinced that social competency habituated by work requirements must be reinforced in the private sector through moral suasion, that is, through an honest and ethically rigorous "subnational" conversation among blacks. Today, when blacks constitute two-fifths of all AFDC recipients and the majority of long-term welfare dependents, such fraternal help, reinforced by private mediating institutions, is imperative.[63] He writes:

Some social tasks are better undertaken through the "mediating structures" of private, voluntary associations. Mutually concerned persons who trust one another enough to be able to exchange criticism constructively, establish codes of personal conduct, and enforce social sanctions against what is judged to be undesirable behavior can create and enforce com-

munal norms that lie beyond the capacity of the state effectively to pro-
mulgate.[64]

Illustrating his understanding of the value of mediating structures,
Loury points to the amazing success of a home for unwed mothers in
Lynchburg, Virginia, run by the church of Rev. Jerry Falwell, where
there have been virtually no second unwed pregnancies—typically,
nearly one-half of teen unwed mothers have a second child out of wedlock.[65] "It should not be surprising," writes Loury, "that churches, or
residential associations, or civic groups are potentially more effective at
changing the underlying values and behaviors of their individual members than the bureaucratic alternative."[66]

The mainspring of Loury's mediating structures strategy for aiding
the underclass is harnessing the talents and "social capital" of the black
middle class. Loury's mediating structures strategy, then, complements
Woodson's. Woodson wants to systematically call attention to, and have
poorer communities learn from, those in their midst who, sharing their
circumstances, have managed to become self-reliant. While not disagreeing with this wise tapping of neighborhood capital, Loury would
also enlist the formidable resources of the black middle class to accomplish what government cannot do—the communication of values
uniquely suited to achievement. Loury regards this class interaction as
a form of "self-reliance."

> It makes sense to call for greater self-reliance at this time because some
> of what needs to be done cannot, in the nature of the case, be undertaken
> by government. Dealing with behavioral problems, with community val-
> ues, with the attitudes and beliefs of black youngsters about responsibility,
> work, family, and schooling is not something government is well suited
> to do. The teaching of "oughts" properly belongs in the hands of private,
> voluntary associations. . . . It is also reasonable to ask those blacks who
> have benefitted from set-asides for black business—to contribute to the
> alleviation of suffering of poor blacks—for without the visible ghetto poor,
> such programs would lack the political support needed for their contin-
> uation.[67]

In opposition to critics' simplistic reduction of self-reliance to atomistic
"bootstraps nonsense," Loury joins other dissidents in imbuing the concept of self-reliance with broad meaning. We have seen two clear senses
of self-reliance in the work of other figures: the existential context of
self-initiative emphasized by Steele, and the idea of neighborhood self-
help stressed by Woodson. In the above passage, Loury introduces a

third sense of self-reliance. This approach relies upon the initiative and fraternal concern of those African-Americans who have attained middle- and upper-class success, and have experienced at first hand the holistic mechanism of personal effort within the sphere of democratic capitalism.

In Loury's mind, without this corporate form of self-reliance, this merging of the economic destinies of middle- and lower-class blacks, no substantive alteration in the condition of the poor will likely be realized, even with "the return of economic prosperity, with the election of a liberal Democrat to the presidency, or with the doubling in size of the Congressional Black Caucus."[68]

Loury sees a conversation about responsibility, initiated by the black middle class, as contributing to the establishment of a larger ethos of responsibility in all segments of the black community. "One of the principle sources of 'social capital' available to any community," says Loury, "is the ability of mutually concerned persons to exchange critical judgments of their fellows."[69]

What would be the nature of this conversation, especially with the young? It would have to address, certainly, a problem that Raspberry—certainly no uncritical booster of black conservatives—raised in one of his columns. The column was inspired by two phone calls, just hours apart, to his home. The first was from a Howard University professor "who just had to talk" of his alarm at the plight of the black underclass and the failure of the black middle class to act decisively in response. The second call came from an engineer friend, who was equally agitated. Lunching at a local restaurant, he had been disturbed by three black youths, he told Raspberry, whose loud conversation filled the restaurant with profanity and obscenity. He continued:

> I'm no prude; my friends and I used some of the same language when I was growing up. The difference is, we would never have said such things in the presence of adults. You'd like to think of trying to help some of these kids find a job or possibly hiring some of them. But the truth is, I'm afraid of them. These kids are going to be lost unless we figure out some way of rescuing them. But what?[70]

Raspberry's recommendation: "a formal organization, locally based, for pairing these disaster-bound youngsters with middle-class adults who could help them develop the academic and attitudinal basis for escaping the underclass: a sort of Big Brothers approach designed to inculcate middle-class values."[71] Raspberry's idea shadows, on a smaller scale, Loury's much larger social strategy. The essential likeness of their approaches lies in the communication and transmission of "bourgeois" values and practical skills through mediating structures.

MISSED OPPORTUNITIES

With Raspberry, Loury would prefer the black leadership to demonstrate creativity and positive fraternal concern, rather than continually engage in a public cataloguing of black failure and its prevalence.

> Remarkably, we think that the mere announcement of the small number of blacks who attain a certain achievement constitutes an indictment of society, and not of us. Thinking thus, we engage in an exhibitionism of non-achievement, hurrying to advertise our every lack of success.[72]

Given the thrust of Loury's thinking, it is likely he would find such an "exhibition of non-achievement" in the protests by a number of black college presidents against a recent National Collegiate Athletic Association's ruling that tightened academic standards for college-bound student-athletes. Responding to the ruling which raised the required GPA from 2.0 to 2.5, on a scale of 4.0, William DeLauder, president of Delaware State University, sounded the alarm, declaring, "This is clearly a discriminatory proposal."

Of course, the ruling does "discriminate," in the dictionary sense that it makes a distinction between low grades and acceptable grades, but just as surely, such discrimination does not penalize black students *as such*. To claim that it does is to posit a rather grand and implausible theory of conspiratorial oppression. Still, the racially tinged criticism of the ruling does not surprise Loury; indeed, in an article published a year before the ruling, he anticipated precisely the kind of mechanical response that did greet it.[73]

The first thing to observe in this episode, from a Lourian perspective, is the mechanical reaction of black leaders—a public affirmation that black student athletes cannot and should not be expected to rise to the challenge of achieving a C+ average. This announcement, as the sole and primary response of the black leadership, forecloses from the outset any creative thinking about solutions to the problem of underachievement. Protesting the ruling does not alter at all the statistics that show black students dropping out of colleges at rates exceeding those for every other ethno-racial group; nor does it address the ill-preparation largely responsible for this dropout rate. The reflexive cry of "discrimination" all but drowns out important questions: Would black student-athletes not be well served by extra study and enhanced academic preparation in high school? Would not the two or three hours a week of extra effort in secondary school to raise their GPAs pay off in enhanced chances for academic success at the university?

We believe Loury would see this as a chance to demonstrate the efficacy of a mediating structures strategy, through competent groups and individuals taking it upon themselves to tutor and train academically deficient students in the skills they presently lack. In this way, the NCAA affair, rather than becoming an occasion for the black leadership to protest alleged institutional hostility against blacks, would offer an opportunity for authentic community building.

Student athletes are often the natural heroes of their fellow students and so, to a critical degree, set the tone of a school. The overall attitude of the student body toward academics could be raised by seeing the extra discipline it would have to exercise to meet the ruling's criteria. In light of the Ogbu and Fordham study, this boost for academics would be welcome. In stark contrast, because of the transvaluation communicated by black leadership by crying discrimination, the mobilization of community that could have resulted, was unrealized. This failure of the black leadership to impose and abide by high educational standards was addressed by Booker T. Washington nearly a century ago: "I would not have the standard of mental development lowered one whit, for with the Negro, as with all races, mental strength is the basis of all progress."[74]

We offer this scenario, not as a plank in Loury's social philosophy, but rather to highlight the predictability of civil rights advocacy as it stands today, and its general unwillingness to embrace unconventional and self-help strategies. In this instance, an opportunity was lost to mobilize the enormous creativity, talent, and energy in black communities everywhere. Loury, who, like other dissidents, would harness these resources in the form of school vouchers, writes of such missed opportunities: "It is politically and morally irresponsible to sit back in disgust, as so many veterans of past struggles are fond of doing, constantly decrying the problems, doing little or nothing to solve them."[75] These opportunities for "subnational conversations" on values, and for fraternal action, must not be allowed to pass, noted only by feckless cries of discrimination, Loury insists. Black dignity requires more.

A thematic summary of much of Loury's thinking is found in the following remarks by Anne Wortham:

[In 1989] I gave two talks at Smith [College]. The first was on individualism in the black community. My basic argument was that whites do not have a monopoly on individualism, that blacks can be individualists, too. To illustrate this point I spoke of my own upbringing, how individualism had been a key element of my father's teaching, and how much of his teaching I could now find in many philosophical works that he himself was unaware of. I told the audience of my father's constant reminder to my siblings and me that he was raising us to be "independent, self-supporting and law-abiding citizens." Later I learned from my studies that he was teaching us a key principle of individualism and the very basis of a free society: that the corollary of political freedom is self-responsibility.

In the middle of this, a black student—a young lady who, I later learned, was to be my hostess the next day—ran out of the room in tears. Why was she crying? Well, I was speaking in a language that was offensive to her. Students told me of the offensiveness of my views during the question period after the talk I gave the next night. They told me, in effect, that I spoke in a language that should not come from someone who is black and female. For they had been taught that my ideas were the same as those used by racists to justify their exploitation of the disadvantaged. One young lady, a white student, condemned me and said I should not have been permitted to speak.[76]

Decades earlier, Glenn Loury, as a college student passionately interested in issues of race and politics, also heard Wortham speak. Though the efflorescence of Loury's thought would follow a different path from Wortham's, owing to their disparate philosophical roots, the unique figure of Anne Wortham did impact Loury's thinking and, we suggest, has been a factor that led him to embrace the aphoristic philosophical fragment that Wortham expressed years later: "The corollary of political freedom is self-responsibility."

As a relatively young man, Loury has many years remaining in which to further develop his ideas and their implications. Their vector and emphasis, as well as his thought here surveyed, suggests that the concept of dignity will continue to predominate in his work.[77] Loury's ongoing intellectual inquiry promises to enrich black advocacy and prod the usual and common thinking about social ethics.

NOTES

1. James Patterson and Peter Kim, *The Day America Told the Truth* (New York: Prentice-Hall, 1991), p. 188.

2. See Paul Sniderman and Michael Gray Hagen's discussion of "symbolic racism" in *Race and Inequality: A Study in American Values* (Chatham, NJ: Chatham House, 1985), pp. 11–12.

3. Kenneth Minogue, *Alien Powers: The Pure Theory of Ideology* (New York: St. Martin's Press, 1985), pp. 144–46.

4. Of course, the civil rights movement even went beyond this, holding that legal and statutory discrimation (e.g., "whites only" water fountains and reserved sections on buses) was immoral, regardless of whether it was the law. This is ultimately an appeal to natural law. Not insignificantly, it also shows the impotence of positivism as a philosophy of jurisprudence, inasmuch as self-evident truths are privileged above legal precedent and code.

5. Glenn C. Loury, "Responsibility and Race," *Vital Speeches*, 15 April 1983. p. 400.

6. Leon Higginbotham, *University of Pennsylvania Law Review* 140: 1005.

7. Glenn C. Loury, "Who Speaks for American Blacks?" *Commentary* 83, no. 1 (January 1987): 35.

8. Ibid.

9. Glenn C. Loury, "Two Paths to Black Power: The Conflicting Visions of Booker T. Washington and W.E.B. Du Bois," a lecture, American Enterprise Institute, Washington, D.C., 13 November 1991; adapted into article form, "Two Paths to Black Power," *First Things*, No. 26, October 1992, pp. 18–24.

10. Ibid., p. 7.

11. Ibid., p. 79.

12. Glenn C. Loury, "Black Dignity and the Common Good," *First Things*, June/July 1990. p. 18.

13. *Media Watch* 6, no. 5 (May 1992): 1.

14. Peter Collier and David Horowitz, eds., *Second Thoughts about Race in America* (Lanham, Md.: Madison Books, 1991), p. 80.

15. Charles M. Sherover, *Time, Freedom, and the Common Good* (Albany: State University Press of New York, 1989), p. 247.

16. Joseph Conti, interview with Glenn C. Loury, 5 June 1992.

17. Glenn C. Loury, Reply to Hendrik Hertzberg, "Wounds of Race," *New Republic*, 4 September 1989, p. 6.

18. Glenn C. Loury, "Beyond Civil Rights," *New Republic*, 7 October 1985, p. 23.

19. "Data In: Multiculturalism Gaining Control," *Campus*, Spring 1992, p. 9.

20. Glenn C. Loury, "The Need for Moral Leadership in the Black Community," *New Perspectives* 16, no. 1 (Summer 1984): 18.

21. Loury, "Black Dignity and the Common Good," p. 17.

22. Loury, "Who Speaks for American Blacks?" p. 35.

23. Ibid., p. 37.

24. Glenn Loury, "Two Paths to Black Power."

25. Mickey Kaus perceptively speaks to this point. "Americans aren't really eager to impoverish their lives by limiting their associations to people of their own economic class or skin color. They are only unwilling to share their society with people who reject its few basic values." *New Republic*, 7 May 1990.

26. Conti interview with Glenn Loury, 5 June 1992. Also, personal letter from Glenn Loury, 23 July 1992.

27. Loury, "Two Paths to Black Power," p. 17.

28. William Raspberry, "Race-Based Advantage Is a Detour," *Los Angeles Times*, 17 March 1991.

29. Michael Eric Dyson, "Melanin Madness," *Emerge*, February 1992, p. 37.

30. Max Weber, in *Protestant Ethic and the Spirit of Capitalism* (1904–1905), explicates the elective affinity between these two systems.

31. Joseph Amato, *Victims and Values: A History and a Theory of Suffering* (New York: Praeger, 1991), p. 152.

32. To digress into philosophical foundations for a moment, it seems to us that the disapproval of moral relativism and the insistence on the intrinsic moral qualities of certain behaviors is justified.

Cultures are comprised of attitudes and propositions about social reality, habits, and institutions, and these things are not value free. Who of us would hesitate to decry Nazi culture? That culture was autonomously derived and massively approved by its participants, yet its axiological base was of the most evil sort. It was, quite simply, based on immoral ideas—and we deliberately use the phrase "immoral ideas," for ideas can and frequently do have a discernible moral character. For example, compassion, justice, and fulfillment of obligations (familial, interpersonal, and political) are all generally accepted virtuous dispositions. Despite the powerful influence of modern social and cultural criticism, with its influential historicist presumption of the inveterate subjectivity of ideas and values, it still cannot be denied that we, as human beings, *operate in moral terms*. We approve of justice and highly esteem the importance of the rights to religious freedom and free speech. We act as if rape, racism, torturing babies, and desecrating the environment are all immoral practices, never morally admirable. This widespread and common assent to the categorical validity of certain general norms implicates an innate knowledge of moral order on the part of human beings. While this conclusion is not consonant with the verdict of contemporary critical studies, its Natural Law thrust is not without its defenders, classically or presently. The significance of this grand tradition for the topic at hand lies in the fundamental claim that moral values—and as a necessary consequence, political and social practices—cannot entirely be a matter of subjective choice. Some are intrinsically better than others.

This idea is, of course, diametrically opposed to the contemporary ethos of moral relativism that holds sway today in both academic and popular circles. But relativism of any form faces the debilitating logical problem of self-refutation. To deny the existence of objective truth is to enter into self-referential incoherence, since if one's denial of objective truth is true, it is necessarily false as well. But a proposition cannot be both true and false at the same time. We cannot on the one hand make absolute claims, and then on the other hand deny the very possibility of absoluteness.

The historicist contention that all values are historically conditioned, then, must itself be a historically contingent assertion, if historicism is to be true. But if the historicist thesis is itself time-bound, we have no reason to accept its transhistorical applicability. It cannot serve as a universal critique of ideas and concepts.

On the basis of this demonstration of the logical impossibility of strict relativism—and on the basis of our lived moral experience—it is reasonable to assert the reality of transpersonal, transcultural moral truth. It is also reasonable to assert the direct human perception of that truth. After all, there must be some ultimately antecedent moral knowledge in human beings, as well as the innate capacity to perceive and categorize moral concepts, or else human moral practice itself could never have commenced. Morally and otherwise, if I did not know some things, I could not reasonably doubt anything, and if I did not know some things without proof, I could know nothing by means of proof. In these ideas lie the epistemological warrant for nonrelativist ethics.

33. Loury, "The Family, the Nation, and Senator Moynihan," *Commentary*, June 1986, p. 24

34. Loury, "The 'Color Line' Today," *Public Interest* no. 80 (Summer 1985): 99.

35. Irving Kristol, address at the American Enterprise Institute, first aired on CSPAN, 7 December 1991.

36. Ibid.

37. Loury, "Black Dignity and the Common Good," p. 16.

38. Loury, "Beyond Civil Rights," *New Republic*, 7 October 1985, p. 25.

39. Loury, "The 'Color Line' Today," p. 95.

40. Loury, "Who Speaks for American Blacks?" p. 35.

41. Andrew Hacker, *Two Nations: Black and White, Separate, Hostile, Unequal* (New York: Scribner's, 1992), pp. 51–52.

42. Loury, "The Need for Moral Leadership in the Black Community," p. 16.

43. Glenn C. Loury, "Black Political Culture after the Sixties," in *Second Thoughts: Former Radicals Look Back at the Sixties*, edited by Peter Collier and David Horowitz (Lanham, Md.: Madison Books, 1989), pp. 145–46.

44. Ibid.

45. *Los Angeles Sentinel*, 7 May 1992, p. 2.

46. Joseph Conti, interview with Glenn C. Loury, 3 June 1992.

47. Loury, "Responsibility and Race," *Vital Speeches*, 15 April 1983, p. 400.

48. Quoted in William Bennett, *The De-Valuing of America* (New York: Summit, 1992), p. 197.

49. Conti, interview with Loury, 5 June 1992.

50. Ibid.

51. Robert Benne, *The Ethic of Democratic Capitalism: A Moral Reassessment* (Philadelphia: Fortress, 1981), p. 28.

52. Conti interview with Loury, 5 June 1992.

53. Lawrence Mead, *Beyond Entitlement: The Social Obligations of Citizenship* (New York: Macmillan, 1986), p. 21.

54. Glenn C. Loury, "Linking Public and Private Efforts in Overcoming Poverty," in *Welfare Reform: Consensus or Conflict?* edited by James S. Denton (Lanham, Md.: University Press of America, 1988), p. 19.

55. Ethelbert W. Haskins, *The Crisis in Afro-American Leadership* (Buffalo, N.Y.: Prometheus, 1988), p. 15.

56. Conti, interview with Loury, 5 June 1992.

57. Collier and Horowitz, *Second Thoughts about Race*, p. 61.

58. Conti, interview with Loury, 5 June 1992.

59. Robert Hilburn, "Beyond the Rage," *Los Angeles Times*, 24 May 1992.

60. Ibid.

61. Loury, "Linking Public and Private Efforts," p. 19.

62. Loury, "Two Paths to Black Power."

63. Lawrence Mead, *Beyond Entitlement*, p. 24.

64. Loury, "Who Speaks for American Blacks?" p. 35.

65. Loury, "Linking Public and Private Efforts," p. 20.

66. Ibid.

67. Loury, "Black Dignity and the Common Good," p. 16.

68. William Raspberry, *Looking Backward at Us* (Jackson: University Press of Mississippi, 1991), p. 145.

69. Loury, "Need for Moral Leadership," p. 18.

70. Raspberry, *Looking Backward at Us*, p. 164.

71. Ibid., pp. 164–65.

72. Loury, "Black Political Culture," p. 142.

73. Loury, "Black Dignity and the Common Good," p. 17.

74. Victoria Mathews, ed., *Black-Belt Diamonds* (New York: Negro University Press, 1969), p. 91.

75. Glenn C. Loury, "A Prescription for Black Progress," *Christian Century*, 30 April 1986, p. 438.

76. Anne Wortham, *Restoring Traditional Values in Higher Education: More than Afrocentricism*, Heritage Lectures no. 316, Washington, D.C., p. 15.

77. At this writing, Loury's first book, *Free at Last? Racial Advocacy in the Post-Civil Rights Era*, is in publication by the Free Press (New York).

CONCLUDING REMARKS

There is an old adage: If you keep doing what you did, you keep getting what you got.

Robert L. Woodson

In the preface we advised the reader that this was a book about more than race. It should now be clear that fundamentally this has been a book about values and the human behaviors they implicate. Values, whatever else they may be, are valued ideas—that is, ideas that for some reason are held to be important and worthy. So on a more general level this has been a discussion of ideas and their influence, for good or ill, on human beings living in society. As such, this work is a normative one, imputing to ideas and their consequences degrees of worth. Inasmuch as it has done so, this book evinces confidence in the ability of ideas to affect or change political policies and social situations, to make an impression on people made newly aware of personal, social, and political realities.

Andrew Hacker, in an article, "The Myths of Racial Division," follows a catalogue of social crises facing the American family with these comments:

Given the ubiquity of absent fathers—black and white—little will be gained lecturing one race on its duties. To call on black Americans to show greater discipline would seem to suggest that only they have deviated from national norms. Black families will become more stable when all households evolve a stronger structure.[1]

For our purposes what is perhaps the most important point to draw from Hacker's remarks is that they reflect the static and reactive position assigned to the black community by today's civil rights establishment and those in academia who, like Hacker, share the establishment's narration of the black experience in America. In his book *Two Nations: Black and White, Separate, Hostile, Unequal*, Hacker catalogs the struggles of African Americans, but, as with other works in the "literature of shame" genre, he unreflectively concludes that hatred on the part of white America is all to blame and that therefore white Americans should tend to their own problems before pointing that historically exercised pale, bony finger of accusation at oppressed black America.

But the New Black Vanguard would say to Hacker, "Why wait? Why should *we* wait for white America to reform before we vigorously address failings in the African-American community? Why should the black community dutifully wait for a national reformation of the family before we overcome our own family problems and become more stable?" Glenn C. Loury says of Hacker's project:

> I don't think Hacker takes black people seriously. . . . If 60 percent of Americans [and not just black Americans, as is currently the case] were born out of wedlock, even Andrew Hacker in New York City would see that that was a catastrophe for this society. But when 60 percent of blacks are born out of wedlock, Hacker says that it's just the inevitable consequence of Americans changing their values. So blacks can be literally littering the streets, dying from gunshot wounds in the chest inflicted by each other, and to Andrew Hacker it is only significant insofar as it reflects what white racism has done to blacks—and the only question is whether an invidious comparison between whites and blacks is being made. For me, the 60 percent figure has vitality and meaning in and of itself. I don't need to know what the number is for whites to know that that's bad.[2]

Sowell, Steele, Woodson, Loury, and the other dissident voices would have African-Americans take the lead and serve as an example to the nation of the possibility of social victory. Today, the civil rights establishment functions as an incredible hindrance to the realization of that possibility. Clint Bolick summarizes its present agenda:

> Many of those who today invoke the mantle of [black] leadership have attempted to transform the nature of civil rights from those basic freedoms we all share equally as Americans into special privileges for some and burdens for others based solely on the same characteristics they once fought to render irrelevant. They have exchanged "color-blindness" for color consciousness; equality of opportunity for forced equality in result;

individual liberty for group reparation; civil rights for social engineering; justice for power. They have abandoned their role as statesmen and assumed the role of politicians; and, in so doing, they have tarnished the rich legacy they inherited.[3]

Political scientist Lawrence Mead spends the last few pages of *The New Politics of Poverty*, one of the most astute and careful studies of political economy in our time, positing black conservatism as *the* key to inaugurating a new era of hope for America's urban underclass. "Progress may wait upon the emergence of a more conservative black leadership, willing to abandon the activists, reject racial liberalism, and enforce orthodox norms in the name of [economic] integration."[4]

The thinkers surveyed in this book are the conservative black leadership to whom Mead is referring. Their rise to political hegemony in the African-American community is not assured, but it certainly is warranted. The current political assumptions in America—regarding discussions about race—are basically distorted and misleading, and ring false to a great many Americans of all classes and ethnicities.

So it is that, in the minds of many, today's popular attitudes about race are like the giant balloons in the famous Macy's Thanksgiving Day Parade, slowly moving down the thoroughfare, demanding and commanding everyone's attention. But like the balloons, attitudes about the inhibiting power of racism are distorted out of all proportion to its real significance. These attitudes are only bloated cousins to the significantly less powerful reality at their core.

The work of the New Black Vanguard represents a vigorous protest against the twisted state of racial discourse in America today. Although their diverse ideas are presented in different philosophical contexts, they clearly exhibit common themes. These include a view of the human person that transcends race, and of national interest that transcends ethnic affiliation; a call for good faith in race relations; renewed attention to the critical role of values in shaping social conditions; a rejection of media-constructed perceptions of who represents black interests and the thinking of most black citizens; a desire to conserve the best of American institutions and democratic capitalism; an emphasis on black dignity, redefined; and the ability of all black Americans, both individually and communally, to superintend their own lives and their own destinies. Moreover, since the dissidents are advancing a point of view that constitutes a trenchant apologetic for democratic capitalism and civic virtue, the New Black Vanguard is actually a vanguard for all Americans, whatever their color, who see merit in such principles.

Reaching for a political humanism beyond race and resentment, the black dissidents replace the civil rights establishment's drive to reduce personal identity to racial classification with the powerful concepts of personal responsibility and self-initiative, demonstrating that a people enhances the common good through the exercise of self-interest, rightly understood.

NOTES

1. Andrew Hacker, "The Myths of Racial Division," *New Republic,* 23 March 1992, p. 21.

2. Joseph Conti, interview with Glenn C. Loury, 5 June 1992.

3. Clint Bolick, *Changing Course* (New Brunswick, N.J.: Transaction, 1988), p. xii.

4. Lawrence Mead, *The New Politics of Poverty: The Nonworking Poor in America* (New York: Basic Books, 1992), p. 259.

SELECTED BIBLIOGRAPHY

Abernathy, Ralph. *And the Walls Came Tumbling Down*. New York: Harper and Row, 1989.

Amato, Joseph. *Victims and Values: A History and a Theory of Suffering*. New York: Praeger, 1991.

Anderson, Digby, June Lait, and David Marsland. *Breaking the Spell of the Welfare State: Strategies for Reducing Public Expenditures*. Cambridge: Social Affairs Unit, 1981.

Bennett, William. *The De-Valuing of America*. New York: Summit, 1992.

Berger, Peter L. *Capitalist Revolution: 50 Propositions about Prosperity, Equality, and Liberty*. New York: Basic Books, 1986.

————. *An Invitation to Sociology*. Garden City, N.Y.: Doubleday Anchor, 1963.

————. *The Precarious Vision*. Garden City, N.Y.: Doubleday, 1961.

Berger, Peter L. and Richard John Neuhaus. *To Empower People*. Washington, D.C.: American Enterprise Institute, 1977.

Bloom, Allan. *The Closing of the American Mind*. New York: Simon and Schuster, 1987.

Bolick, Clint. *Changing Course*. New Brunswick, N.J.: Transaction, 1988.

————. *In Whose Name? The Civil Rights Establishment Today*. Washington, D.C.: Capital Research Center, 1988.

Butler, John S. *Entrepreneurship and Self-Help Among Black Americans*, Albany, N.Y.: State University of New York, 1991.

Butler, Stuart M., and Anna Kondratas. *Out of the Poverty Trap: A Conservative Strategy for Welfare Reform*. New York: Free Press, 1987.

Buzzard, Lynn, and Paula Campbell. *Holy Disobedience*. Ann Arbor, Mich.: Servant Books, 1984.

Collier, Peter, and David Horowitz, eds. *Second Thoughts about Race in America* Lanham, Md.: Madison Books, 1991.

————, eds. *Second Thoughts: Former Radicals Look Back at the Sixties*. Lanham, Md.: Madison Books, 1989.

Cone, James H. *Black Theology and Black Power*. New York: Seabury, 1969.

Crouch, Stanley. *Notes from a Hanging Judge*. New York: Oxford University, 1990.

Dash, Leon. *When Children Want Children*. New York, Morrow, 1989.

Denton, James, ed. *Welfare Reform: Consensus or Conflict?* Lanham, Md.: University Press of America, 1988.

Detlefsen, Robert. *Civil Rights under Reagan*. San Francisco: Institute for Contemporary Studies Press, 1991.

D'Souza, Dinesh. *Illiberal Education*. New York: Macmillan, 1991.

Efron, Edith. *The News Twisters*. Los Angeles: Nash, 1971.

Gerth, H. H., and C. Wright Mills, eds. *From Max Weber*. New York: Oxford University Press, 1946.

Gilder, George. *Wealth and Poverty*. New York: Basic Books, 1981.

Gutman, Herbert. *The Black Family in Slavery and Freedom, 1750–1925*. New York: Vintage, 1977.

Hacker, Andrew. *Two Nations: Black and White, Separate, Hostile, Unequal*. New York: Scribner's, 1992.

Haskins, Ethelbert W. *The Crisis in Afro-American Leadership*. Buffalo, N.Y.: Prometheus, 1988.

Institute for Contemporary Studies. *The Fairmont Papers: Black Alternatives Conference, December 1980*. San Francisco: Institute for Contemporary Studies Press, 1980.

Jencks, Christopher, and Paul E. Peterson, eds. *The Urban Underclass*. Washington, D.C.: Brookings Institution, 1991.

Kimball, Robert. *Tenured Radicals: How Politics Has Corrupted Our Higher-Education*. New York: Harper and Row, 1990.

Kozol, Jonathan. *Savage Inequalities*. New York: Crown, 1991.

Lemann, Nicholas. *The Promised Land*. New York: Knopf, 1991.

Lester, Julius. *Falling Pieces of the Broken Sky*. New York: Little, Brown, 1990.

Matusow, Alan. *The Unravelling of America*. New York: Harper and Row, 1984.

McFadden, Robert et al. *Outrage: The Story Behind the Tawana Brawley Hoax*. New York: Bantam, 1990.

Mead, Lawrence. *Beyond Entitlement: The Social Obligations of Citizenship*. New York: Macmillan, 1986.

———. *The New Politics of Poverty: The Nonworking Poor in America*. New York: Basic Books, 1992.

Murray, Charles. *Losing Ground*. New York: Basic Books, 1984.

Niebuhr, Reinhold. *Moral Man and Immoral Society*. New York: Scribner's, 1932.

Novak, Michael. *Free Persons and the Common Good*. Lanham, Md.: Madison Books, 1989.

———. *The Spirit of Democratic Capitalism*. New York: Simon and Schuster, 1983.

Patterson, James, and Peter Kim. *The Day America Told the Truth*. New York: Prentice-Hall, 1991.

Patterson, Orlando. *Ethnic Chauvinism*. New York: Stein and Day, 1977.

Pinkney, Alphonso. *The Myth of Black Progress*. Cambridge: Cambridge University Press, 1984.

Pohlman, Marcus D. *Black Politics in Conservative America*. New York: Longmans, 1990.

Raspberry, William. *Looking Backward at Us*. Jackson: University Press of Mississippi, 1991.

Rector, Robert. "Strategies for Welfare Reform." Heritage Lectures no. 378. Heritage Foundation, Washington, D.C., 1992.

Rusher, William. *The Coming Battle for the Media*. New York: Morrow, 1988.

Ryan, William. *Blaming the Victim*. New York: Vintage, 1976.

Sachar, Emily. *Shut Up and Let the Lady Teach!* New York, Poseidon Press, 1991.

Sandel, Michael. *Liberalism and the Limits of Justice*. Cambridge: Cambridge University Press, 1982.

Schuyler, George S. *Black and Conservative: The Autobiography of George S. Schuyler*. New Rochelle, N.Y.: Arlington House, 1966.

Sigelman, Lee, and Susan Welch. *Black Americans' Views of Racial Inequality*. Cambridge: Cambridge University Press, 1991.

Sleeper, Jim. *The Closest of Strangers*. New York: Norton, 1990.

Smith, James, and Finis Welsch. *Closing the Gap: Forty Years of Economic Progress for Blacks*. Santa Monica, Calif.: Rand Corporation, 1986.

Sowell, Thomas. *Black Education: Myths and Tragedies*. New York: McKay Publishing, 1972.

———. *Civil Rights: Rhetoric or Reality?* New York: Quill, 1984.

———. *Compassion versus Guilt*. New York: Morrow, 1987.

———. *A Conflict of Visions*. New York: Morrow, 1987.

———. *The Economics and Politics of Race*. New York: Quill, 1983.

———. *Knowledge and Decisions*. New York: Basic Books, 1981.

———. *Pink and Brown People*. Stanford, Calif.: Hoover Institution Press, 1981.

———. *Race and Economics*. New York: Longmans, 1975.

Steele, Shelby. *The Content of Our Character*. New York: St. Martin's, 1990.

Teague, Bob. *The Flip Side of Soul*. New York: Morrow, 1989.

Williams, Constance. *Black Teenage Mothers: Pregnancy and Child Rearing from Their Perspective*. Lexington, Mass: Lexington Books, 1991.

Williams, Walter. *All It Takes Is Guts*. Washington, D.C.: Regnery-Gateway, 1987.

———. *The State against Blacks*. New York: McGraw-Hill, 1982.

Wilson, James Q. and Glenn C. Loury. *From Children to Citizens*. Vol. 3. New York: Springer-Verlag, 1987.

Wilson, William Julius. *The Truly Disadvantaged*. Chicago: University of Chicago Press, 1978.

Woodson, Robert. *Black Perspectives on Crime and the Criminal Justice System*. Boston: G. K. Halla, 1977.

———. *On the Road to Economic Freedom*. Washington, D.C.: Regnery-Gateway, 1987.

———. *A Summons to Life*. Cambridge, Mass.: Ballinger, 1981.

———. *Youth Crime and Urban Policy*. Washington, D.C.: American Enterprise Institute, 1981.

Wortham, Anne. *The Other Side of Racism*. Columbus: Ohio State University Press, 1981.

———. *Restoring Traditional Values in Higher Education: More than Afrocentricism*. Heritage Lectures no. 316, Washington, D.C., from a lecture given on 22 February 1991.

INDEX

90; responsibility, 14, 30, 73, 76,
174, 207–9; values, 31–32, 69–70,
202–7, 215–16

McLittle, Emmanuel, 8, 191 n.86
Malcolm X, 23, 45, 204
Malveaux, Julianne, 89–90
Maritain, Jacques, 131
Marshall, Kenneth, 172
Marshall, Thurgood, 111
Matusow, Alan, 174
Mead, Lawrence, 47, 50, 53, 80 n.90,
80 nn. 93, 94, 102, 191 n.69, 213,
216, 229
Media: attitude toward black
dissidents, 61, 153; bias in, 24–25,
27–28, 38, 57, 123, 181, 184, 199;
racial protocol in, 24, 27–28, 32, 38–
39, 54, 70
Mediating structures, 72–73, 168–72,
216–20. See also Woodson, Robert
L., voluntary association
Mencken, H. L., 87
Meredith, James, 86
Minimum wage, 80 n.93
Minogue, G. Kenneth, 120 n.33, 202
Mismatch theory, 46–47
Morality: bartering in, 152; relativism
and, 43, 144–45, 206, 223 n.32. See
also Values
Moynihan, Daniel, 25–26, 32, 81
n.124, 137, 206
Moynihan thesis, 25–26, 32
MTV, 36
Murray, Charles, 34, 36, 81 n.110,
137, 212, 216
Myers, Michael, 13

National Association for the
Advancement of Colored People
(NAACP), 2, 4, 58, 111, 126, 146,
160, 170, 173, 197
National Center for Neighborhood
Enterprise (NCNE), 25, 65–66, 173,
180, 185
Neuhaus, Richard, 171, 176–77, 179
New Black Vanguard: antecedents of,
3–4, 63, 85; attacked by critics, 10–

11, 21–23, 25, 27, 39, 46, 52, 68–69,
119; dissent from civil rights
establishment, 21; diversity of, 8–9,
21, 76; positive proposals of, 68,
72–76; themes in ix-x, 3, 9, 21–76;
228, 229–30. See also Black
dissidents
Niebuhr, Reinhold, 98, 120 n.31, 126,
131, 134
Novack, Michael, 11, 131, 154 n.27,
183

Ogbu, John, 37, 72, 159, 176, 220
O'Hare, William, 34
Operation Cul de Sac, 149–50
Opportunity, 26, 30, 34, 196–99, 220;
denigration of, 35–36, 38–39, 41,
48, 57–58, 67–68, 70–71

Page, Clarence, 135, 189 n.4
Parker, J. A. "Jay," 8
Patterson, James, 145, 194–95
Patterson, Orlando, 8, 25, 31, 128,
132, 134–37, 149, 207
Perception, 100–101, 114
Peterson, Jesse, 8, 32–33, 35, 40, 96,
145
Picus, Lawrence, 55, 81 n.125
Pinkney, Alphonso, 33, 105–6, 201
Pluralism, 25, 43–44, 46, 135
Potter, David, 127
Poverty: industry, 49, 73; programs,
49–50, 72. See also Woodson,
Robert L.,"poverty pentagon"
Powell, Adam Clayton, 23
Pozner, Vladimir, 158–59
Prager, Dennis, 33, 43, 120 n.37, 213
Pragmatism, 108, 175
Preference falsification. See Public
"truth"
Preferential treatment. See
Affirmative action
Pregnancy: among black teenagers,
30, 33, 52, 54, 61, 116; out of
wedlock, 2, 5, 29, 32, 50, 52, 58–60
Public Enemy, 35, 37–38, 163, 214
Public opinion polls: black public, 24;
nomination of Clarence Thomas,

About the Authors

JOSEPH G. CONTI earned a Ph.D. in Social Ethics at the University of Southern California, where he did research in media culture, the psychology of race relations, and comparative religion.

BRAD STETSON also holds a Ph.D. in Social Ethics from the University of Southern California, where he focused his study on religious and political philosophy, as well as on the ethical implications of American cultural pluralism and racial diversity.